Striking Out

Critical Texts in Social Work and the
Welfare State

General Editor: Peter Leonard

Published

Pete Alcock and Phil Harris: WELFARE LAW AND ORDER

Ragnhild Banton, Paul Clifford, Stephen Frosh, Julian Lousada, Joanna
Rosenthall: THE POLITICS OF MENTAL HEALTH

Paul Corrigan and Peter Leonard: SOCIAL WORK PRACTICE UNDER
CAPITALISM: A MARXIST APPROACH

Ian Gough: THE POLITICAL ECONOMY OF THE WELFARE STATE

Chris Jones: STATE SOCIAL WORK AND THE WORKING CLASS

Paul Joyce, Paul Corrigan, Mike Hayes: STRIKING OUT: SOCIAL WORK
AND TRADE UNIONISM, 1970–85

Peter Leonard: PERSONALITY AND IDEOLOGY: TOWARDS A MATERIALIST
UNDERSTANDING OF THE INDIVIDUAL

Chris Phillipson: CAPITALISM AND THE CONSTRUCTION OF OLD AGE

Forthcoming

Lena Dominelli and Eileen McLeod: FEMINIST SOCIAL WORK

Peter Leonard: A CRITICAL HISTORY OF SOCIAL WORK THEORY

Mike Oliver: THE POLITICS OF DISABLEMENT

Goran Therborn: WELFARE STATES AND ADVANCED CAPITALISM

Series Standing Order

If you would like to receive future titles in this series as they are
published, you can make use of our standing order facility. To place a
standing order please contact your bookseller or, in case of difficulty,
write to us at the address below with your name and address and the
name of the series. Please state with which title you wish to begin your
standing order. (If you live outside the United Kingdom we may not
have the rights for your area, in which case we will forward your order
to the publisher concerned.)

Customer Services Department, Macmillan Distribution Ltd
Houndmills, Basingstoke, Hampshire, RG21 2XS, England.

Striking Out

Trade Unionism in Social Work

Paul Joyce, Paul Corrigan
and Mike Hayes

MACMILLAN
EDUCATION

First published 1988

Published by
MACMILLAN EDUCATION LTD
Houndmills, Basingstoke, Hampshire RG21 2XS
and London
Companies and representatives
throughout the world

Printed in Hong Kong

British Library Cataloguing in Publication Data

Joyce, Paul, *1952–*
Striking out : trade unionism in
social work. — (Critical texts in
social work and the welfare state).
1. Social service — Great Britain
2. Trade-unions — Great Britain
I. Title   II. Hayes, Mike   III. Corrigan,
Paul   IV. Series
361.3′0941   HV245
ISBN 0–333–38815–1 (hardcover)
ISBN 0–333–38816–X Pbk (paperback)

Contents

List of Tables

Acknowledgements

Over the years, many trade unionists in social services departments have helped us by agreeing to talk about their experiences and perceptions. Because of their generosity, we have been in a position to analyse the particular circumstances of, and developments in, social work trade unionism. Many of the quotations in this book, which have been taken from our conversations with them, testify to the rich and vigorous ideas and arguments which have informed social work trade unionism. We would like to thank them all for their patience and kindness.

The final structure and arguments of this book owe a great deal to the comments and criticisms of Peter Leonard, the editor, and Steven Kennedy at Macmillan. We are also grateful for the helpful criticisms of an anonymous reviewer, whose suggestions and comments led to a number of changes. Of course, any faults or weaknesses that persist are entirely due to us.

We would also like to thank Lucy McAuley, who typed the manuscript. And, inevitably, we must acknowledge the essential support of family and friends.

P. J.
P. C.
M. H.

Editor's Foreword

To be both a social worker and a trade union activist in the late 1980s is to experience defeat at almost every turn. Major structural changes are under way in British society of a kind which would be unimaginable even in the 1970s. Under the leadership of a determined and ruthless right-wing government radical change is taking place in many of the institutions, policies and practices which were established as a result of the long struggles of the Labour movement during this century. Although battles continue to be fought, the terrain is increasingly defined by a white male ruling class which every day shows its contempt for both trade unions and welfare services and has the capacity and ideological clarity to act upon these deep-seated emotions.

The consequences of this historic crisis for the Labour movement, for feminists, for anti-racists and for other progressive forces are profound. It is not difficult to sink into despair when faced with such a decisive shift in class forces, a shift which is designed to be *permanent*, leaving Britain with a social and cultural order dominated by a market liberalism fashioned to the management of a declining economy and massive unemployment. The superstructural characteristics of this new order are a strong authoritarian central state apparatus, a profoundly weakened local government and a minimal level of public sector health and social services grudgingly provided for the poorest and most defenseless segments of the population. Such a society, all the elements of which are already in place, requires, as a major precondition, the termination of a strong trade union movement which would otherwise be a significant source of resistance.

One alternative to despair and disillusionment is to engage in a critical, often painful, re-examination of the assumptions upon which the political practices of the Left have long been based. Have the material conditions which generated past political struggles changed to a degree which requires completely new forms of practice? Has the class structure of our society undergone such transformations as to demand a rethinking of the most basic taken-for-granted assumptions about 'the class', its composition, and its role in future political struggle? Can the forces of the Left so transform themselves that they can simultaneously confront the oppression of gender, racism and class without destructively prioritising one over the others?

For social work trade unionists, the present political crisis and the questions which it raises point to very specific dilemmas. As the central state becomes more authoritarian in its attempt, aided by media-assisted moral panics, to control 'deviant' populations and victimise social workers for the devastating results of structural inequalities, where does one turn for support, for defensive cover, for collective action?

Two possibilities have presented themselves. One is to turn to professionalism and to professional associations as the ground upon which to stand and demand a degree of autonomy in relation to state power and present the challenge of liberal professional values against punitive social policies. But social work professionalism, even when it has been at its most progressive, has proved to be too weak on its own to withstand prolonged assault. The radical Right has little patience with liberal professionalism, seeing it as an interference with cost-effective management and as one reason why social workers are difficult employees.

The second possibility, not necessarily incompatible with the first, is to turn to active trade union work, to militancy, as the means by which the particular needs of social workers, and possibly their welfare clients, can be most effectively defended. Here again, many problems have presented themselves. What kind of trade unionism is most appropriate to public service workers has been the source of many debates, and for social workers within NALGO has always been seen as difficult issue. As professionals engaged in a labour process which, despite contradictions, produces concrete benefits for people, the traditional model of trade unionism has been often experienced as ineffective. Industrial action involving the withdrawal of labour has invariably been a painful process, full of personal conflicts for social workers and problems for at least some welfare consumers.

These issues, and many similar ones, lie at the core of *Striking Out*. The authors grasp hold of the essential dilemmas of social work trade unionism and have produced an extremely important book, critical to the political situation of the last years of the 1980s and I believe the beginning of the 1990s. Based upon a foundation of empirical research, the book places social work trade unionism in the context of manual and white-collar unionism and charts its history in the 1970s and 1980s. The result is a book which uses history to ask central theoretical and political questions, and it is this which makes it so impressive. The most important question which is raised by this book has to do with the need for different sections of the trade union movement to develop forms of struggle most appropriate to their particular conditions. On the basis of careful analysis, Paul Joyce, Paul Corrigan and Mike Hayes argue that social work trade unionism during the 1970s and early 1980s made the mistake of adopting forms of struggle appropriate to other more traditional parts of the trade union movement and that it became, for a time, vanguardist and sectional in its whole approach to industrial relations. Such an approach, though understandable, failed to take full account of the contradictions within social work practice – its oppressive and beneficial elements – the particular nature, in other words, of the *labour processes* of social workers.

Because this is an intensely political book, reflecting the author's commitment to both trade unionism and progressive forms of social work, the research, the questioning and the analysis leads, towards the end of the book, to a set of practical proposals for the way forward for social work trade unionism.

This is bound to be an extremely controversial book, especially so far as the Left is concerned. Arguments will be especially fierce over the problems and possibilities of "rank-and-file' militancy and over the likelihood of large trade union organisations ever becoming political instruments for progressive change in the present historical period. Debates amd

arguments over the issues raised by this book and the solutions offered, the attempt to 'learn from history', are of central
importance at the present time. This is a book which looks at
our recent history, including the experiences of defeat, in a
non-defeatist way. It is what we need now.

McGill University   PETER LEONARD

Introduction

In this book we study the problems and dilemmas encountered by social workers as trade unionists, the distinctive
aspects of social work trade unionism, and the way that the
experiences of trade union struggle teaches social workers
about trade union methods, tactics and strategies. The aim is
to develop an understanding of the practical trade union
experiences of social workers which allows the real basis for
the strength and importance of social workers and their union
organisation to be grasped. We should stress that this book is
not a history of trade unionism in social work, although major
aspects of that history will be covered by us. Neither is it an
academic treatise on trade union organisation amongst social
workers, although we have found it necessary to study the
organisation, methods, tactics and aspirations of social work
trade unionists. And, finally, it is not a disinterested study of
social work trade unionism, because we believe that there
needs to be a broad growth of trade union consciousness
amongst social workers, thereby providing a powerful impetus
to the regeneration of all welfare work in Britain.

It is our intention in this book to deal with what may have
appeared as the surprising emergence of social workers' trade
unionism in the 1970s and the subsequent developments in
the early 1980s, the main phases being outlined below. Until
the 1970s social workers employed by local authorities were
often members of the National and Local Government Officers' Association (NALGO), the main union for non-manual
staff in local government, but they did little to attract the
attention of the trade union world. In this period, their
identity as trade unionists was merged with the general identity

1

of the non-manual local government trade unionist, an identity, therefore, not associated in popular conception with aggressive trade unionism or radicalism.

A major dispute in 1978–9 changed this. The dispute, which was over the right to negotiate social workers' grades locally, involved a small number of NALGO branches taking very determined and, in some cases, very lengthy strike action which resulted in a colossal loss of working time: with hindsight it is possible to see that trade union activism had been growing and maturing in the new social services departments of the post-Seebohm era. Although initially narrowly-based in certain types of local authority, this activism began to express itself in workplace union organisations that seemed to be moving closer and closer to the shop steward form found in the private manufacturing sector. Official trade union approval was given for these changes in 1977: when the main union, NALGO, issued a circular to its branches giving advice on the introduction of shop steward systems, thereby formally marking the arrival of the shop steward movement. In the wake of this growth of workplace activism and militancy, there was talk of the transformation of NALGO and of the 'new unionism', which was an allusion to a period in the nineteenth century when semi- and unskilled workers, who had previously been outside the ranks of organised labour, joined trade unions during a phase of heightened labour militancy (see Maybin, 1980).

In the 1980s the trade unionism of social workers has felt much less insurgent, but there was a major dispute in 1983, this time involving residential social workers, who were not regarded as being in the forefront of social work trade unionism. In this dispute, which ended rather barrenly from a trade union point of view, there seemed to be very little real union strength behind the action. It did nevertheless show the continuing advance of a trade union consciousness in social work and may have helped to push this advance further along. In the period since 1979 there has been a move towards greater involvement in mainstream work for NALGO by social work activists, a growing strategic and tactical sophistication and, in some places, a new interaction between social work trade unionism and professional ideas. All in all, the period since 1979 has been a complex and interesting one for social work trade unionism.

But knowing the recent history of social workers' trade unionism is not the same as understanding it. Indeed, it is all too easy to take the events of the last fifteen or so years of social work trade unionism and force them into the conceptual categories supplied by traditional ideas of trade unionism, categories that have been mainly used to understand manual trade unionism. To understand the trade unionism of social workers it has to be studied in its specificity, appreciating what is peculiar to it, analysing what is the result of its location on a public services terrain, and taking into account the significance of professional ideas and organisation for trade union practice. It is not easy to approach the study of social workers' trade unionism in this way, but it is indispensable for a realistic understanding of it. We have found a number of themes and arguments to be essential to this more 'grounded' approach and we provide an outline of them in the following sections of this chapter. We conclude with a brief discussion of our research methods and a short guide to the structure of the book.

THEMES IN THE STUDY OF SOCIAL WORKERS' TRADE UNIONISM

In our study we have been concerned with recognising and tracing the implications of the fact that social workers are, in historical terms, 'young'. By this we mean that, both as a section of the labour force and as a fraction of the working class, social workers are a new force. This concentration with their 'newness' raised questions for us about the forms of trade union struggle they would use and about how, in practice, they related to older fractions of the working class.

Forms of struggle are created, adapted or improvised by the trade union movement in specific economic, political, legal and social conditions. Thus in the nineteenth century there was a period when a number of trade union leaders became convinced of the advantages of the method of mutual insurance. Judged in the abstract, this conversion may seem like an abdication of responsibility by cowardly union leaders, but there is another point of view that stresses the practicality of this change where conditions were extremely unfavourable to more overt forms of struggle, such as, for example, collective bargaining. Similarly, different sections of the trade union movement have to develop those forms of struggle most appropriate to the conditions they face.

For social workers the question was whether they, as members of a new fraction of the labour movement, would develop new and specific forms of struggle representing their uniqueness or whether they would copy forms of struggle of the past. As we will show, they got into the paradoxical situation of representing their newness and growing power by trying to take on board forms of struggle which had emerged in different times and with different labour-processes. It became their badge of honour to be called 'shop stewards' rather than representatives, since this meant they were in a real 'union'. And when they were in dispute, taking part in strike action became the test of whether they were part of a proper union.

Our view of this paradox is a sympathetic one. Even if copying an old form of struggle is a mistake, any tendency to be critical on our part would have to be tempered by the knowledge that trade union struggle is not easy to mobilise. Furthermore, critical comments regarding the trade union practice of the 1970s may be inappropriate if the social workers involved believed that the only possible form of struggle was an old form and if the credibility of the form of trade union struggle was itself crucial for mobilising trade union action amongst social workers.

We have also been interested in the issue of how social workers have related and should relate to older fractions of the working class. What we found was that, as a young fraction (not only of the working class but also of a young and growing organisation called NALGO), they fought very hard for their specific interests. We believe that initially they made the mistake of seeing their own fractional experience as in some way representing the 'whole union', and once or twice even the whole working class. This at times manifested itself in a sectionalism that was vanguardist and unconcerned with forming and maintaining alliances. More often it manifested itself in a sectionalism that appeared unable to see why its issues and problems could not be expected to dominate branches and unions or the rest of the class. This could be seen on occasion when a few very new trade union social work members viciously attacked their sisters and brothers (who may have been building the union for decades) for 'not supporting us'. Exploration of these modes of relating to older fractions of the working class has involved us in studying the phenomenon of rank-and-filism in social workers' trade unionism, which we recognise is a trade union ideology which only a very few people practice in anything approaching its pure, uncompromised form. However, we would suggest that a significant number of social workers when coming into trade unionism for the first time believe that rank-and-filism is what 'real' trade unionism is all about.

Other trade unionists in local government sometimes accuse field social workers of being arrogant and it is only a short step from this to blaming their arrogance for the failures of social worker trade unionists to build and maintain alliances. We think it is fruitless and harmful to identify arrogance as the culprit. The real problem is located in the mistake of seeing a fractional experience as representing the whole experience of the people who form a trade union or a class. And this mistake is a 'normal or everyday' experience of consciousness. For the world view of the working class is fragmented and, consequently, when fragments of the working class are in struggle or conflict they see their issues and forms of struggle as representing the whole class.

In any case, the analysis has to be driven deeper into the social relations which underlie the trade union behaviour of social workers. And this analysis has to deal with a set of questions that are generally overlooked. How can we explain this new and, in its own terms, important fraction expressing its importance and its newness through forms of struggle which are most obviously 'old' and not its own? Why is power expressed in this way? And, more importantly, what can be done to ensure that social worker trade unionists continue to develop as a part of the union as a whole?

The answer to these questions must lie within the difficulty of recognising contradictions in the social work experience.

One in particular is expressed in the tendency of many social workers to veer between seeing their labour-process experience as either very important and central, or totally unimportant and marginal. This matches their oscillation between their experience of trade union power as one of either strength or weakness. We believe that both aspects are true at once. It is undoubtedly the case that the labour-process of social workers – that of professional, organised social care – is of importance to society as a whole and especially to disadvantaged and oppressed groups. It is obviously the case that the role of social workers in carrying out functions around, for example, child abuse or the organisation of community care, have great social importance. However, at the same time, analysed in terms of the 'industrial muscle' view of the importance of labour, social workers are weak. This, of course, can be put in some perspective by the outcome of the miners' dispute of 1984–5 which has shown that, faced with a powerful state, the industrial muscle measure of the importance of labour renders nearly all labour as 'weak'.

The importance of the labour-process and the specific form it takes in the democratically-controlled public service sector of the British economy are important themes in our study and, for us, provide a key to understanding the experiences of social work trade unionists. The developing trade union consciousness in social work has to be seen as the result of trade union struggles over issues and problems that have their origin in the social relations which are part and parcel of the labour-process in social work. These struggles provide the experiences which can, and often do, teach lessons to social worker trade unionists. In talking of the lessons taught by the experience of trade union struggle, we are moving on to the arguments we have developed in the course of this study.

THE ARGUMENTS

A key argument of this book is that it is possible to develop an understanding of the recent past which increases the real experience of strength and importance of the labour-process of social work to society. Therefore, it is not necessary to build the strength and importance of social work on an historically outmoded and inappropriate set of beliefs. Furthermore, this understanding comes out of the experience of social workers. Indeed, perhaps the single most important point we make is that experience teaches people about trade union methods, tactics and strategies. It is not so much intellectual or political criticism that achieves this as the real, historical experience of coming into struggle and, mainly, losing set piece battles. As will be seen, a very different social work trade unionism has emerged from the harsh teaching of history.

We have tried to stress the difference between the traditional private sector experience of trade unionism and that of the white-collar public sector. Given our commitment to public sector trade unionism, we do recognise, of course, that, for workers, the public sector is firstly an employer. Whilst the interests of employer and employee are, of course, different, it is a mistake to interpret these differences as ones that are inevitably and always antagonistic. It is undoubtedly true that, within the reality of local authority corporate management, all managers have great pressure put upon them to act as if they were in the private sector. It remains the case, however, that they are *not* in the private sector. And to treat every team leader or head of home as if their every action was antagonistic to the interests of the workers has proved unhelpful. It may prove a useful way of fostering an antagonistic consciousness amongst white-collar workers to draw such sharp and sure lines. It does, however, mean that those who are on 'our' side (that is, the workerist side) of that line are fatally weakened in their fight for the importance of the labour-process of social work.

This is not to say that it can be safely assumed that the interests of managers will coincide with those of the workforce in social services. But it is equally absurd to make the opposite mistake of believing that they will always be antagonistic.

So, where do these arguments lead? Struggles for local democracy in the early 1980s highlighted the alliances that must be built from amongst all the workforce in local government, together with the politicians as democratically elected leaders. These struggles, we believe, indicate a unity of purpose around some issues of local democracy. The prospects for

alliances involving the 'enemy' managers are favourable despite the ideology of antagonism, partly because they are
usually in the same union and because their commitment to
social service work is usually high.

A second argument which is crucial to our analysis is that
social work trade unionism expresses both the difference of
social workers from other local government white-collar staff
as well as their similarity to them. It is, in fact, the specific
relationship between their difference and their similarity at
any moment which defines the nature of their trade union
consciousness.

The difference of social workers was very dominant in the
1970s. We will show later in this study how they constructed
their trade unionism in the context of their membership of
NALGO, which was, and still is, the main trade union organisation for British social workers. Their activity in this period,
although undertaken by a relatively small number of social
workers, distinguished and set social workers apart from many
other groups because it was aimed at producing changes in
NALGO that would make it better suited, as they saw it, to
the purpose of providing for their collective representation. It
is this self-activity which, more than anything else, allows us
to talk meaningfully of social work trade unionism. In the
1970s their difference was objectified in the character of their
trade unionism, which was activist, militant and sectionalist.

It will be seen that we tend to lay great stress upon the
importance of integrating the trade union experience of social
workers within the wider experience of their union, however
'sluggish' or slow the union may appear. Whilst it may seem
the opposite of common sense, integration of their trade union
experience within the broader experience of their union is
important because it can lead to a wider realisation of the
value of the social work labour process. And we would argue
that it is one-sided to dwell on the dangers of integration into
the union because of fears that such a development would
liquidate social workers' trade union activism and militancy.

In this book we attempt to get to the heart of the dilemmas
and problems for social work trade unionism, but, as we have
argued above, this involves making the connection between
the strength (or weakness) of their trade unionism and the

importance (or unimportance) of the role of social work in
society. It requires an analysis of the relation between their
trade union consciousness and their changing experiences of
the social work labour-process in democratically-controlled
public services. And it needs an understanding that there are
two distinct and different sets of alliances to build. Firstly,
those alliances between the different fractions of the working
class that must be formed within each sector of the economy.
Secondly, those alliances that must be formed from fractions
that are located across different sectors of the economy.

RESEARCH METHODS

It will be obvious from the preceding discussion that we were
interested in understanding the contradictory and difficult
processes involved in the development of trade union consciousness and practice amongst social workers. We were also
interested in this development as it had unfolded in the 1970s
and 1980s. And we wanted to understand as much of the
richness and diversity of social work trade union practice as
we could encompass in a study that was trying to analyse as
well as describe; elaborate arguments as well as report facts.
In consequence, we have relied on interviews, formal and
'unstructured', with social workers, their trade union officials,
and, on occasion, their managers. Many of these were carried
out in the 1970s and involved questionnaires. Some were
taped. More interviews were carried out in recent years and
again we used tape recorders wherever possible.

We have made a good deal of use of the interview data,
partly because the accounts of social work trade unionists
interested us, especially with respect to the ideological aspects
of the growth of trade unionism in social work. We were also
concerned to record the attitudes and views of social workers
at various moments in the development of social work trade
unionism. As we have stressed, experience teaches powerful
lessons and accounts and positions change accordingly. Statements made at various times therefore provide 'snapshots' of
developing trade union consciousness. These interviews have
provided us with many of our quotations and, because they

are exact excerpts from conversations we had with social workers and others, they have a roughness and difficulty which some people may find off-putting. This did cause us concern but we have decided to include them in the text because of their richness, authenticity and subtlety. They also contain different perspectives and shades of opinion from our own that we think are useful because they inject into the study tensions with our own arguments. We welcome this because we do not agree with privileged accounts of the world, because we cannot provide 'positive' proofs of everything we conclude, and because we expect our arguments to draw responses from those who do not accept them.

In addition to data obtained from interviewing social workers and their union officials and managers, we have used a range of documentary materials and the results of a survey of NALGO branches we carried out in 1982.

OUTLINE OF THE BOOK

In this introduction we have been concerned with defining the themes and arguments which have guided us in, and emerged from, our study of the growth of trade union consciousness and practice amongst British social workers in the 1970s and 1980s. We have, additionally, provided a brief outline of some of the key aspects of the recent history of social workers' trade unionism and indicated the research methods we have used.

In Part I of the book we discuss the existing intellectual debates about trade unionism. These debates are taken from the industrial relations literature, a voluminous literature which is the product of the efforts of intellectuals (academics and others) whose research work and theorising has its own language and objectives, and whose concerns are best seen as occasionally overlapping with those involved in the literature of social work. Consequently, there is an incipient problem in this area of trying to mediate between two very different intellectual traditions – industrial relations and social work. Both traditions may try to discuss the motivation and experiences of social workers' trade union action, but they do so in very different ways. The segmentation of different areas of intellectual life shows up here as the difficult problem of communicating about trade union issues across two intellectual traditions.

Because the industrial relations literature is so extensive, we have had to be both selective and single-minded in addressing those aspects of the debates which are relevant to our concerns. And in recognising the uniqueness of social workers, we have found ourselves looking critically at current theories and concepts of trade unionism. We have, therefore, engaged a wide range of contributions to the theory of trade unionism and, as will be seen, we have often found gaps and ambiguities in the existing body of theory. This should not be regarded as surprising. The enterprising and vigorous trade union action of social workers threatens to bring them to the notice of the trade union world. It further threatens to upset the established pecking-order of the labour movement, which ranks groups of trade unionists according to their power, influence, status and visibility. These are new realities, demanding new explanations which go beyond the thinking of the industrial relations orthodoxy.

In Chapters 2, 3 and 4, which form Part II of the book, we use our empirical evidence to study the practical trade union experiences of social workers. We examine, in Chapter 2, the material conditions facing social workers and we explore the character and dilemmas of sectionalist trade union activity. The focus of Chapter 3 is rank-and-filism in social workers' trade unionism, which is partly explored through an analysis of the dispute in 1978–9 over local bargaining rights with respect to the grading of social workers. Chapter 4 considers some of the various trade union methods developed by social work activists in the context of the attack on local government by the Thatcher governments of the 1980s. In this second part of the book we do draw conclusions, as well as indicating the way in which social workers who are active in union affairs come to terms with their experiences. The overall conclusions are, however, left to the third and final part of the book.

In Part III we consider the main conclusions which emerge from our study of the practical experiences of social workers to date and we propose a trade union programme to build upon the achievements of social workers' trade unionism. In Chapter 5 we explore and clarify our understanding of the theoretical concepts necessary to make sense of the trade union experiences of social workers and Chapter 6 looks in detail at the contemporary political context of social workers' trade unionism. Finally, Chapter 7 summarises our programme for social workers' trade unionism, based on our understanding and analysis of the growth of a trade union consciousness in social work.

Part I
Theories

1

Theories of Trade Unionism

One of the longest strikes in post-war Britain began in August 1978. It lasted some forty-two weeks and resulted in over a quarter of a million working days lost.

The dispute, at a superficial glance, had some strange features. Firstly, the workers involved were social workers and it had been, and still is, comparatively rare for professional workers of any type to take part in strike activity. Secondly, many social workers took seriously the idea that they were engaged in professional practice, and indeed their professional body – the British Association of Social Workers (BASW) – had adopted a professional code of ethics in 1975, and yet the very duration of the strike activity seemed likely to ensure considerable suffering for the clients of social services departments. Professional ethics, which invariably require that practice should be orientated towards the welfare of the client, seemed, therefore, to be at odds with self-interested industrial action. Thirdly, some social workers had been organised in trade unions for a long time, well before the formation of unitary social services departments in the 1970s, and yet they 'burst' into industrial unrest towards the end of the 1970s. It seemed strange that there should be such a time lag. Finally, while they were by no means the only public sector trade unionists to take their first major strike action in the 1970s, their motivation seemed on the surface to be quite different. In the 1970s major industrial action was taken by local government manual workers (1970), gas fitters (1973), hospital manual workers (1973), firemen (1978), public service workers (1979) and civil servants (1979). Many of these disputes were, ostensibly at least, about pay increases and had been, arguably, provoked by the state's policy on pay. In contrast, the social workers' dispute had resulted from the refusal of local authorities to negotiate social work gradings on a single-employer basis.

Union membership in the public service unions grew rapidly in the 1970s and large scale stoppages in the public services showed that these weren't just paper members. But the 1978–9 dispute suggested that social workers were a group particularly worthy of serious study because of the complex issues involved in professional grades of employees in the public services becoming active in trade unionism. A series of questions regarding the social workers were prompted by the strike action:

(i) What was going on? Were economic grievances the mainspring of the militancy? Or had there been a shift in their consciousness – either politically or professionally?

(ii) What type of trade unionism was social work trade unionism? How did it relate to trade unionism amongst other groups of workers?

(iii) How was the trade unionism of social workers likely to develop in the future? Would it settle down and mellow after a youthful period of militancy? Or had it passed into a permanently militant phase?

Obviously, detailed and concrete study is needed to answer questions like these, but where should we start looking to find the answers? The current literature on trade unionism should be able to provide us with some guidance.

Analytically, we can identify four types of theory of trade unionism, and in principle all the influential studies in this area can be allocated to one or other of them. First we must distinguish between those studies that have focused on the individual union members, with the implicit or explicit purpose of explaining union character in terms of their motivation and intention, and those that have focused on social institutions, such as collective bargaining or the state, to explain union behaviour. Next we must distinguish between those that methodologically use an empirical approach and seek to explain differences believed, or observed, to exist empirically and those which take as their starting point a well worked out theoretical system. This second distinction, combined with the first, yields four types of trade union theory.

TABLE 1.1 Types of theory of trade unionism

| | Type of approach | |
Focus on	Empiricist	Theoretical system
Individual union member	1	2
Social institutions (e.g. collective bargaining, the state)	3	4

The individual–empiricist theories

The work on white-collar trade unionism often fits quite well into the first type of approach. The problems addressed by this branch of academic endeavour include the identification of the reasons why white-collar workers join unions (Strauss, 1954; Cook *et al.*, 1976), what factors determine union growth among white-collar workers (Bain, 1970), and whether or not their position in the social structure has any bearing on their militancy (Lockwood, 1958; Bain *et al.*, 1973).

In some ways this approach could be said to be somewhat mysterious in terms of its antecedents. It is tempting to anchor it in the descriptive approach which was the general hallmark of early British social science and studies of industrial relations in particular (typified by the more academic work of the Webbs and G. D. H. Cole). In describing British trade unions, it has been usual to identify two or three types in terms of their membership, methods, financial strength, union government, degree of reliance on full-time officials, and so on. The classification in the past tended to consist of three principal types of trade union – the craft union, the industrial union and the general union. The craft unions were unions that had a policy of recruiting only workers who had served apprenticeships; and so the less skilled were excluded. The industrial unions organised all workers employed in an industry or in a group of related industries irrespective of their skill or grade.

The general unions were defined by the absence of any underlying principle in their recruitment policy – they neither
excluded workers because of their skill grade nor restricted
recruitment to specific industries. They sought to be all-
inclusive.

A theory of trade unionism can be built on the empirically
derived classification. Lane (1974), for example, suggests that
many differences in organisation and methods between craft
unions and the later trade unions of labourers were linked to
the labour market:

> But all of these things that set the new unions apart from
> the old were directly related to the labour markets in which
> they operated. Lacking the possession of scarce skills as a
> bargaining counter, they had to try to organise into mem-
> bership all those who could possibly be used as blacklegs
> against them. Organising low-paid workers they had no
> choice but to charge low subscriptions, and low subs could
> not bear the cost of benefit funds for pensions, sickness,
> unemployment, etc. They had to retain a large staff of
> full-time officials to keep up with shifting employment so
> characteristic of the general labourer. (p. 111)

Inevitably, changes in trade union membership have made
the older classifications of trade unions look obsolete. In the
late 1960s white-collar union organisation expanded. According to Hawkins (1981):

> Between 1964 and 1974, by contrast, white collar union
> membership increased faster than the white collar labour
> force . . . The penetration of white collar unionism was
> particularly impressive in manufacturing industry, where
> density rose from 12.1 per cent in 1964 to 32.0 per cent in
> 1974. (p. 80)

And so, when Hyman and Fryer (1975) described British
trade unionism they found that the threefold typology was no
longer adequate. Not only was it difficult to find 'pure' examples of industrial and craft unions, the picture, they said, had

also become further complicated by the growth of white-collar trade unionism.

It might be thought that it would be a relatively easy process to add a fourth type of union – the white-collar union – to the existing classification and to identify its distinctive characteristics. The characteristics could then be related to the labour-market position of white-collar workers; or to some other factors if the labour market approach to explaining trade union types is not favoured. In fact, influential writing on white-collar trade unionism has not followed this line at all. Instead, studies of white-collar workers as a whole, or studies of specific sections of white-collar workers, seem to be more concerned about the similarities and differences in behaviour of white-collar and blue-collar workers.

Common to many of these analyses is an assumption that white-collar workers join unions or pursue militant trade union methods when their income deteriorates or fails to match their aspirations for a 'middle-class' life style. Thus Strauss (1954) has argued: 'White-collar workers join unions, not because they reject their middle-class aspirations, but because they see unionism as a better way of obtaining them' (p. 81). Vic Allen (1971) has claimed that the rise of trade unionism amongst white-collar workers was caused by their loss of status, which was itself a result of inflation, full employment and mechanisation. He believes, for example, that inflation caused substantial reductions in their real incomes compared with those of manual workers. Pursuing a different line of argument, Lockwood (1958) was convinced that the more privileged position of clerical workers in terms of income and job security accounted for their relative lack of militancy compared with manual workers.

Perhaps one of the most common features of work in this area is the view that the aspirations, attitudes or class imagery of white-collar trade unionists are reflected in the character of their trade unionism. Thus it may be argued that the white-collar union is seen by its members as a means of realising their middle-class aspirations and so it takes on aspects of the professional society (Strauss, 1954). Or white-collar workers are seen as only partially reconciled to the use of militant

methods, causing the white-collar trade union to appear equivo-
cal and hesitating or biased towards non-conflictual methods of
pressing demands (Allen, 1971).

The distinction between white-collar and blue-collar trade
unionism obviously appears to have some foundation in reality. Price and Bain (1983) report that white-collar trade
union density, at 44 per cent in 1979, was still a lot lower than
that of manual workers, which was 63 per cent, despite the
rapid increase in union membership amongst white-collar
workers since the late 1960s. And Creigh and Makeham's
study (1980) of official dispute statistics from 1966 to 1973
showed that over this period strike action was lower in most
non-manual occupational groups than in the manual groups.
These are very important objective facts, delineating important differences between blue-collar and white-collar workers.
However, in themselves they are insufficient to justify the
vulgar stereotypes that are often drawn on in arguments about
categories of trade unionism. These distinctions have much
greater weight in the field of ideology. Indeed, the distinction
drawn by both blue and white-collar trade unionists is one of
the main themes of this book. We believe it exists much more
in the arena of the emotions than in material reality.

The need for some caution in this area is suggested by a
study of nearly five hundred men in Liverpool carried out by
Cook *et al.* (1976). They interviewed a random sample of men
and found that 65 per cent of white-collar workers were in
trade unions, staff associations or professional type associations, as against 80 per cent of blue-collar workers. In other
words, collective organisation is very common for both categories of worker, notwithstanding the fact that only 36 per
cent of the white-collar workers were in TUC unions. This
comparison was made somewhat problematic by the differential coverage of the closed shop. Half the blue-collar trade
unionists said they had joined a union because of the existence
of a closed shop as against only a quarter (23 per cent) of
white-collar trade unionists. Whilst it seems that the presence
of the closed shop is a major factor in the extent of union
membership, the presence of the closed shop is probably a
function of management as well as worker attitudes. And so it
must be remembered that management is more prone to see

the closed shop as appropriate for blue-collar than for white-collar workers.

Their study also casts doubt on the existence of ideological differences between white-collar and blue-collar trade unionists. When they excluded those people who had joined a union because of the closed shop, they found that the majority of people in both categories, white-collar and blue-collar, had joined their union to pursue occupational interests. And exactly the same percentage (15 per cent) of both referred to ideological or ethical reasons for joining their union.

Overall, the following assessment by Nicholson *et al.* (1981) seems a fair one:

> From the well established (and common sense) observation that people's attitudes and beliefs are contextually dependent, and that the type of work people do, their social roles, and their social background create systematic differences in people's goals, attitudes and aspirations, then some major differences between the approach to trade unionism of different groups is to be expected. However, it would be naïve to expect these to divide along the simple boundary between white and blue collar occupations, and not because the boundary is in some places hard to locate (which it may be) but rather because the differences within either group are as great or greater than they are between the groups. (p. 25)

The individual-theoreticist approach

Theories of proletarianisation, which have been developed and applied in recent years, represent the second approach to the theory of trade unionism. They have been articulated specifically to account for the allegedly distinctive qualities of the trade unionism of workers whose proletarian status is for some reason considered doubtful. The aim behind the use of proletarianisation theories is to relate trade union character to the class position of the union membership.

Originally the concept of proletarianisation referred to the process whereby elements of a new petty bourgeois class consisting of tradespeople, shopkeepers and handicraftsmen

– who were also described by Marx and Engels as 'intermediate classes' – were constantly passing into the proletariat (Marx and Engels, 1942). These classes had a small amount of capital and so they weren't without property, or forced to sell their labour as were the proletariat. But the size of their capital was not enough for an assured, independent existence. Modern industry, owned by large capital, outcompeted the petty bourgeois class and constantly introduced new systems which made the production methods used in the petty bourgeois sector obsolete. Petty bourgeois victims of the competition posed by modern industry sank into the proletariat: they were proletarianised.

In the 1970s Rosemary Crompton (1976 and 1979) suggested using the idea of an ambiguous class situation to explain variations amongst white-collar workers in their propensity to participate in trade unionism. In this frame of reference, proletarianisation is no longer a movement of people into the proletariat but a movement towards an unambiguously proletarian class position. As such it is used by her to explain shifts towards trade union forms of collective action by white-collar workers.

In her 1976 discussion of approaches to the study of white-collar trade unionism she sets out her conceptual framework, stated at a highly abstract, theoretical level. This is based on her interpretation of Marx's account of the capitalist mode of production. She suggests that the capitalist mode of production is dominated by a 'capitalist function' and a 'labour function'. Central to her argument is the proposition that the form of the capitalist function has been changing. In the early stages of capitalist development the capitalist function was embodied in the owner-entrepreneur or the entrepreneurial extended family. As capitalism develops, Crompton argues, differentiation occurs *within* the capitalist function. So, middle-class employees are needed to develop and administer new techniques to raise relative surplus value (for example, work study and personnel management). Also, 'the many and varied tasks and operations within the capitalist function – the provision of finance, marketing, supply of raw materials, control of the labour force, etc. – have increasingly been dealt with by specialized sectors dealing with a particular aspect of the capitalist function' (Crompton, 1976, p. 414).

She then argues that the middle class has a class situation which is structurally ambiguous. Firstly, white-collar workers without property are agents of the capitalist function. This means, says Crompton, that they cannot be unambiguously identified with either the proletariat or the bourgeoisie. Secondly, employees in specialised sectors such as accounting, advertising, banking and insurance are in an ambiguous class situation because they are agents of the capitalist function *and* because they do not create surplus value. This means that they cannot be exploited in the manner of the proletariat, but they are oppressed since they have no discretion over the use to which their labour is applied. Thirdly, Crompton argues that white-collar workers who both carry out the work of co-ordination and technique necessary in any complex production process and who perform the work necessary to extract surplus value are carrying out both a labour and a capitalist function. They are, therefore, also in a class situation characterised by structural ambiguity.

Crompton uses an already published study of technicians to illustrate her approach to the understanding of trade unionism. She argues that the technicians have been affected by rationalisation, which has caused a drastic reduction in their participation in the capitalistic function:

As the class situation of technicians has become less ambiguous – as they have been truly 'proletarianized' – so have their market and work situations changed in the manner described. It is not surprising, therefore, that the technicians have shown ambivalence or outright antipathy towards company-oriented schemes of consultation and company-encouraged staff associations' and have chosen instead to join trade unions. (Crompton, 1976, p. 421)

Where the class situation of white-collar workers is ambiguous, there is, according to Crompton, conflict over the best form of collective action: some white-collar workers apparently seeing staff associations and co-operation as appropriate, others favouring trade unions.

What about public services employees? Where do they fit into all this? Is there a necessary material distinction between public and private sector employees? Crompton does refer to public sector workers, but it is clear that they were on the periphery of her concerns. She notes that 'the increasing productivity of the capitalist mode of production generates a more widespread demand for other services – the cost of which is met out of the increasing mass of surplus' (Crompton, 1976, p. 416). In the technical sense of the word, they are, therefore, 'unproductive'. So are these employees – in medicine, education and administration – in ambiguous class situations? The answer from Crompton on this point is not clear. She says:

> The development of the state, and its increasing involvement in the processes of production and distribution, is a characteristic feature of the development of monopoly capitalism . . . because the state is an integral part of monopoly capitalism, the class situation of state employees parallels that of employees in the private sector – state employees are variously productive, unproductive, exploited (and exploiter), oppressed (and oppressor), etc. – a similar mode of analysis of the class situation of state employees can be applied as above. (Crompton, 1976, pp. 425–6, footnote)

This is a very creditable attempt to respond theoretically to historical changes in the economic structure of Britain and to develop a more differentiated view of workers using a class analysis. There are, however, problems, as far as we are concerned, with this particular elaboration of class analysis. Crompton's later attempt to apply her framework to insurance workers shows, in our opinion, signs of a lack of robustness in her concepts.

In her 1979 article she defines a composite process she calls 'double proletarianization'. This is where the planning and discretionary elements in a job are reduced (deskilling), whilst, at the same time, aspects of the job which are related to the capitalist function are also attenuated. In fact, the deskilling aspect and the removal of work of the capitalist function are not clearly separated in her analysis of the changing class situation of insurance workers:

Mechanization and computer technology now perform the clerical work for which it was once worthwhile to employ steady, reliable and loyal servants. Insurance work is now split between, on the one hand, a mass of semi-skilled data processors and machine feeders, and on the other, a (much smaller) stratum of managerial positions – in short, the function of capital within the industry has been progressively concentrated in recent years. (Crompton, 1979, p. 414)

This alleged change in their class situation is said to have precipitated a very rapid increase in trade union membership. It seems that the proportion of insurance clerks in TUC affiliated unions went up from 13 per cent to 28 per cent over the period from 1965 to 1975, although some of this was due to ASTMS taking over staff associations.

It is apparent that the class analysis in this approach to the study of trade unionism is in danger of collapsing into an analysis of the locus of control. Crompton herself says at one point: 'Has the function of capital – briefly control – been centralised within the organisation as a consequence of the introduction of computers? (1979, p. 415). The class analysis, in other words, has been swamped by the deskilling debate which was popular in academic circles in the late 1970s. That it could be swamped may point to some inherent flaw in the framework.

This examination of proletarianisation theories can be rounded off with a brief look at Kelly's (1980) study of British civil servants. This group of workers, like social workers, are not regarded as part of the mainstream of the British labour movement, even though civil service unions have been established for a reasonably long time and are affiliated to the TUC. The ambiguities of their position within the trade union movement are confounded by the intellectual and political difficulties of locating their class position. All these intellectual factors, though, are overdetermined by the historical and cultural reality based upon the feeling that such people are not 'real workers'. This history still affects the view that 'real workers' are male, manual and in manufacturing.

Kelly's approach to the study of proletarianisation is to

investigate variables that are familiar from Lockwood's research into clerical workers: pay relativities, the extent of feminisation, the extent of recruitment of working class people, the extent of bureaucratisation, and the extent of mechanisation. In other words, the focus is on the market and work situations of civil servants. This orientation is reflected in Kelly's view of the causes behind the growth of civil service unions early in this century:

> By the outbreak of the First World War Civil Servants were joining trades unions or other protective associations in increasing numbers. The major impetus to this growth was the steadily growing bureaucratization of the Service because this had led to the concentration of Civil Servants in larger work groups, and the application of rational management principles led not only to a similarity of work experience for many civil servants, but also to a similarity of experience of grievance. The major source of grievance was low pay. At the same time conditions in society at large were becoming increasingly favourable to the growth of trade unions in so far as legal recognition had been granted gradually in the last quarter of the nineteenth century. (Kelly, 1980, p. 94)

It is also evident in his assessment of the development of trade unionism in the civil service and in his accounts of industrial action by civil servants:

> I have argued that the single most important factor in bringing about these changes has been pay, and therefore the income proletarianization . . . seems to have been vital in this respect . . . But pay alone would not have been sufficient. Certain other factors have created conditions favourable to the development of instrumental unionism, viz. demographic change, bureaucratization and mechanization. (1980, p. 125)

On the positive side, the analysis provided by Kelly is useful because it identifies non-class variables that are important in explaining unionisation and militancy. It fails, however, as a class analysis and there is an implicit recognition of this by Kelly himself. Although he uses the term 'income proletarianization', which he defines as a relative or absolute fall in income, he is aware of the fact that level of income is not a criterion of class:

> Marx states that class is not necessarily determined by level of income so we cannot therefore, using this evidence, legitimately argue that the class position of white-collar workers has changed. We can say that for some white-collar workers erstwhile financial advantages have disappeared and in that sense, and that sense alone, can we talk about proletarianization. (1980, p. 133)

In spite of the useful bringing together of material on civil service trade unionism, Kelly's study can be criticised for further muddying what was already muddy water, although we recognise that muddiness itself may be a necessary component of analysis. Calling a relative or absolute decline in income a measure of proletarianisation serves to confuse.

One aim of this book is to be part of a critical appraisal of proletarianisation theories and there are several issues which need particularly close attention. Firstly, Crompton assumes that there is a connection between the market and work situations of employees and their class position, also that this is useful for understanding white-collar trade unionism; a class analysis, however, may be important for reasons other than this. There is no need to see everything as determined by class position in order to believe in the value of a class analysis. Non-class variables may be useful for explaining variations in union behaviour amongst workers in the same class. Secondly, it may be time to return to a more traditional interpretation of proletarianisation – an interpretation which sees the process as being the movement of individuals from one class to another due to the effects of competition between large-scale private capital and other forms of social production. Thirdly, there may be a need to return to the traditional definition of class which emphasises ownership (or non-ownership) of the means of social production for classes involved in the capitalist system (that is, a class is not defined according to whether it is involved in the control of labour or acting on behalf of capital). Fourthly, class analysis would need to be developed to recognise the existence of competing forms of social production; this would also involve elaborating the traditional class analysis to deal with workers in the public sector. Class relationships in the public sector are in need of urgent study in the light of the fact that so much employment and social capital is involved. The second section of our book, dealing as it does with the practical experiences of social work trade unionism, provides the empirical base for this refutation. Its theoretical underpinnings are discussed in Part III.

The institutional–empiricist approach

The third type of approach, one that starts with established empirical differences in trade unionism and then seeks to account for them in terms of the effects of social institutions, has not, as far as we know, been applied to public sector trade unionism. Or, if it has, it has not been used in a substantial study.

The potential of such an approach is hinted at by Thomson's (1983) sketch of industrial relations differences between the private sector and the two public sectors. As can be seen in the table below, his work suggests that there are sharp contrasts in trade unionism, including strong differences in density of union membership, nature of organisation and forms of struggle and conflict.

These kinds of global generalisations are difficult to validate and explanations can verge on the totally speculative. Thomson's view is that the differences in industrial relations reflect underlying economic and political factors. For example, unionisation may be greater in the public than in the private sector because, while there has been a *government* policy to encourage union membership, there was no *public* policy to institutionalise union membership.

Clegg (1976) has reviewed international evidence to support his theory of trade unionism according to which differences in trade unionism are explicable by variations in the institution of collective bargaining. Thus he observed that

TABLE 1.2   An inter-sectoral comparison of British trade unionism

	Public services	*Public market sector*	*Private sector*
Manual union density	very high	very high	variable (e.g. low in services)
White-collar union density	high	high	low
Union structure	relatively clear occupational jurisdiction	generally clear jurisdiction	highly complex with competitive unions
Extent of informal organisation	little	limited	frequent
Nature of bargaining relationship	traditionally co-operative through the Whitley system – but trend towards adversary	adversary	adversary
Industrial conflict	relatively few strikes	occasional large strikes	few large official strikes – many unofficial plant or workgroup strikes

SOURCE: Adapted from Thomson (1983).

trade union density was generally higher in the public sector than in the private sector and argued that it could be attributed to the greater extent of collective bargaining coverage in the former. In the United States, where union density is lower in the public sector, he points out that public sector collective bargaining has continued to be very patchy in its coverage. Other arguments by Clegg, although not concerned with inter-sectoral comparisons, suggest the possibility that the limited development of workplace bargaining and the distinctive strike pattern of the public sector (that is, relatively few strikes or occasional large strikes) have been a result of centralised collective bargaining. But however much potential there is in this type of approach, theory construction along these lines has scarcely begun.

The institutional–theoreticist approach

Finally, we come to studies of trade unionism which have begun with theory and which have sought to explain trade union behaviour by reference to the effects of social institutions. Contemporary theories of trade union incorporation fit into this category. Some of these emphasise incorporation of the union movement by state institutions at national level; for example, it is often argued that involvement in corporatist tripartite bodies (such as the National Economic Development Council; the Advisory, Conciliation and Arbitration Service; and the Manpower Services Commission) has a debilitating effect on the trade union movement. There is another brand of incorporation theories that has focused on the dangers to trade union independence and effectiveness of reformed collective bargaining institutions at workplace level. More complex variants of incorporation theory have been based on the thesis that state institutions have contradictory effects. Hyman (1975), for example, has argued that monopoly capital depended increasingly on the state for grants, subsidies and the training of the workforce, which caused increased government spending and an increased tax burden for workers. To counter the tax effects, workers required larger pay increases – which were necessarily inflationary. According to Hyman, the state then responded to the union pressures for pay increases with incomes policies. But the incomes policies have been uneven in their impact – partly because the government was in a position to veto 'excessive' pay settlements in the public sector – and thus disrupted traditional pay relativities, causing hitherto passive groups of trade unionists to become militant.

There are innumerable other theories which purport to explain trade union behaviour in terms of social institutions. Some even attempt to place trade union behaviour in the context of the development of the entire complex of social institutions which go to make up a social formation. In the most recent times there has been a concern with the durability of social democratic societies based on the welfare state and the consequences for trade unionism of the political shifts to the right which have threatened them. As Claus Offe (1984) has written:

> The welfare state is based on the recognition of the formal role of labour unions both in collective bargaining and the formation of public policy. Both of these structural components [state provided welfare services and the formal role for trade unions] are considered to limit and mitigate class conflict, to balance the asymmetrical power relation of labour and capital, and thus to overcome the condition of disruptive struggle and contradictions that was the most prominent feature of pre-welfare state, or liberal, capitalism. (p. 147)

The welfare state, then, entailed recognition and legal rights for trade unions – rights for the individual member as well as for the collectivity – and there is some evidence (Hibbs, 1978) to support Offe's view that the trade unions' new relationship with the state during this period did produce appreciably greater industrial harmony. The conservative argument, which developed in the Britain of the 1960s and 1970s, largely in response to the conditions produced by the welfare state under the ascendancy of social democratic politics, was that the power of the unions had depressed profits and, therefore, made investment unattractive. The threat to the welfare state became serious in the 1970s when there was, in northern Europe as well as in Britain, a political resurgence of the Right which claimed a mandate to reduce the burden of the welfare state. They also promised, in Britain, to reduce the excessive power of the unions. No one is really sure what will happen to industrial conflict when the recession finally passes, but the chances are that the dismantling of the welfare state, and the deliberate exclusion of the trade union movement from participation in state policy making, will lead to a return to a period of more bitter industrial warfare, unless, that is, a new role is offered to the trade unions by a government of a different political complexion.

CHOOSING A THEORY?

All the theories above *can* be made to yield speculative
answers to the questions we asked earlier on. But in some cases
the theories are built on sand (for example, theories of white-
collar unionism), or little progress has yet been made (for
example, institutional–empiricist theories), or a critical reap-
praisal is needed of key postulates (for example, proletarianisation theories), or they are at such an abstract level that they
give only the broadest of hints about the line of enquiry to
pursue (for example, theories of the welfare state).

We are not saying that they can all now be dismissed as
being of no account. In our view all the theories and work we
have looked at have some ideas to offer. The theories of
white-collar trade unionism are probably right to stress the
importance of income levels, job security and other substan-
tive working conditions. They are probably right to stress the
effects of bureaucratisation on the similarity of experience,
and mechanisation on the nature of work. The proletarianisation theories are right to pay attention to class, although
perhaps class relations should have been looked at instead of
class positions. And it would scarcely be wise to ignore the
institutional context formed by collective bargaining arrangements and industrial relations dispute procedures – even if
Clegg has over-emphasised their importance in explaining
union behaviour. Finally, the theories of trade unionism that
have focused on the role of the state and the welfare state
suggest there is a need to take into account the nature of the
state, its relations to the capitalist private sector, and the
consequences of both for the treatment by the state of its
employees.

We are not going to indulge now in a bout of grand theory
building, as we think that would not be very productive. The
theories we have reviewed above have been useful to us as a
starting point, but the theoretical explanations which will
gradually emerge in the course of this book have been developed by us in the course of our research. We have discussed
the data as we have gone along, argued amongst ourselves
about what it means, hypothesised, and in the end decided on

an interpretation which we think matches the empirical experiences of at least some social work activists. The second part of our book is an empirical exploration of some of these ideas – so we will return to them.

Part II
Issues Facing Trade Unionism in Social Work

Part II

Introduction

Some 'veteran' social work activists take the late 1970s as their benchmark for measuring the vitality of social work trade unionism. For them it represents the period in which determined struggles were fought against the traditional methods of negotiation with employers, the bureaucratic centralism of their union, and old ideas of the limits of proper trade union action in local government. But, in fact, each stage in the development of social work trade unionism needs to be appreciated in its own terms and at its own pace. At each stage, social work activists found themselves in a distinct set of circumstances, these circumstances providing both opportunities and problems. And at each stage their trade union activity raised, more or less distinctly, specific issues and dilemmas.

Highlighting the historical path of social work trade unionism can, inadvertently, create a misleading impression about the salience of various issues and dilemmas at a given point in time. In some social services departments the spread of trade union consciousness and practical trade union activity was later than the 1970s. And many social work activists are part of a younger generation for whom the events of the 1970s are known only as a secondhand experience. There are also the NALGO branches where the veteran activists are still struggling with issues and dilemmas that emerged in the 1970s, principally due to the specific social relations in the branch and the interventions of political 'masters', which have combined to retard the development of social work trade unionism in their locale.

The historical line of development of social work trade unionism is not obliterated by these 'deviations', but it means that the issues and dilemmas of trade union action are continually being experienced for the first time by newly-active individuals and by newly-active social services workplace organisations. To express the same thing differently, social work trade unionism is subject to uneven development, with the result that all the issues and dilemmas studied by us exist and are being faced by contemporary social work trade unionists somewhere today.

The real beginnings of social work trade unionism (which is not the same as the start of trade unionism amongst social workers) occurred in the early 1970s, when newly-established social services departments were set apart from other departments as centres of union activism. But great care must be taken not to exaggerate the spread of this emergent activism; it was largely confined to field social workers in local authorities in London and other cities. The first cases of industrial action were typically locally based and small-scale. In the first few years of the 1970s, there were disagreements between councils and trade unions over night-duty teams in field work services. In at least one local authority, failure to agree satisfactory pay arrangements for these teams led to social workers refusing to provide this service. Then there were disputes over issues such as the grading of social work posts and homelessness. One dilemma confronting the social work activists of NALGO, the main white-collar union, was whether or not to act independently of their fellow union members. Whilst acting autonomously allowed them to take the initiative and to act in a bold and vigorous manner, it denied them the added strength provided by the support of other members in the same branch. A related issue was the character of this trade union activity. Where this activity focused on issues primarily of specific concern to social workers – issues in other words which were linked to the nature of the service being provided to clients – this created obstacles to a united front with other trade unionists. The latter were inclined to view with suspicion the extension of trade union activities to

matters of council policy. This could be seen as too radical –
even too political. And, of course, it is important to recognise
that many local authority staff, up and down the country, still
see things like this.

In the closing years of the 1970s, social work trade unionism
entered a new phase when the significance of industrial action
became different. Industrial action was then part of a mobilisation by social work activists to challenge the centralised
negotiating arrangements of Whitleyism. We will examine the
nature of Whitleyism shortly (in Chapter 2), but we can
usefully note here that in this period it was its manifestation in
a national form that was the chief target of the social work
activists' offensive. Not only was the ending of Whitleyism
forced on to the agenda at NALGO's annual delegate conferences in 1977, 1978 and 1979, but also a number of branches
took all-out strike action to enforce local claims on the pay and
grading of social workers in 1978–79. The struggle to end
Whitleyism, certainly in some NALGO branches, led to long-
drawn-out trials of strength. The issue it raised, and this was
an issue that was clearly perceived by some activists, concerned the capacity of social work trade unionists to compel
individual employers to abandon Whitleyism, even when led
by energetic and capable shop steward committees. The dilemma these experiences posed for social work activists arose
from the fact that an all-out strike was seen as the most
powerful mode of expressing trade union power and yet there
were councils who had withstood this action. Why, some were
asking themselves, hadn't the strikes hurt the councils more
than they did? Many social work activists are still asking this
question following their own experiences of industrial action
against their own employers.

The late 1970s were also marked by developments in the
relationship between NALGO and the main professional body
for social workers, the British Association of Social Workers
(BASW). The latter body appeared to be threatening NALGO's
position as the main union organisation for local authority
social workers. In 1978, BASW was involved in the decision to
set up the British Union of Social Workers (BUSW), which

was established in 1979 as a new and independent union for social workers. Not surprisingly, NALGO resented BASW's activities and responded by severing a formal relationship with the professional association through a joint consultative committee. This dislocation of the relationship between the two organisations signalled the emergence within trade union circles of a debate about the union role in professional matters. A number of branches set up working parties or working groups to look at policy issues. At national level, NALGO began in the 1980s to present a union viewpoint on policies for the personal social services. In 1982 it responded to the Barclay Report and in 1984 there was a National Executive Council Working Party report dealing with personal social services generally.

Following the election of a Conservative government in May 1979, the development of social work trade unionism faced an increasingly difficult set of conditions. It was not just the crisis created by the collisions between the central government's policy of cutting public expenditure and the policies of Labour controlled local authorities. It was not just the changes made in the legal framework, which were denounced by the British trade union movement as aimed at undermining union organisation and the union movement's capacity to take effective industrial action. It was also, crucially, the loss of confidence among the ordinary union members which was compounded by a loss of initiative by the union leadership at all levels of the movement. The post-war styles of leadership, adapted to full employment and a relatively favourable bargaining position, suddenly seemed inept. And, many argue, they still are.

At first glance, the developments of this period seem to lack coherence. We have already noted the broadening of the union role to encompass more explicitly the professional issues of social services policy, both at branch and national level. Then there was the first national action of residential social workers in 1983, which began in the September with an overtime ban and a ban on admissions of clients to residential homes, and ended in December with about 1500 social workers on strike. Importantly, but much less sensationally, there was a widespread movement of social work activists into positions of responsibility in NALGO. And, at the local level, the activists were grappling with the issue of the development of new methods that would be effective now that all-out strikes seemed to be definitely out of the question. A number of union organisations in social services departments are currently at this stage of evolving methods and tactics to replace all-out strike action.

So we see in this brief introduction that different issues and dilemmas have come into the foreground at different stages. Social work trade unionism is very unevenly developed and all the issues and dilemmas are still to be found somewhere: sometimes affecting particular individuals, and sometimes whole union organisations in social services departments. In the chapters that follow it will be our task to explore these issues and dilemmas in detail. But before we proceed with this task there is one final point that we must make clear. We must stress that the rise of social work trade unionism within NALGO was not an isolated development. It coincided with, and was intertwined with, the growth of greater militancy in other sections of the NALGO membership. Moreover, within the NALGO of the 1970s, there was an upsurge of interest in a more active form of union democracy. These are things that have to be taken into account in order to form a proper assessment of the significance of social work trade unionism. There have been occasions when the relatively faster growth of activism and militancy in a social services department led social workers to the false conclusion that change was only occurring in their department. This helped to foster divisions within NALGO branches where there was resentment of the implication that activism and proper trade union consciousness was a monopoly of social services shop steward organisations.

The next three chapters, then, discuss what we see as the three main issues that have faced, and still face, social work trade unionism. These are, firstly, the sectionalism found amongst some social workers who in practice confine their union solidarity to their immediate colleagues in the social services department and fail to pursue solidarity with other union members in the same trade union branch; secondly, the rank-and-filism which weakens the national solidarity of trade

union members in local government and is another form of
sectionalism; and thirdly, the struggle to find better methods
of fighting for membership interests, especially in the context
of the attack on local government and local democracy by the
state when all-out strike action may be counter-productive.

2

Radicalism and Sectionalism

INTRODUCTION

Social work trade unionism was born in the early 1970s, apparently the offspring of the Seebohm-instigated reorganisation of personal social services in local government. The first signs of the 'new trade unionism' was the emergence of workplace activism in the newly constructed social services departments of local authorities in the big cities. And then, also in these same departments, industrial action began to happen.

The events in local government of the early and mid-1970s are not easily fitted into the usual scenarios of union growth and surging militancy, in which groups of workers undergo rapid unionisation at the same time as there is a wave of militancy. Indeed all periods of substantial union growth in British history have happened alongside periods of labour militancy. The three episodes which stand out in this connection are the wave of 'new unionism' in 1889–91, the decade of working class mobilisation which began in 1910 and finished around 1920, and the period from 1968 to the early 1970s. In each of these cases aggregate union membership in Britain grew rapidly and the number of strikes soared. But in social work it was not so much that there was a growth of union density, as that the activities of social workers as trade unionists were no longer merged and indistinctive in NALGO activity generally.

Furthermore, there have been lingering confusions and uncertainties over the character of social work trade unionism. Rightly or wrongly, it is usually assumed that white-collar workers turn to militant trade unionism as their market position deteriorates. In particular, it has often been assumed that declining income differentials over manual workers pushes white-collar workers reluctantly into industrial action. But in the case of the social workers, their pre-1960 history was characterised by low salaries and they appear to have suffered no sharp reduction in salaries in the late 1960s or early 1970s that would account for the outbreak of industrial militancy. So was, and is, the explanation really to be found in the growth of radical political ideas amongst social workers? Or, is it right to argue, as some have done, that a militant form of professionalism has developed because the professional bodies representing social workers have not been able to achieve the type of professional control over social work activities that, say, doctors' organisations have secured in medicine?

Some of these confusions and uncertainties undoubtedly stem from the difficulties which are consequent on trying to apply categories such as 'political' or 'professional' to behaviour in the local government terrain. If 'political' social workers embark on collective struggle to change the policies of social services departments and thereby improve the quality of services provided to working-class clients, the action may be termed political because of their motivation. It is also true, however, that such struggles will be seen as political because they lead to the social workers challenging priorities that have been determined by democratically elected councillors. But then again, if 'professional' social workers attempt to use trade union organisation and methods to achieve professional goals, they will also be acting politically. Professionals are concerned about occupational self-control, nominally in the clients' interest, but if they are employed in local government there is obviously a conflict between this and democratic control of services by the elected members of the council. It is evident, therefore, that in the local government context, it will always be difficult to separate, accurately and completely, the effects of radical political ideas and the effects of militant professionalism.

In this chapter we begin by looking at the material conditions facing social workers. The most critical of these have been the changing organisation of social work as a labour-process, the organisation of local authorities, the reorganisation and reform of local government, Whitleyism, and the changing nature of NALGO. We will then be exploring the character of the early social work trade union activity, and the issues and dilemmas which this activity posed to the activists in social services departments. Finally, we will be looking at the results of this activity, not only the changes produced in the situation of social workers, but also the lessons that these experiences taught.

THE CHANGING LABOUR-PROCESS

The labour-process in social work may be conceived, as a first approximation, as an activity which is carried out on a 'raw material', which consists of people in various degrees of 'distress' and, very broadly, people who are judged incapable of sustaining themselves in and through the existing forms of 'ordinary' social life (for example, people with a mental handicap, or with a mental illness, some old people, and young children without 'proper' parents). The product of the labour-process is people whose distress has been eased or who have been placed in situations or institutions so that they are now supported to an extent that they are able to sustain themselves or, more minimally, so that their physical survival is extended.

Social work as a labour-process has historically taken various forms – and continues to do so at the present time. It has manifested itself as activity by family, friends and neighbours. It has manifested itself as private sector voluntary work by individuals and organisations. In more modern times, the state has increasingly stepped in as the organiser of this labour-process and in doing so has brought this activity well and truly into the social economy. This labour-process is now being carried out very often by labour that has been hired specifically by the state to do this work.

The consequences of bringing the social work labour-process into the state sector of social work, both in the short term and in the long term, are not well understood and are disputed. Irrespective of this, the numbers of social workers paid by the state has continued to grow over forty or more years and seems to be irreversible, even though governments of different political persuasions come and go. Indeed, the tendency seems to be all the time in the direction of 'society' expecting more from social workers, especially when things go wrong and 'scandals' of one sort or another hit the headlines. Whilst politicians may stress the responsibilities of families and communities in dealing with social work problems, in practice the state's responsibility for social work increases, and continued to do so under the Thatcher governments of 1979 and 1983. Politicians do not appear to understand the social and economic forces that are leading inexorably in the direction of public sector forms of social work.

This is not to say, however, that the state is eagerly pumping more and more resources into generously funded social work activities. Fiscal planning of welfare services by the state is always under pressure, albeit varying amounts of pressure, by demands to reduce the burden on the profit-making sector of the economy, and by demands to cut excessive levels of taxation on the private citizen. The budgetary problems of social work due to these pressures are affected, in their timing at least, by the division of the state into a part that determines the state's income from taxation (that is, central government) and a part that administers the delivery of social services (that is, local government). In consequence of conflicts between these two parts of the state, there are times when pressures to reduce expenditure on welfare services are not successfully transmitted from central to local government. The pressures may be diverted to other services or may be delayed. So whilst the continued expansion of state social work goes ahead, it is fitful and jerky, and it is contingent on the balance of forces inside and outside the state.

It is against this background that we should understand the development of the labour-process in state social work and the various and contradictory attempts by the state to reorganise social work to make it more effective. As well as this background, we also have to recognise that the labour-process in state social work is controlled and regulated directly by the state, and that social workers have various collective organisations to represent their occupational interests. This labour-process can only be understood in terms of contest. Therefore, understanding the position of labour in state social work involves understanding the intersections of three more sets of social forces. Firstly, we have reorganisations of the labour-process by the state under the influence of shifts in its social policies. Secondly, we have the actions of social workers through their collective organisations. And thirdly, we have interventions by the state which are guided not by its social policies but, at a deeper level, by its attempts to manage and pacify social workers as state employed labour. These intersecting social forces have to be placed against the background we have outlined above. Evidently, the analysis of the development of the labour-process in state social work is very complex. We would go further than this and say that this sketching of the factors involved in the development of the social work labour-process suggests that it is materially different from the development of labour-processes in the private sector and therefore any generalisation from the latter to the former should not be done unguardedly.

The labour-process in state social work currently reflects the results of over thirty years of change under attempts at state control. In the 1950s and 1960s, social work took place within quite separate branches of the public sector. This division of labour was reflected in the diverse labels used to describe state social workers: there were almoners (medical social workers) in hospitals, probation officers, and a very small number of psychiatric social workers; in local government, but separated into different departments, were health and welfare officers, child care officers (whose numbers increased markedly in the early 1960s) and education welfare officers; and there was a large, and almost totally unqualified, workforce in residential homes. There was little co-operation between these various groups of social workers in the delivery of their services.

It is interesting to note what this shows about the nature of the 'product' of the labour-process in social work at that time, which was, of course, defined by the state. Putting to one side the clients of the services who were placed in residential homes, social workers were specialising in specific types of social distress. Up to that time, therefore, the state had been accumulating responsibilities for specific distresses in an *ad hoc* sort of way. It had still to develop a generalised responsibility for social problems. Also, these services did not have to interrelate because of the very special nature of the raw material being worked upon – that is, people. If the various types of specialised labour in car production do not co-operate and interrelate, the product (in this case, a car) is not produced. This is not so in social work because the raw material/product is an active element in the labour process. This is significant because it logically implies that pressures to develop co-operation between different types of social workers are state induced and not due to an intrinsic requirement for the completion of the labour-process.

A major development in the labour-process of social work was brought about by the Local Authority Social Services Act of 1970 which required local authorities to set up social services committees at council level, to employ Directors of Social Services, and to establish social services departments to carry out the policies of the new committees. The new departments came into being in England and Wales in 1971, whilst in Scotland similarly comprehensive departments had already been set up as a result of an Act passed in 1968.

In the wake of this legislation, some of the previously separate branches of social work were brought together in the new social services departments. Initially, social workers specialising in child care and health and welfare services were combined; in Coventry, for example, social workers were drawn from the children's department, the welfare department and the education department to form the new social services department in 1971. Later, in 1974, the employment of hospital social workers was transferred from the National Health Service to the new social services departments, although they often retained their offices in hospital premises.

The cause of the reorganisation was a change in the state's policy on social work which was reflected in the report of the Seebohm Committee published in 1968. The report signalled two important changes of policy: first, the policy became one of offering a, theoretically speaking, comprehensive service with respect to social problems; and, secondly, the policy required greater co-operation amongst social workers. These fundamental changes were articulated in the report as proposals for new unified departments which would provide the range of services currently carried out by separate children's departments, welfare departments, and so on. The report called for a community-based and family-orientated service which would be available to all. Importantly, the report called for comprehensive, area-based teams of social workers, managed by senior social workers. The field social workers in the area teams were to specialise to some degree but each family or individual was to have a key social worker. This point meant that the Committee envisaged that social workers would specialise but would also have a generalist dimension to their social work practice. In fact, the departments set up after the 1970 Act sometimes went much further than this in breaking down specialist distinctions and went a long way towards developing truly generic social workers.

Obviously, this reorganisation of the labour-process in the early 1970s still left a number of branches of social work as separate and isolated specialisms – for example, education welfare officers and probation officers. But for many social workers this was a major transformation of their labour-process. Alongside this change there was also a strong annual growth in the numbers of local authority social work staff. In 1968 there had been about fifteen social workers per 100 000 population in the local authorities of England and Wales. By 1971, the ratio had increased to twenty-five per 100 000 (Younghusband, 1978, p. 294). In summary, the development of social work in the state sector had resulted in increased numbers of social workers, who were working in larger employment concentrations in the new departments, and who were less divided by specialist skills and knowledge. These trends were very favourable for the growth of a stronger collective consciousness among social workers.

Trends towards concentration were further reinforced by a massive reorganisation of local authorities in England and Wales in 1974 which left local government with a smaller number of larger authorities. This had been preceded by a similar reorganisation of London's local authorities in 1965 and was followed by reorganisation in Scotland in 1975. The differential timing of reorganisation of local government may partly explain the earlier development of trade union activity in some of the London councils. Indeed, the sequence of developments in London, specifically the occurrence of local government reorganisation prior to the Seebohm reorganisation of social work, may have helped to avoid the integration problems some social workers report where separate social services departments were combined in 1974. This matter is confused, however, by the geographical dispersion of social services workforces in county departments outside London. For whilst large numbers of social workers who are employed by the same local authority may be said to be in a situation of employment 'concentration', a situation which is often thought to be conducive to unionisation, they may not experience concentration if their work organisation is geographically dispersed. Therefore, both the disruptive effect of the 1974 reorganisation and the inhibiting effect of geographical dispersion may be important in the pace of development of trade union activity in the county councils.

There was no *inevitable* reason why the development of conditions favourable to the strengthening of the collective consciousness of social workers should have been linked to an upsurge of trade union consciousness and activity, let alone militancy. The changes in the labour-process might have instead promoted involvement in professional associations. Terence Johnson (1972), for example, argues as follows:

> Professionalism is associated with a homogeneous occupational community. Homogeneity of outlook and interest is associated with a relatively low degree of specialisation within the occupation and by recruitment from similar social backgrounds . . . However, the culturally divisive tendencies of specialisation may be contained within an occupation already characterised by professional institutions. (p. 53)

In fact, professional associations in social work appeared to anticipate the formation of a homogeneous occupational community. In 1970, just as the Act requiring the setting up of new social services departments was passed, the British As-

sociation of Social Workers (BASW) was formed by amalga-
mating a number of specialist social work bodies. The
organisations which became part of BASW were the Association of Psychiatric Social Workers, the Society of Mental
Welfare Officers, the Institute of Medical Social Workers, the
Association of Child Care Officers, the Association of Family
Case Workers, the Moral Welfare Workers Association, and
the Association of Social Workers. The fact that the reconstruction of the professional representation of social workers
occurred prior to the setting up of the new social services
departments is an important argument against seeing occupational bodies as merely an outgrowth of a collective consciousness shaped by a shared occupational activity. There is
obviously some scope for choice and room for manoeuvre on
the part of those who control occupational bodies. And, of
course, individual members of social work professional associations could probably see advantages in a single body in a
post-Seebohm world, in which case their specialist activities
did not prevent them from developing a view of their joint
interests which transcended their current differences in
specialism.

The newly formed BASW saw itself from the beginning as
specifically representing the more highly 'skilled' social workers. In BASW's memorandum, articles and bye-laws it was
stated that membership was restricted to qualified social
workers and people occupying posts 'in which in the opinion
of [BASW's] Council a qualified social worker would appro-
priately be employed'. Its claim to be a body representing
professional workers was, however, severely impeded. Unlike
doctors, there was no state guarantee of a monopoly for social
workers by means of a requirement to have a licence to
operate (except in a few legal aspects). Furthermore its own
status as a professional association could not be boosted by
becoming a qualifying body with its own training and education system to award qualifications to social workers.
(Much of the Institute of Personnel Management's status as
the professional body for personnel specialists, for example, is
based on being the qualifying body.) This was because responsibility for training was given to the Central Council for
Education and Training in Social Work (CCETSW), which

was set up as the qualifying body for all social work training in 1971.

If the Seebohm reorganisation was going to boost professional activity, a substantial increase in membership should have been expected after 1971 when social services departments were set up. When BASW was formed in 1970 it had about 10 000 members. It gained members and in 1973 its membership exceeded 11 000, but after that it fell back and for most of the late 1970s its membership was slightly below 10 000 (if we ignore free members). In the early 1980s the fortunes of BASW deteriorated and membership fell below 9000, reaching a low point in December 1982 with only 7845 members.

The other professional association of the early 1970s was the Residential Child Care Association, which catered for social workers in the residential setting, but this was much smaller than BASW. In 1974, when it became the Residential Care Association, it had some 3000 members. It has remained the smaller body in the 1980s when it has changed its name yet again to become the Social Care Association.

The subsequent development of the social work labour-process is dealt with here only briefly, but it can be usefully noted that changes in state policy on social work and hospital care after 1979, as well as changes in budgetary allocation processes in local government resulting from attempts by central government to change the scale and pattern of public expenditure, have fostered the introduction of greater specialisation in field work. Although this represents, in a sense, the reversal of the trend towards generic social work under Seebohm, the difference this time is that it is occurring inside the social services department. Two other changes which occurred for quite different reasons were the introduction of a three-level job hierarchy for the main body of social workers in social services departments and the move towards decentralised services in some progressive councils.

These are all very contradictory developments. Much of the impetus behind specialisation comes from the community care policy which, since 1979, has resulted in the movement of children, people with a mental handicap, and people with mental illnesses out of residential homes and hospitals ('institutions'). Certainly for the latter groups this has involved developing support systems for individual clients because the community's capacity to care for such people is inadequate. To a degree, therefore, there has been a swing back to the pre-Seebohm era of focusing on individuals and specialising in particular forms of social distress. On the other hand, decentralisation in progressive authorities has continued the See-bohm report's concern with a community service to all and has continued the emphasis on generic social work practice.

The introduction of three pay grades (referred to as levels) for the main body of social workers in 1979 had different effects on the social work labour-process, depending very much on the actions of local trade unionists. In some places trade unionists have insisted on automatic progression up through the three levels and, consequently, the labour-process has been unaffected. In other local authorities, it seems that managers have used Level 3 as a professional grade and have thus ended up moving the division of labour inside their departments towards a relatively small number of highly 'skilled' social workers and a relatively large number of less skilled staff. That is, the division of labour in social work has been developed in a more hierarchical direction. Whilst this has caused concern amongst some social work activists, for it is usually assumed that more hierarchical organisations retard trade union consciousness and activity, there has been no systematic assessment of the consequences of the changed pay structure for social work trade unionism.

It is clear that changes in the organisation of the social work labour-process have been on a massive scale and must be considered in any analysis of the emergence and development of social work trade unionism. Now we will look at another important factor shaping the circumstances of trade union activity and that is the organisation of local authorities.

THE ORGANISATION OF LOCAL AUTHORITIES

Few people with any knowledge of local government would deny that state social workers work in a bureaucratic organisational framework, or that this has very important implications for their trade union activity. But rarely is the specific nature of the bureaucratic context of social workers probed to any extent. In general the word bureaucratic is used to describe one or more of the following characteristics: the hierarchical nature of control; a proliferation of 'red tape'; the slowness of the departments to respond to any change of policy or the emergence of any need in the local community; and a tendency towards some kind of impersonal 'officiousness'. These characteristics are commonly associated with bureaucracies, and no doubt are to be found in local government. The point is, however, that when we look more closely at local government we see that it is not a typical bureaucracy (if there is such a thing) but that it has distinctive features which need to be understood.

Social services departments are, like other departments in local authorities, run on very hierarchical lines. But that just means that social workers have bosses. The key question concerns the locus of decision-making in the hierarchy. Are all the decisions being taken at the top, at the bottom, or somewhere in between? To make any progress in this area we need to make two distinctions with respect to the types of decisions involved. First we must distinguish decision levels, especially between day-to-day, operational decisions, and decisions concerned with the overall strategy or policy. Secondly, the making of decisions on employment-related matters tends to be handled quite differently from decision-making in service-related matters. In effect, the issue of how centralised is decision making has to be judged in at least four major areas (see Table 2.1).

TABLE 2.1 Decision-making in the hierarchy

	Employment related	Service related
Strategy/policy level	1	2
Day-to-day operational level	3	4

Where employment related matters are concerned, for example, recruitment, selection, staffing levels, discipline and grievances, it is common to find considerable involvement by elected members and highly formalised and standardised procedures which severely constrain and limit the discretion of staff at all levels of the hierarchy. Alan Fowler (1980), writing on personnel management in local government, has expressed the following view about this close involvement of elected members:

> Member involvement in employment matters is a unique feature of local government. In no other large-scale employment sector do elected representatives of the public at large, working voluntarily, part-time and unpaid, and with no formal training or experience for this specific role, act as 'managing employers' to the considerable extent which has become normal in most local authorities. (p. 66)

In the case of service related matters, when the early social work activists first started seeking recognition from senior social services management, they found them reluctant to discuss council policy. There were meetings over individual issues and day-to-day operational issues, but policy matters were embargoed as being the prerogative of the council.

Trade union activists in social work are often dubious about the real control exercised by councillors. As one field worker put it:

> Ultimately the most important decisions are taken at the council level, although in most cases the recommendation from the Director will form the basis of any council policy. So councillors, although they can quibble about the total amount of finances, are not really in a position to argue about the whys and the wherefores. Because they haven't got the experience. They are amateurs.

There can also be real confusion about exactly who is in control. Social work shop stewards often complain that the senior management have blamed the relevant council committee for a bad decision, or no decision, or say that senior management have said that they can't make a decision because it is a matter of council policy. And at the same time the council committee blames the senior management for decisions made or not made. The decision eventually gets made, but social work activists are left none the wiser as to who is really in charge.

Whatever the situation, policy related to service matters tends to be decided at, or near, the top of the hierarchy, presumably reflecting the public accountability of the elected council members for service policies. In contrast, operational decisions of a day-to-day nature are often made at the bottom of the hierarchy. The obvious explanation for this would be the strong emphasis on social work as a professional occupation. According to most notions of professionalism, the professional is an expert who knows best and is trusted to act ethically and in the best interests of the client. Thus there is no need for close surveillance by supervisors nor is there a need for the discretion of the social worker to be hedged by rules and procedures. This professional rationale for operational discretion may be regarded as merely a self-serving occupational ideology. And it could be argued that there has been a recent development of more procedures and controls in some areas of social work, such as child abuse casework. It is still true, however, that the work activities of social workers in their generality are not bureaucratically structured, which is to say, not subjected to close circumscription by rules and procedures (Davies, 1986).

So, to sum up the key points of the argument so far, the bureaucratic nature of local government is most pronounced in relation to employment related matters, whereas on the service side, decision-making on policy is centralised rather than bureaucratic. It can be said that in local government in general and in social work in particular, there is bureaucratic control of labour, not of the labour-process.

These specific characteristics do have an impact on trade unionism in social work. Firstly, the procedures and local agreements in the industrial relations area are extremely detailed and formal by comparison with many other parts of the British industrial relations system. How this detail and formality reacts back on the social relations in local government is difficult to say authoritatively, but there is certainly a strong tone of constitutionality in dealings between the two sides. Secondly, the centralisation and ambiguities of social services policy-making frustrates attempts by social services activists to take up policy issues with their social services management, although individual, day-to-day matters may be easy to take up. This can lead to demands by social work activists to have local machinery through which they can meet, and maybe negotiate, with their real employers, by which they mean elected members.

Another aspect of bureaucratic organisation which has been remarked on is its tendency to stratify occupational groups and 'formalise incipient cleavages' (Johnson, 1972, p. 80). How, if at all, does this manifest itself in the specific case of social workers? Are they stratified and split? Even before the late 1970s and the introduction of the Level 3 social work grade, social work was highly stratified. In the field work services of one London borough there were at least four grades of social workers in the non-managerial strata: ancillary, assistant, social worker and senior social worker. The senior social workers were not always seen as non-managerial staff; the exact line between management and workers depended to some extent on personalities.

This stratification should not be seen as following in any systematic way the gradient of skill, knowledge or responsibility distributed amongst social services staff. Social workers on lower grades may be doing as much responsible work as, or more than, others higher up the career structure. And the movement up the job scale may have as much to do with the numbers of experienced social workers in an area as it does with the skills, knowledge and capacity for responsibility of an individual.

In a highly stratified occupational group such as social workers in local government, the boundary between management and workers is not intrinsic to the stratification. It may even be deliberately constructed. This may be done using various means – for example, by taking staff off the standard pay scales, making changes to job descriptions and job titles, putting pressure on senior staff to join unions other than NALGO, or suggesting that an active role in NALGO is incompatible with senior status in local government. It may also result from senior grades of staff belonging to professional associations. In some social services departments, the cleavage between managerial grades and non-managerial grades has been caused or reinforced by the development of 'managerial professionalism' (see Stewart, 1983, p. 217 for one definition of this term).

Stewart has examined the relationship between management and professional values and largely sees it as mediated by the hierarchy:

> A professional ideology will come to be influenced or even replaced by management values as the professional ascends the management hierarchy . . . Few senior officers drawn from professional ranks would ever admit they had modified their professional stance . . . While emphasising their own 'wider' professionalism senior officers within the service will, however, tend to be critical of the 'narrow' professionalism of some of their staff. (Stewart, 1983, p. 104)

In the case of social workers, the relationship actually varies from one locale to another. In some local authorities, the identification with professionalism is made by the managerial grades and vocally rejected by field social workers. The membership of the professional association is a must for the hopefuls who would join the managerial grades and membership subsequently confers a degree of prestige which buttresses managerial authority. In this case it would be wrong to see the movement up the career ladder as corrupting pure professional values; joining the professional association is a shrewd and instrumental move by those who would be upwardly mobile.

In many areas where a strong trade union consciousness has developed, the professional dimension may be almost totally invisible. Social work activists are hard put to think of any BASW members and there is no overtly professional activity or organisation. Indeed the activists never even think about BASW and certainly do not worry about the relationship between them and BASW members. In their view, trade union activity is automatically concerned with professional issues about the quality of the service being offered to clients. And in some departments the activists see no inconsistency in being in dual membership of NALGO and BASW, seeing the former as important for occupational representation and the latter as useful for its publications and the diffusion of the latest knowledge on social work skills.

From a trade union point of view, stratification, managerial professionalism, and even some sets of professional values can be a nuisance and cause aggravation to social work activists. But it has to be recognised that professionalism in all its guises – organisational and ideological, visible and invisible – has been a continuing force in social work and is not going to go away.

REORGANISATION AND REFORM

In the years between 1965 and 1975 the whole system of local government in Great Britain was restructured, starting with the London authorities in 1965, then the rest of England and Wales in 1974, and ending with the Scottish authorities in 1975. This was enormously important because of its consequences for the structure of employment in local government, but also because, particularly in 1974, it opened the door to the simultaneous restructuring of local government management. In the 1974 reorganisation many new councils attempted to move towards a management structure based on a corporate approach and a stronger development of the personnel function. These developments were proselytised in the Bains Report, which was produced in 1972 by a working party set up to consider the management structures of the new local authorities. In the 1980s the reorganisation of local government was extended down to the operational level by a trend towards decentralisation of services, especially social services and housing. This decentralisation has not been a homogeneous phenomenon and has been undertaken by councils for very different reasons in very different circumstances. But like the other reorganisations and reforms mentioned, it has been important in changing the conditions in which social work trade unionism develops.

In the early 1960s the administrative apparatus of public power was subjected to a critical and searching review. There is more than one possible explanation for the timing of this review. It may be that the continuing decline in the British economy, which caused politicians, including Conservative ones, to look more favourably on a strengthened role for the state in economic planning, led them to see the need to bring about a general modernisation of the administrative machinery. An alternative view is that the attempts to negotiate an entry into the European Common Market had stimulated a questioning of the British approach to administration. It is probably also significant that modernisation was a major theme of the Labour Party's campaign in the general election of 1964. The early 1960s were, therefore, a period in which there was a surge of confidence in the ability of the state to steer the economy to achieve faster growth and, simultaneously, a growth of critical attitudes about the administrative capacity of state structures. The most important restructuring of local government in this century began against this background, even if not directly caused by it.

After the reorganisation of local government, England and Wales were left with a two-tier structure of councils in London, in the metropolitan areas and in the non-metropolitan areas. The distribution of functions between the two tiers differed. The social services function was carried out by the lower tier councils in London and the metropolitan areas and the upper tier councils in the non-metropolitan areas. In 1986 the structure of local government was again changed, involving the abolition of the Greater London Council and the metropolitan counties, but this has left undisturbed the distribution of responsibilities for social services.

The size and local significance of the social services non-manual workforce, which includes field workers, residential workers, day centre staff, administrative workers and others, does seem to be closely correlated with this tripartite employment structure. (Some residential and day centre workers, it should be noted, are not included in the non-manual category.) As Table 2.2 shows, whilst the average non-manual workforce is considerably bigger in the social services departments of non-metropolitan counties, it is, in fact, the London boroughs which have a relatively large number of social services personnel when compared to the total non-manual workforce or when compared to the population covered by the local authority.

TABLE 2.2   Non-manual social services workforce in English and Welsh
local authorities, 1984

Type of council	Number of councils	Average number of non-manual social services employees	Social services employees as a percentage of all non-manual employees	Ratio of population to social services employees
Non-metropolitan county	47	1254	8.6	533
Metropolitan district	36	782	8.9	404
London boroughs and the City	33	768	15.8	271

SOURCE: Adapted from *Joint Manpower Watch Quarterly*, 37 (LACSAB) 25 June 1984.

There are innumerable other differences which accompany
these statistical contrasts but we can usefully refer here to the
differences in the political complexion of councils, in the
degree of workforce dispersion, and in the social and economic
environments. Generally it is the social workers in the non-
metropolitan counties that find themselves in the most un-
promising conditions for trade union organisation. Whilst
they are employed in very large departments, the territory
they cover is much greater than that covered by their counterparts in the other two types of council. This makes the
development of vigorous and well functioning union organisation much more difficult to achieve. Their employers are more
likely to be Conservative councils whose attitudes towards
trade unionism are hostile or, at best, neutral. Moreover, they
work in regions with quite different social structures from
those found in urban environments and where the dominant
forms of economic activity are associated with weaker trade
union traditions. Also, despite their numbers, social workers
in the shires are a smaller proportion of the membership in
their local union branches than are their London counterparts
and this seems, at times, to be reflected in a less influential
role in the making of branch policy.

'Corporate management' has been introduced in local
government over this period. Stewart (1983) has suggested

that the corporate approach was developed as a critique of local government management and policy-making, which were both seen as very uncoordinated because of the strength of the departmental approach and the direct linking of individual departments and council committees:

> It was not merely that local authorities were divided into departments but that the departments were matched by committees and their boundaries marked by a dominant profession. While the critique did not deny the need for departmentalism, it argued that differentiation must be matched by mechanisms capable of integrating the work of the authority. . . . (Stewart, 1983, p. 167)

This critique says that each council had multiple hierarchical control structures and this led to a fragmentary approach to local government. The corporate management proposals were aimed at remodelling the control systems of individual local authorities into single, unified hierarchical structures. Three mechanisms were suggested to overcome the lack of co-ordination: the introduction of a policy and resources committee to co-ordinate council policy-making; the creation of an authoritative chief executive to head the council staff; and the formation of a management team of chief officers to pull the senior strata of officers together.

In certain respects, the promotion of the idea of corporate management suggested that a convergence with private sector management structures was being planned. This appearance was definitely reinforced by the introduction of the job title of director instead of the older title of chief officer. The fact that these changes in management were introduced and consolidated just at the time that the Labour government, elected in 1974, was announcing and planning public expenditure cuts seemed to many as strong circumstantial evidence that corporate management had been introduced for sinister reasons and was a very retrograde step.

The Bains Report, which set out the ideas of corporate management, also proposed the replacement of establishment officers by personnel specialists. Before 1974 there were few personnel specialists and the existing establishment officers concerned themselves with staffing numbers rather than the full range of personnel management activities. It could be argued, therefore, that the local authorities were neglecting the human resources that their workforces represented, and were failing to develop and improve the value of those resources through the use of personnel management techniques and programmes. The advocacy of the introduction of personnel management, like support for corporate management, seemed to many to be an argument for 'borrowing' management forms from the private sector. And also like corporate management, the widespread setting up of personnel functions in local authorities coincided with cuts in public expenditure and thus seemed to confirm the alien and hostile nature of this import from the private sector.

In the years that followed 1974, personnel specialists found themselves spending more and more time on industrial relations. It was this aspect of their role which more than any other showed a marked tendency to increase. It may have been due to the legislation of the social contract era which created important rights for individual workers and trade unions. And local government certainly became very conflict-prone in the late 1970s with industrial action becoming a common weapon in use by manual and non-manual trade unionists alike. Many of the personnel specialists themselves identified the critical factor as being the growth of negotiating and consultation processes at local level. This was undoubtedly connected with the development of incentive payment systems for manual workers and the increasing significance of workplace representation amongst manual and non-manual staffs.

Nowadays, personnel specialists are involved at all levels of local authorities, usually as advisers, although sometimes as negotiators on behalf of the local authority. Their influence is often considerable, their discretion in some councils has become very wide, and, on balance, they are still gaining in importance in employment related matters. When asked, personnel specialists will admit that they are satisfied with their level of influence over the councillors: their advice is usually accepted on employment issues and some are finding councils becoming more receptive to their advice.

The emergence of strong personnel departments has not changed the bureaucratic approach to the management of labour in local government. Indeed, if anything, it has reinforced the traditional approach. This can be particularly the case where personnel departments have brought in job evaluation systems to determine 'objectively' the allocation of non-manual jobs to the grading structure. The process of grading labour has, in consequence, become more standardised and more formalised. This has caused problems on the industrial relations front by frustrating attempts by local union representatives to negotiate the interpretation and application of nationally agreed grading structures. The personnel specialists advise the elected members of the results of the job evaluation, and where these are accepted as authoritative by the elected members, there is less disposition to haggle over regradings with local union representatives. The bureaucratisation of labour under personnel management is, however, a general feature of local government and is certainly not just expressed through the use of job evaluation. While the personnel specialists blame the law for growing bureaucratisation in the handling of local industrial relations, it seems quite clear that they themselves are an active factor in this process.

The effects of corporate management and personnel management on trade union activity in local government have been important but very contradictory. In the 1970s, just as workplace trade unionism developed amongst manual and non-manual workers, precedents were being created by local authorities for introducing private sector forms (that is, corporate management and personnel management). This helped to legitimise the arrival of shop stewards, a form of organisation that was unusual in local government and popularly associated with the private sector. In fact, it is sometimes said that personnel specialists foster the growth of shop stewards and shop stewards foster the growth of personnel specialists. The encouragement of systems and procedures by personnel specialists provide legitimised roles for shop stewards and thus stabilise their organisation. On the other hand, whilst local trade unionists wanted direct access to elected members, whom they identify as their employers, they increasingly found management, and sometimes personnel specialists in particular, blocking their access or pre-empting their negotiations. The policy and resources committees, where they took off, also made life difficult for local union negotiators because joint committees were increasingly unable to arrive at agreements until approval by these committees had been obtained.

Finally, brief mention must be made of another reorganisation of local government that has been occurring in varying degrees in the 1980s – decentralisation. Some councils are using this principle to completely overhaul their services and many other councils are also involved in decentralisation but on a piecemeal basis. For a small number of left-wing councils this decentralisation has been inspired by a desire to bring about a full-blooded and positive form of local democracy. These councils are not content with a passive democracy based on the electoral process: they want services which are responsive to the needs of local people because local people are involved in a more continuous way in evaluating services and expressing the priorities to be pursued. Decentralisation of services into 'mini town halls' is seen as necessary for this fuller form of democracy to be realised. This does not involve breaking up councils and increasing the numbers of council bodies, but involves reorganising the field work services in social work, housing, and so on. This type of decentralisation must be distinguished from apparently similar decentralisations carried out by Conservative councils which have led to stronger control by professional managements rather than more involvement of local citizens.

Decentralisation does have a strong effect on social work trade unionism, not least as representation systems are reorganised to give the various field work services (that is, social workers, housing workers, and so on) channels to express their common interests as 'mini town hall' workers. This may be as an adjunct to their representation on a departmental basis, but in time it may replace departmentally-based systems of representation.

The discussion above shows that local government reorganisations and reforms have had complex, multiple effects on the situation of social workers. Although difficult to comprehend because of their complexity and multiplicity, their existence helps to explain many of the particularities of the local experience of social work trade unionism.

WHITLEYISM

The history of Whitleyism is interesting, not least because of its conception in a very militant phase of British industrial relations during the First World War, and because of its development into an industrial relations practice for much of the public sector. But in understanding the position of social workers in local government in the 1970s, and in the 1980s, we need to analyse it as a collective bargaining structure, drawing out some of the implications of that structure for trade unionism.

The Whitley machinery covering most non-manual workers in local government, and that means more than half a million workers, is technically very impressive, certainly by comparison with the ramshackle negotiating machinery in many other parts of the British economy. It comprises a national joint committee, known as the National Joint Council for Local Authorities' Administrative, Professional, Technical and Clerical Staff (NJC–APTC), a number of what are called Provincial Councils, and, in most local authorities, local Whitley committees. What makes it impressive, however, is not its comprehensive, three-tier structure, but its effectiveness in making collective agreements, applying them, and sorting out disagreements and disputes.

What are the major characteristics of the structure of collective bargaining? Firstly, both sides in the negotiating relationship are, in numerical terms, strongly representative of their respective constituencies. High levels of trade union membership on one side are matched by almost all British local authorities being in the relevant employers' association on the other side. Employees are represented by NALGO (which has by far the biggest membership amongst non-manual local government staff), National Union of Public Employees (NUPE), Transport and General Workers Union (TGWU), General, Municipal, Boilermakers and Allied Trades Union's

(GMBATU) White-collar section, and Confederation of Health Service Employees (COHSE). The English, Welsh and Scottish local authorities, are represented by the Association of County Councils (ACC), the Association of Metropolitan Authorities (AMA), the Association of District Councils (ADC), and the Convention of Scottish Local Authorities (COSLA), the last of which is not directly represented on the NJC–APTC.

Secondly, the scope of the national agreement is very broad. The trade union and employer representatives on the NJC–APTC have negotiated a very detailed national agreement, which is known as the 'purple book' matters covered by the agreement include salary and grading structure, sick pay, appointment and promotion of staff, post-entry training, hours and leave, maternity leave, expenses and allowances, disciplinary rules and procedures, health and safety, appeals against salary grading, grievance procedures and trade union membership. The national agreement sets minimum standards in the key areas of terms and conditions of employment, although it should be noted that in the case of Scotland different pay scales apply which are negotiated by a Scottish Whitley Council. The scope of the national agreement makes it one of the most comprehensive collective agreements in British industrial relations.

The actual negotiations on the NJC are carried out by, on the staff side, national union officials and staff side representatives from thirteen Provincial Whitley Councils and a Scottish Whitley Council and, on the employers' side, representatives of the employers' associations and the employers' sides of the Provincial Councils and the Scottish Council. It is, therefore, a very centralised system of collective bargaining.

A distinctive feature of the Whitley constitution is that it requires a majority of *each* side of the NJC to approve a decision before it can be regarded as carried. This appears to bolster the cohesiveness and solidarity of both the trade unions and the employers since it rules out the possibility of the minority unions or small sections of the employers doing deals with the other side against the wishes of the majority of their own side.

The Whitley machinery is very impressive in terms of the authority of the national agreement. In the 1970s and the early 1980s nearly all local authorities closely followed the national agreement. Practically all local authority white collar staffs found the major source of pay increases came from national negotiations. There were a few local authorities where local bargaining over pay had on occasion been very important, but in most cases local bargaining mainly functioned to obtain improvements in areas such as leave, gradings and hours of work. In other words, the national agreement provides a very strong framework for local government terms and conditions of employment.

The conciliation procedures, which are based on the three-tier structure, so that differences are referred from local joint committees at individual local authority level to the Provincial Councils and then up to the NJC, also seem to have a fair degree of authority. Whilst not always able to resolve problems, the Provincial Councils will often settle grading appeals and disputes referred to them from the local level.

Notwithstanding the authority of the centrally-negotiated national agreement and the relatively effective conciliation arrangements, there is a considerable potential for single-employer negotiations by branch and other local union officials due to the need to administer the national agreement, especially with respect to the agreement of gradings for specific jobs. There can be an enormous involvement of branch officials and representatives in negotiating upgradings of jobs, which thus provides an alternative source of increases in income to national pay settlements.

In summary, the Whitley machinery for white-collar workers in local government is a highly centralised, very representative collective bargaining structure, which produces agreements that are very broad in scope, authoritative, and backed up by relatively effective conciliation procedures and local bargaining about the application of agreements.

Given such a strongly centralised collective bargaining structure, what are the implications for trade union action? One effect of centralisation is to impose fairly standardised terms and conditions. From a certain viewpoint, this may be seen as a virtue because it produces consistent treatment for the workers covered by agreements. Another effect is to make active involvement by the rank and file membership in the negotiating process both unnecessary and difficult. This non-involvement may be appreciated by workers who for one reason or another have no desire to be active. It can, however, be the source of intra-union conflict where more say in the collective bargaining process is wanted by local trade unionists.

Also, the centralised bargaining structure probably 'frees' local authorities from some of their industrial relations responsibilities. The individual authority is left with the task of applying an agreement that has been settled nationally, and national agreements are by definition very general. Therefore, provided the local union is not 'bargaining aware' and insists on negotiating the interpretation of the agreement, the local authority can be left with a relatively free hand in the allocation and utilisation of labour. It may be significant that the real shift towards centralised agreements in local government occurred after the inter-war depression when labour was stronger and more capable of challenging local authorities at the local level.

In many cases, the collective bargaining structure of an industry seems to be reflected in the structure of the trade unions that organise the workers covered by it. So, where collective bargaining is centralised, there is a tendency for power in the trade unions to be concentrated centrally. What is really difficult to know is the extent to which trade unions have adjusted to, or been moulded by, a bargaining structure, and the extent to which they have shaped it. Related to that is the question of whether trade unionists who do not like a bargaining structure are able to act effectively to change it. These seemingly theoretical questions were turned into practical questions by social work activists in the 1970s when they attempted to change the Whitley structure.

Finally, in charting the conditions of social work trade unionism, we turn to a brief examination of the union to which most social workers belong.

CHANGING NALGO

We must bear in mind that NALGO as a whole went through a great period of change in the 1960s and 1970s. It was as late as 1961 that a NALGO conference introduced a strike clause into the rules. Only in 1964 did the union join the TUC. It was even more recently – in 1970 – that the union's first official strike occurred; and that was a very small strike in Leeds Corporation. After this the union started to gear itself up for a more mainstream trade union role. In 1971 policies and procedures for industrial action were settled at the union's conference, and the special reserve fund for strikes was increased.

The changes in NALGO showed that in the union there was an increasing readiness to use the traditional weapons of industrial warfare. However, the attitude towards political activities and objectives was quite a different matter. In 1973 a NALGO delegation at a special Trades Union Congress voted in opposition to a one-day strike protesting against a statutory wages policy. At this and other times NALGO attempted to maintain a policy of strict political neutrality. On the other hand, this policy did not prevent the union taking apparently radical positions if the membership's interests were at stake. Thus in 1966, at the TUC, NALGO seconded a TGWU motion opposing the pay freeze and the Prices and Incomes Act of the Labour Government, which was being backed by the TUC General Council. And in 1971 the NALGO conference voted to make privatisation a strike issue. So, whatever the ideology of the union and its leaders, the policy of political neutrality was not a pretext for total inaction, even on what were quite political issues.

The shifts by NALGO away from its traditional relationships to the trade union movement and to militant forms of trade union struggle led, in 1974, to its first major dispute in local government. The dispute took place in NALGO's London district and concerned a claim for an increase in the allowance for the greater costs of working in London (which was known as London Weighting). In this particular dispute, the adherents of the NALGO Action Group (which was usually referred to, not inappropriately for a pressure group, as NAG) were busy gingering up support for a militant line.

The 1974 dispute was part of a definite trend in NALGO. The workload of the union's Emergency Committee, a committee of the National Executive Council (NEC) with the formal authority of the union to make industrial action official, increased substantially in the 1970s. Between 1968 and 1972, it considered an average of eight cases per year; whereas between 1973 and 1976 this figure increased to thirty. This trend towards militancy was urged on by NAG supporters, who were very influential at the union's conferences in 1972 and 1973.

The growing militancy seemed to be rewarded by even higher rates of membership growth. In 1975, the membership of NALGO increased by an astonishing 15 per cent, which was the biggest annual increase in the whole period from 1970 to 1985 and more than double the average annual increase for the 1970s. Of course, there may have been several contributory factors in this booming membership growth. The reorganisation of local government had various consequences which were probably important. Not only did it increase the scale of employment, it also destabilised pay relationships and upset private expectations, and calculations, of upward career mobility at the local level as a result of the merging of staffs from separate authorities. Then there were the effects of inflation and the pay explosion of 1975 which probably swept many people into the protective net of trade unionism. And the election of a Labour government in 1974 also meant that the trade union movement gained in status and legitimacy, which are important assets for the more pragmatically minded recruits to trade unionism, as well as for the more timid ones.

But there were reminders to the activists of NALGO that the meaning of this militancy was not to be misconstrued. At the 1975 conference of the union, the Manchester branch failed to get the required support for a motion instructing the NEC to investigate affiliation to the Labour Party. The following year the same message was repeated. The Islington branch proposed a ballot on affiliation, but this was also lost. In other words, the NALGO membership had become more willing to take part in, and support, industrial action; it had not decided to become politically aligned with the left.

The social work trade unionist of the early 1970s needed to understand two things, above all else, about NALGO. Firstly, the union was not an immobile, conservative social force. It was changing, and changing rapidly. Secondly, it was fast becoming more militant, but not by any means radical in a political sense. At least, it was not becoming more radical in any overt or explicit way. But, as we have seen, the union taking a position on the basis of membership interests could, on occasion, lead to it siding with apparently left positions on issues such as incomes policies and privatisation.

EARLY STRUGGLES

Whilst NALGO was taking note of a new mood amongst some of its members, especially its younger members, social workers were becoming active as trade unionists. The activity was directed at social services managements but it led to conflict with the branch. The conflict was not seen by social workers as being with the ordinary branch members, who were regarded as very apathetic and passive, but with what they often saw as 'right wing' branch officers who tended to be mainly drawn from senior grades of the non-manual workforce and who controlled branch life.

The trade union activism was centred on field work staffs and only exceptionally were residential workers and day centre staff part of the early developments. Indeed, it seemed as though the activism in the field work sphere was mainly confined to social services departments in inner city areas which faced major economic and social problems and which were afflicted by high rates of staff turnover. These economic and social problems looked as though they were going to be exacerbated by the fiscal problems of welfare state capitalism which were leading to spending cuts. This phase of development of the welfare state, directed by a Labour government apparently in the grip of monetarist economic doctrine from late 1974 onwards, seemed to many social workers a betrayal of the inner city poor. Although the numbers of social workers had been increasing, unfilled vacancies were running in some departments at very high levels and social work activists saw the looming dangers of frozen posts and chronic understaffing.

It is important to note that the acute sense of dilemma experienced by many social workers was partly due to the success of the Seebohm Report. After the report, it was generally accepted that social work was not just an amalgam of the responsibilities previously carried out by the former child care officers, almoners, psychiatric social workers, and so on. The task had become, in effect, the solution of all social problems. So, events had conspired to place social workers in an impossible situation: they felt they were expected to solve all the problems of their local communities, but, from late 1974 onwards, the signals coming from central government intimated a crisis in the ability of the state to pay for welfare state services. It could be argued that this sharpening contradiction exposed the remoteness of the social work situation from occupational self-control, which was the traditional definition of professionalism. The social workers were neither in control of the means of delivery of the service nor were they dictating the needs to be met. Both of these were matters over which they seemed to have little influence.

Social work activists were often told that if they had grievances or differences with their managers, they should use the proper procedures, which meant referring matters to the local Whitley committee for consideration by employer and staff representatives. In fact, Whitleyism theoretically offered an alternative channel to professionalism for social work activists to gain leverage over their situation. But the Whitleyism they saw did not fill them with enthusiasm. It was often said by them that real negotiations did not occur on the local Whitley committees, which were 'talking shops' in which senior, trusted staff were consulted by the councillors. Relations between the two sides were peaceful, co-operative and, some said, 'cosy'. The problem was not only the nature of Whitleyism. The activists were also critical of the attitudes of their own branch officials which helped, in their view, to produce this cosiness. A London NALGO member who had been on a local Whitley committee was very critical of the secrecy that had surrounded this way of doing things:

There used to be a hell of a lot of secrecy about what happened between staff side and council. And this was true about [1970] when I think the majority of staff side resigned because they felt they were ineffective. But part of that ineffectiveness came from their own attitude – what we would now call an outdated and even reactionary attitude towards their dealings with the council. They felt a sense of honour about what went on at joint committees, that things were secret, and that staff shouldn't know what was going on until things were finalised.

The branches were often run by a few branch officials, who had a marked tendency to be from senior grades in the council workforces. These officials formed small, élite groupings which relied on departmental representatives to keep them in contact with the membership; but this appears to have been a misplaced reliance in as much as they actually were very isolated and remote:

> I can only go back to when I first came to work for the borough and within a comparatively short time I became an officer of the union but the impression I got at the time was that people saw the trade union committees, especially the staff side [of the local Whitley committee], as remote as the council committees as regards contact.

In many circumstances, sticking to procedures is a principle which is important for the maintenance of trade union unity and strength and is not an unreasonable demand on sections of a union. Rightly or wrongly, the early social work activists challenged this constitutionalism on the basis that, not only was Whitleyism irrevocably bureaucratic, but also that oligarchic tendencies were well advanced in NALGO branches. And so the early struggles of social work trade unionism often rejected the approaches of traditional professionalism and of Whitleyism, containing instead an element which was anarchic and challenging to existing power structures.

The early struggles often reflected the concerns of the social work activists with a good quality service to their local communities. This made their actions challenging in a second sense. The activists were often expressing dissatisfaction with the quality of the local authority services, which they said was an important issue for their members. Of course, many trade

unionists in social services rated good pay as the most important priority, and many wanted work which was interesting,
but, said activists, social work trade unionism had to address
the concerns of social workers for the quality of services. A
London social work activist said of his members in 1976:

> They're concerned about the implications of their job for
> other people – for the community at large. And that I think
> is the only way that in a social services department type
> setting that you can really get people involved in the union
> because they are inclined to be much less concerned about
> their personal problems.

The plight of homeless families, and the way they were
dealt with by welfare services, came to be a high priority issue
for many social workers in the 1970s. In the London borough
of Tower Hamlets in 1972, radical social workers produced a
report criticising their council's housing policy, in which they
investigated the facts regarding housing, homelessness and
fair rents, and made recommendations for, amongst other
things, action by Tower Hamlets council (Tower Hamlets
Case Con, 1972). In another London borough, Islington,
social workers arranged demonstrations, protests and meetings in a campaign to alter the council's housing policy as it
affected squatters. The social workers involved saw themselves as forming an alliance with the squatters in a bid to
confront the council and force a change of policy. They
believed that the management of social services had to be
by-passed, as did the formal structures, if problems of poverty
and poor housing were to be dealt with. In Liverpool, a few
years later, social workers threatened a one-day strike following a move by councillors to discipline social workers who had
placed homeless families in hotel accommodation which was
considered too good. And there were other instances of trade
union action by social workers to force changes in the policy
on homeless families.

In the early years of the 1970s, the developing consciousness of the newly unified social workers had a strong element
of radicalism which expressed itself in demands and chal-
lenges to councils to change their policies. It was a radical

consciousness that took as its priority the problems of local disadvantaged people and blamed their social environment for the problems. It was a radical consciousness that believed that part of the solution to these problems lay within the reach of councils, if only the councils could be stirred to action. Organisationally, this radical consciousness had its base in Case Con, which was an important socialist body of social workers, and, somewhat ambiguously, in local NALGO branches. As the 1970s progressed, however, the trade union base for radicalism gained in importance, no doubt because the emergent workplace union organisation in social services departments provided a more organic link to local NALGO branches. But the increasing significance of a trade union base for radicalism contained issues and dilemmas for the activists. We can see these best if we look in detail at one case.

Tower Hamlets – a case study

The London borough of Tower Hamlets is not a beautiful sight, unless you happen to be an industrial archaeologist, or an urban sociologist, although people who have grown up there often feel a strong sense of loyalty and affection for the area. In the 1960s, when the borough was formed, it bore a strong 'working class' character, if by that you mean manual working class. It had lots of terraced back streets, estates and new (now despised) blocks of flats. It was never a single community, but was rather a collection of localities grouped together into an inner city borough.

Culturally as well as physically the area had been shaped by the development of the London docks, the population of Tower Hamlets providing a major source of dock labour for decades. In the 1960s the effects of containerisation, and the consequent switching of activities from the centre of London to Tilbury and other container-handling facilities, triggered a crisis in the local economy. The movement of population out of the borough to the suburban periphery was never rapid enough to match the decline of economic activity and by the mid 1980s the borough had one of the worst unemployment rates in Britain.

The borough's field social workers in the 1970s perceived

the area to be poor, deprived and derelict: they described it as one of the most poverty-stricken areas in Britain. Some of them had definitely come to Tower Hamlets because of the poverty and the social problems. Whatever their motivation, few of the field social workers were local people. A social worker in an area team told us:

> Most of the social workers don't come from this area at all. This reflects on education in the borough. Social workers tend to be more educated in terms of their having been to university and having got qualifications. Similarly with the residential workers.

In fact, residential social workers were more likely to see themselves as being local and could be very bitter about the 'foreignness' and educational superiority of the field workers.

The social services department had been formed in the wake of the Seebohm report by reorganising into one department the social workers who had been in the children's department, welfare, mental health, and so on. And as in many other local authorities, extra social workers had been recruited and the social services department had expanded. By the mid-1970s, the expansion phase was over and the financial crisis of the welfare state was expected by some social workers to put developments into reverse. Some were unsure whether there would be compulsory redundancies. As one field worker put it, 'Whether cuts will mean that local authorities won't replace staff or actually reduce the number of staff is one of the things we are not certain about.'

The work of the social services department covered the usual range of clients and problems. The department looked after the welfare of old people and people with a mental handicap, ensured that disabled people received the proper aids, helped with family crises, took children into care, handled the hospitalisation of people having mental breakdowns, tried to prevent electricity being .cut off to families who had not been able to pay their bills, and negotiated with various agencies on behalf of clients. The field work services had been set up, in line with Seebohm, on the basis of area teams of generic social workers. Usually the social workers in area teams were divided into those working on short-term cases and those working on long-term cases, and there were many scattered establishments providing residential and day centre services.

The party representation on Tower Hamlets Council was described by one social worker as '100 per cent Labour since time immemorial'. This captures the spirit of the Labour Party's dominance in the area, even if it is not strictly correct. In the 1920s, local Labour councillors became famous for their militant political stand in refusing to cut relief payments to the unemployed. After the Second World War the area continued its association with left political traditions by electing a number of Communist councillors to one of the borough councils. By the 1970s, however, the reputation of local Labour politicians was under attack from trade unionists on the left in the council workforce. This included some social work activists who saw the Labour councillors as undemocratic, unaccountable and, deep down, uncaring. The following analysis of the council was offered by a field worker in 1976:

> It's never been challenged in the council chamber. It's not used to being challenged outside it either. It doesn't like publicity. It's embarrassed by it ... The people in this borough have been almost totally inarticulate in terms of running things. The council know that and I therefore doubt very much whether there will be a tremendous great revolution in Tower Hamlets. Because year after year they get in on a 13 per cent poll and they've got away with it for so long.

The local Labour politicians could not be expected to do the right thing, there was no confidence in the formal democratic process, and publicity and embarrassment were all that stood between the councillors and total non-accountability. As it turned out, the Labour Party grip on the area was not as strong as this analysis suggested and, a decade later, Labour lost control of the council. With hindsight, the seeds of this political transformation may be uncovered. In 1976, the scenario of political defeat for Labour was unbelievable.

Despite their poor reputation with left-wing trade unionists in the council workforce, the Labour council had been behind the closed shop which had operated until the Conservative Industrial Relations Act of 1971 made it illegal. Even after this, the council had given strong encouragement to trade union membership amongst the council staff, with the result that trade union membership was very high amongst all grades of employee. On the non-manual side, amongst the 'officers' as they were called, the main trade union was NALGO. It had organised the vast majority of staff, although there were some who belonged to NUPE, TGWU and GMWU (now the GMBATU).

The NALGO membership in the council all belong to the same branch. In the mid 1970s, there were some 500 NALGO members employed in the social services department, including field workers and residential workers. They constituted the largest section of membership with well above one-third of the entire branch membership.

The three key union activities in the branch in the early 1970s were local policy-making, negotiating and consulting with the council on the application of the national agreement and other matters of local concern, and keeping communications flowing between the executive and the membership. These activities were undertaken by different people in the branch. Policy-making was the province of the executive which consisted of officials elected by the branch membership. Negotiations and consultation with the council were carried out by eight staff-side representatives who were elected by the entire branch membership; this, it should be noted, was not based on a constituency system. In practice, the staff-side representatives, who regularly met with elected council members in the local Whitley committee, were under the control of the executive; they were ex-officio members of the executive, they made reports to it, and received recommendations and requests from it. Departmental representatives were used to link the executive and the membership. In theory, the departmental representative had no negotiating or consulting role with management or the council – the workplace bargainers were the staff-side representatives. This, then, described the official local union structure of NALGO in the early and mid-1970s. And it was inside this structure that social work trade unionism found itself growing. How did this occur and with what consequences?

The first expression of social work trade unionism in Tower Hamlets was through the development of a social services departmental representatives' committee (DRC). It consisted of ten departmental representatives elected by and from the social services department and the branch officers who were from social services. This committee began to function from approximately 1972 and for at least five or six years was the only departmental representatives' committee operating in the NALGO branch.

Unlike the traditional departmental representatives who had acted as representatives of the members at the branch executive, and who thus were in effect carrying out an intra-union role, the social services DRC represented social services members in meetings with management. In this respect, the social services representatives were functioning as shop stewards by taking up issues with management, whereas traditional departmental representatives do not strictly merit the term. By 1976, meetings between the social services DRC and social services management were scheduled on a six-weekly basis. Although these meetings steered clear of straight salary issues, which were seen as a national question, and the director of social services refused to discuss matters outside his discretion, a very broad range of matters was still discussed and negotiated. The DRC negotiated on, amongst other things, acting-up money, working conditions (for example, ventilation and heating), the work load and duties of social work assistants, and payments to clients.

Of course, there was more to the operation of the DRC then the meeting with the director and his team. There was a meeting of the committee by itself every week, there were departmental meetings of the social services membership of NALGO, the circulation of minutes and publicity material, liaison with the branch secretary, and matters to be referred to the branch executive and to be explained to the branch. On occasion, the DRC played a supporting role to the staff-side representatives, as in an early dispute over pay for night duty teams, when it put forward recommendations to the staff side. All this activity was co-ordinated and led by a secretary elected by the DRC. The secretary and other representatives in social services found themselves working very hard to keep the whole thing running. In those early years, they spent an enormous amount of their time communicating: talking in meetings with each other, talking to individual members, handing out union newspapers, information sheets, minutes of meetings, and so on. Indeed, the branch magazine was also a crucial focus of their activity, providing as it did an important channel for persuading and arguing with other NALGO members about trade union issues. Negotiating agreements and taking up issues on a day-to-day basis with management did not loom large in their activities.

This growth of activism in the social services department caused concern in some parts of the branch from the very beginning. The branch had decided in favour of allowing departmental committees to be formed because it was hoped that they would dispel the general state of apathy in the branch amongst ordinary members. (The anxiety and the fight against apathy are to be found in most branches of most unions irrespective of the 'objective' level of apathy reigning.) The concern seems to have been partly due to the sponsorship of representatives' committees by the NALGO Action Group, which had many local supporters in a number of council departments, and partly due to fears that these committees would grow in influence and challenge the authority of the branch executive.

Because the social services' DRC did become established and because it was very visibly active, the fear of sectionalism continued to exist in some parts of the branch. To some extent this fear was nourished by factors that may seem emotional rather than rational. The branch seemed at times to dislike social services representatives. A day centre worker thought this was partly because 'there's a generation gap, [and it is felt that] all social services representatives are long-haired graduates or long-haired student types, which isn't actually true'. But, as a field worker said, the mere fact of being active was enough to arouse these fears:

> We are organised as a reps committee, we function and we meet and no other department has got that. The result of

that is that we are the people who put up resolutions, we are the ones likely to be involved in industrial action. There is always something going on in the social services side of the [branch] executive. There are always social services resolutions at the branch meetings. People get a bit pissed off with that, I suppose. There is a lot of talk of élitism, which I don't really understand.

The fact was, however, that this fear of the growing influence of the social services' DRC, and the weakening of branch authority, was not ill-founded. The social services' DRC did, on occasion, act independently. As one social services' representative put it, the difficult relationship with the branch was in part because 'the social services [DRC] tries to go it alone'.

This sectionalism of the social services DRC really became an issue in an ill-fated dispute over the council's homeless families policy in 1975. It was not the first industrial action undertaken by Tower Hamlets social workers, and it could be argued that it was earlier success that led to a serious miscalculation of tactics in the homeless families dispute.

In the earlier industrial action, which was also in 1975, social workers forced the council to advertise two senior posts at a higher grading than originally planned. The social services department was about a quarter under strength and it was believed that substantial cuts were planned by the council in the social services budget. Social workers in area teams were very concerned about overwork, high staff turnover and shortages of qualified and experienced staff. At the end of January 1975, area teams had begun unilateral closing of their offices for portions of the week corresponding to their level of understaffing; this was legitimated in terms of a new branch policy not to carry out work associated with unfilled vacancies. When two senior posts became vacant in an area office, the social workers decided to apply pressure to get the posts upgraded so that good applicants would be attracted. They said that they would not be able to function without a senior and they refused to accept managers drafted in to cover the vacancy on a temporary basis. More pressure was applied by a one-day strike of 230 social services members, during which offices were picketed, leaflets were distributed to the public, and an open air meeting was held in a local park.

One of the social workers involved in this action stressed that this was a 'departmental thing' and totally successful:

> This was a purely departmental thing. What happened was for the first time that I can remember as departmental rep, with a member of staff side, the secretary of departmental reps committee, met a councillor . . . and we negotiated . . . It was agreed that we as workers would not start full work until we got the seniors actually installed . . . It was also agreed that the post would be upgraded. It was a total success.

As the departmental representative also said: 'People like NALGO departmental representatives don't negotiate directly with the council. There is this force in between.' That force was, of course, Whitleyism. The social services' DRC had completely by-passed that machinery. The representatives had attracted masses of media attention with their strike and other action: the issue had been covered by newspapers, television and radio, and the result had been acute embarrassment of the council. A field social worker explained: 'The only weapon we've got in local government is publicity because we can't make our employer lose money.'

Although the director of social services refused to see the DRC for a period of six months as a result of the dispute, it was generally regarded by the social workers as a very satisfactory first experience of industrial action. The DRC had not even considered, prior to the dispute's commencement, whether branch support was needed. The DRC's secretary thought afterwards that if the action had failed, the DRC might have considered the need to involve the branch. So although they were part of NALGO, they had not felt it necessary, or indeed had thought about, getting wider support.

In this first action of the social services' DRC, the trade union action stemmed from the problem of understaffing and the fears of spending cuts, and was motivated by a concern for the service. Of course, terms and conditions of employment are not unconnected with the volume and quality of the service. Thus a problem of understaffing not only leads to a reduction in the standard of service, it also tends to cause a worsening of terms and conditions of employment as social workers find that they are under pressure to increase their efforts to cover vacancies. But the service issue was uppermost in this issue and the action by the social workers should be seen as a manifestation of radical trade unionism.

Radicalism was even more evident in the second major action by the social services' DRC, which also took place in 1975. The issue was the council's policy for dealing with the homeless. The treatment of homeless families by the council's housing department had been a source of concern to social workers for some years. In 1972, radical social workers in Tower Hamlets Case Con had published a report calling on the council to grant homeless families the opportunity to transfer from substandard properties at the end of a probationary period, to provide a transfer system, to modernise substandard property, and to take various other steps to improve the situation (Tower Hamlets Case Con, 1972). In 1975, the social workers attempted to use their trade union organisation to forcibly change the official policy, but this time the issue was the use of hotels to provide temporary accommodation for homeless families. A field social worker centrally involved in the dispute made it clear that social workers were reacting strongly to their own feelings of compassion and distress aroused by their first hand experience of the plight of their clients:

> It used to be the responsibility of every area team to receive families who were homeless in the borough, forward them to some sort of hostel or accommodation or short-life housing in preparation for them to be rehoused. Since about 1972 the use of hotels, none of which were in this area, they were out towards Finsbury Park and King's Cross, were becoming more and more popular, being used more and more by our Homeless Families Section because they found difficulty in getting other accommodation. The conditions in these hotels was appalling. Often families of six or seven were in one room. Often you had to leave the lounge by 9

o'clock in the morning. They were thrown out at 10 o'clock in the morning. When you've got young kids and trying to live on social security its really difficult. Outbreaks of dysentery occurred in the hotels – so-called hotels, bed and breakfast in fact. Social workers coming into contact with families in these situations were getting quite uptight by it all.

The social workers began by raising their objections to the policy of using hotels with social services management: 'for a couple of years there had been representations to the Director that these be phased out. Continual assurances came from the Director: 'Yes, hotels were going to be phased out'.

When the policy continued, the social services DRC could have taken the matter to the branch or to the staff side. It did neither. Instead it acted on a sectionalist basis:

> The reps committee held an open [social services] depart-
> mental meeting which decided on a policy that all those
> families with children under one year, to begin with, should
> be offered housing accommodation – short-life housing
> accommodation – and not hotel accommodation. This was
> to be the first stage of putting pressure on management. If
> management refused to comply, then what we were to do
> was squat families in our offices, getting maximum pub-
> licity.

The social services' DRC believed that the use of the hotels was unnecessary. There was plenty of vacant accommodation in Tower Hamlets and using hotels was very expensive. It was, in fact, noticeable that the social work activists, many of whom were strongly motivated by socialist beliefs, tended to see conflicts between themselves and social services manage-ment as mainly caused by the latter's incompetence and arbitrariness. So the position they took up here was based on the view that trade union action could bring real improve-ments in services to needy and poor clients by pressurising an incompetent management to abandon irrational policies.

Whilst the social work activists had no doubt that they were pursuing a legitimate trade union issue, there was an increasing awareness in the course of this dispute that many NALGO branch members, including substantial numbers of social services staff from outside field work, did not share this perception. That is, for these many NALGO members not in social services field work, homelessness was just not a trade union issue. It was apparent afterwards that the sectionalist approach to the dispute caused a tension between the NALGO branch and the social workers and that this had been compounded by wariness felt in the branch about the strongly radical aims of the dispute.

The social workers did not work out detailed tactics beforehand. They had in the backs of their minds certain ideas, but much of what happened was a response to the situations that developed. They were pursuing a clearly sectionalist line since they chose not to secure prior branch backing and approval. But this does not mean that they were opposed to branch support or had no hopes of some support as the dispute developed. But the support of the branch was not a central concern at the planning stage. As a field worker expressed it, branch support was a matter 'that certainly crept into our considerations'.

Their tactical thinking was essentially the same as in their previous action and very straightforward. They hoped that squatting homeless families would get a lot of media attention and embarrass the council into giving way on the policy of using hotels. As far as they knew, never before had social workers squatted families in social services offices and so the action was reckoned to be very newsworthy. While the tactical thinking was very simple, it must be remembered that the previous action in the very same year had been based on precisely the same tactics and had apparently worked without a hitch. This success had meant that there was no pressure on the social workers to doubt or review their tactics, or to refine them in any way.

The day after the social services departmental meeting, a homeless family was squatted in an area office. The action almost immediately escalated to a walk-out in response to a threat by social services management that the family would not get a short-life property unless they went into a hotel. The social workers in the area team were outraged by this attempt to threaten the family and walked out, and other social workers and social services staff struck in sympathy. Although the strike action only lasted half a day, militancy again seemed to work for the social services' DRC. Management offered the family accommodation and the squat ended after just one day!

Up to this point the initiative had lain with the social workers in Tower Hamlets. They had chosen the issue, the time and the methods. The earlier dispute in the same year must have taken the council by surprise, and barely had that been settled than the second-ever dispute was under way. The social workers had moved speedily and with resolution. A departmental meeting one day, a family squatted the next, and instant strike retaliation when management tried to threaten the family. The methods of the social workers, direct and unconstitutional, made them unpredictable. But in the same way that the trade union consciousness of workers undergoes changes, and just as workers learn to organise in order to protect themselves and achieve some security, so too do the employers and managers of social workers change and learn. The employers and managers were initially unprepared for the social services disputes, but the experiences were changing them and long before the dispute over the homeless family policy was finished they emerged quite changed in outlook – no longer likely to crumble at the sight of a display of militancy.

The change in the other side became apparent only a short time after the first incident, when a second family was squatted in another area office. This time management refused to find housing accommodation and instructed the social workers to turn the family, a pregnant woman and her husband, out of the office. The social workers stuck to their action but it was soon apparent that an early victory was not on the cards. After ten days of squatting by the family, the social workers conceded defeat and found accommodation for the family through a housing association.

The initiative now passed from the social services' DRC. The assistant director of social services called seventeen social workers for disciplinary hearings because they had disobeyed management instructions. It was from this point onwards that it became obvious that the leaders of the social work trade unionists were no longer able to provide the direction necessary to win the conflict. It is clear with hindsight that this was due not to any lack of intelligence on their part, but to their lack of experience. They were simply not prepared for the events that now followed.

In the subsequent phases of the dispute, the leaders of the social workers were unable to identify the practical steps needed to extricate the social workers from the dispute in a well-organised way with minimal loss to morale and self-confidence. Their willingness to do whatever was possible was there, but they began to pay the price for the shortcomings of a sectionalist strategy. Their inability to resist the retaliatory acts of management meant that the failure of their campaign was compounded and turned into a defeat for their union organisation. The calibre of the trade union leadership in the social services' DRC was, however, shown by their willingness to learn the lessons of experience, which meant acknowledging the shortcomings in the sectionalist line they had taken and considering what changes would be needed in future. But this willingness to learn for the future did not save the social workers from the repercussions of their defeat.

Initially the social workers attempted to counter the disciplinary action by calling a one-day strike for the day of the hearings. Some two hundred social workers, mainly field workers, took part. The strike was strongly approved by those involved but there was little confidence that it would dissuade management from carrying out the disciplinary action in the end. In the main, it was an expression of sympathy and solidarity and showed that trade union consciousness was highly developed amongst the field workers. The disciplinary hearings were boycotted by the social workers and so a second set of disciplinary hearings were arranged. These were again ignored, and a petition and lobbying was well supported by social workers. But this was merely postponing the ending of the dispute and not really effective.

After the second set of hearings were ignored, social services management referred the matter to the council, and branch officials were brought in to represent the social workers. The problem was, however, that the sectionalist approach had caused a rift in the branch and some social workers were concerned by the lack of enthusiasm in the way the cases were taken up. Whilst the branch had given retrospective approval to the half-day walk out by social workers, there was nevertheless considerable annoyance with the 'opportunism' of the social workers. They were accused of expecting branch support, and dragging the branch into a dispute, without being willing to consult, and be constrained by, the branch. In effect, they were being accused of wanting the benefits of branch strength without being prepared to accept the authority of the branch.

Eventually the social workers were formally disciplined, although they succeeded in their insistence that they be disciplined as a group and not as individuals. They, to their regret, agreed to be represented by a union official: 'We finally agreed to go along and be seen and disciplined as a group. This was unprecedented in the disciplinary procedure. The council gave ground in that area. We gave ground in agreeing to be represented by a district officer of NALGO.' The social services' DRC in the meantime were unable to think of anything that could be done once the petition and lobbying had been attempted. A leading union activist explained their perplexity as follows: 'We were prepared to consider anything which might turn the tide a bit – but we wouldn't have any backing from the rest of the branch and under those circumstances it seemed a lost cause. The [branch] exec had no real interest in it.' Further significant strike action seemed unlikely to be supported: 'People were keen on the petition. They lobbied enthusiastically. But after that what? You could have a half-day strike. People don't like day strikes unless they can see because of this we are going to get it sorted out.' In this dispute the social services' DRC had tested the strength of their organisation to its very limits. And they found that it wasn't enough. And as the lessons of the experience were learnt it was realised that social workers could not depend on themselves alone but needed the extra strength of their fellow workers in other departments.

The branch resentment of the 'go it alone' style, the sectionalism of social services, came out into the open in various ways. There were public denunciations at meetings and in the branch magazine of the opportunism of the social workers. There was also an incident in which a social services representative complained to the branch of victimisation by management only to be told he should resign because of alleged intimidation by some of his members of an external candidate for a job. The representative, who was a field worker in the area office where the second family had been squatted, had applied for a job which would have represented a promotion but failed to get it. The job was instead offered to an external candidate. This external candidate refused the job following contact with social workers from the area team. A letter from management to NALGO's district office accused his members of intimidating this candidate. The branch requested the representative's resignation and were apparently furious:

> They said he had no control over his members and his members had been intimidating potential employees who would have been NALGO members. So he really got the kicks for the whole lot. There was a real explosion of fury against us. Well, he said it wasn't his job to control his members – it was to represent them . . . All we could do was to support him in relation to the [branch] exec . . . It was a good example of the branch getting split by straight management effort. They can't have expected that one letter would achieve all it did. Really angry exec – it was a wonder we weren't all asked to resign really.

But, of course, management's letter merely exploited a split created by sectionalism; the split wasn't created by management.

The union activists in social services had learnt some painful lessons but it was to their credit that they did learn from their failures. This learning was condensed into the following terse formulation by one of the field social workers: 'There has been a growing awareness of the need to involve the branch. Going it alone works at first because of shock tactics but people learn lessons.' In other words, sectionalism was seen as deficient. Their experiences had taught them that they needed to build a strong alliance with other non-manual workers outside social work – social workers were not self-sufficient.

And experience had taught them that publicity had provided a short-lived advantage which quickly lost its value as councillors and managers had become used to it.

In the period that followed, the social workers at Tower Hamlets set about strengthening their own departmental union organisation as well as building the possibilities of united action with the rest of the branch. In 1976 they undertook the formation of a shop steward system, which they hoped would develop a wider and firmer base in the whole social services department than had the departmental representatives system. The density of representation was greatly increased and each steward was accountable to a specific constituency (a 'shop'). The rationale offered by the leading social work trade unionists was that membership activism was dependent on the quality of representation, which they believed had suffered under the peculiarities and vagaries of the departmental representative arrangements. At the end of 1976 there were twenty-six shop stewards and within a short period there was evidence of issues being brought forward from sections of social services that had been hitherto neglected.

In 1977 branch officials and social services shop stewards were represented on a working party to examine the relationship between the branch and the shop stewards. So much progress was made in repairing relations inside the branch that in 1978 the retiring branch president felt able to praise the social services convener of the shop stewards' committee for his constructive efforts in maintaining branch unity. He told the branch's annual general meeting that the unity of the branch had been preserved despite the growth of the shop stewards' system in social services.

As events were to show in the years after 1976, the move away from sectionalism did not spell the end of vigorous trade unionism, nor for that matter the end of social work militancy. Of course, the transition from sectionalism to branch unity was not always smooth. In 1976, social workers were engaged in a series of one-day strikes over a social worker who had been demoted despite a recommendation by an industrial tribunal that he should be reinstated (the council were refusing to change their decision to implement the tribunal recommendation). Whilst there was dissatisfaction amongst

some social workers over the control of tactics and the decision
to end the dispute, the social services' DRC and the branch
were able to work together and achieve reinstatement of the
social worker.

RESULTS AND LESSONS

Social work trade unionism in its sectionalist and radical form
rarely leads to substantial changes in the conditions facing
social workers. The power that can be mobilised by social
work trade unionism dominated by a politics of sectionalism is
too little for such changes.

The deficiencies of a sectionalist strategy are really only
apparent when the strength of the employer has been underestimated and the sectionalist union action has not been
powerful enough. With the union organisation committed, the
sectionalist character of the action makes sympathetic, sup-
portive action by other groups more difficult to obtain. The
result can be that the sectionalist organisation, already isolated, becomes stranded and then prey to retaliatory actions,
which may, in extreme circumstances, lead to the destruction
of the patiently-built trade union consciousness and organisation of groups of workers. Obviously, sectionalist action does
not lead inevitably and on all occasions to this result. Some of
the risks of sectionalism can be minimised by intelligent
leadership which selects the time for action carefully so as to
pick the most opportune moment in terms of the relative
strengths of the two sides.

But sectionalism is a difficult course even where there are
intelligent leaders. This is because it is not easy for the union
in advance of industrial action to be sure just how much
strength the other side has got. Indeed, it is mainly during a
dispute that the union is able to assess employer strength. And
for a group of workers with limited experience of industrial
action, tactics to maximise union power and exploit employer
weakness may be worked out in advance only to a limited
degree. The launching of sectionalist action is thus a highly
uncertain enterprise. Issues of timing and tactics are practical

considerations which must concern all local trade union leaders, notwithstanding beliefs that the workers united would be
an unstoppable force. In practice, nearly all departmental
representatives or shop stewards in social work know that they
are going to have to be content with mobilising only a fraction
of this theoretically unstoppable force. And thus, in practice,
there is always a danger that the strength of the employer has
been underestimated.

But the balance sheet for sectionalist trade unionism is not
entirely negative. Provided the leading departmental representatives or shop stewards in social work have the capacity
and willingness to learn from experience, and provided they
can translate these lessons into practical measures for strengthening departmental and branch organisation, sectionalism
can be an enriching experience. For example, industrial action
undertaken by social workers without consulting and involving the branch sooner or later runs into difficulties and shows
the importance of social workers trying to build alliances with
other local government officers. Moreover, attempts to gain
the support of these other local government officers for
radically-inspired action brings into sharper focus the differences, as well as the shared interests, amongst groups of
workers. Hazy ideas of worker solidarity have to be replaced
by more concrete understandings of the constellation of interests within the ranks of the working classes. This leads down
the path of shaping union demands which will secure and not
fragment the unity of different groups of workers.

Where the lessons have been learnt, the main lasting result
has been the development of NALGO branches which are
more cohesive and which have moved in the direction of a
stronger trade union consciousness amongst the membership.
Where the lessons have not been learnt, the branch has
remained divided, and therefore weaker, and the social work
activists have not been in a position to profit from the strength
of the branch, but have consoled themselves with their accusations that the branch is right wing, or incorporated, or not so
principled as are the social workers. In some places the
capacity and willingness to learn has also led to departmental
union organisations that are inclusive and thus represent all

social services staff. In others the sectionalism has been based
on a parochialism that comes close to an exclusiveness remi-
niscent of the old craft unions; in these cases the social work
trade unionism has stayed within the boundaries of field work
services.

3
Rank-and-Filism and the Need for Alliances

Social workers have used a variety of tactics and strategies to develop their trade union experience within NALGO. One of the most significant has been the approach of 'rank-and-filism'. Whilst very few social workers would espouse all the ideas and practices that we outline under the heading of rank-and-filism in chapter 6, we believe that a great many did, and some still do, experience much of their trade unionism in relationship to such a set of ideas. For the most part there were, and still are, tensions between social work activists and some branch officials. Sometimes this tension would be caused by overtly different political positions, more often by anxieties and disagreements stemming from those who saw the whole branch as NALGO as opposed to those who were primarily interested in the activists or sectionally in the social workers.

However, these tensions are often resolved and some social work activists learn that branch support is the most powerful resource and set about sorting out the organisational difficulties in their branches. Sometimes it is possible to negotiate an understanding which improves relations within the branch. Sometimes the retirement from union office of key personalities amongst the old branch leadership brings an improvement in relations between social workers and the rest of the branch. The difficulties are sometimes only settled, or eased, as a result of fights and conflicts within the branch.

But the branch is not the only focus of this activity. Social work activists are amongst those members of NALGO who are most critical of bureaucratic tendencies in the union and of possible remoteness from members of the bargaining process under Whitleyism. It therefore seems natural that they should have backed the campaign in the mid- and late 1970s for steward systems and supported the constitutional attacks, through NALGO's conference, against Whitleyism from 1977 onwards. But the early experiences of local trade union activism by social workers must have strengthened this backing and support. These early experiences showed that they were able to achieve only limited strength by acting completely independently. They needed allies. They needed NALGO as a whole. And recognition of their workplace organisation by the local branch is crucial if alliances with others in NALGO are to be encouraged. So the movement of social work trade unionism into the whole business of union reconstruction was given impetus by those early experiences, which had led some social work activists to reassess the value of alliances.

ALLIANCES BOTH WITHIN NALGO AND WITH OTHER GROUPS

Social workers have considered or urged alliances with various groups and the possibility of an alliance with clients has held a special fascination for them. This partly stems from wishing to avoid the paternalistic and authoritarian relationship of social worker and client, but also derives from the discomfort experienced by social workers who perceive their clients as stigmatised by the service they receive. These feelings have led to proposals that clients should have more control and to suggestions that client committees be set up which would have a say in the management of services.

The call to form an alliance with clients can also be located inside a radical frame of reference which places the 'class struggle' at the centre of its prescription for social work. According to this position, the clients are not merely the consumers of a service provided by social workers, they are, much more importantly, part of the working class. Since social workers are also part of the working class, the clients and the social workers should fight together. The enemy in this case is identified as the state, both national and local, which is a capitalist state, so radical social workers should engage in struggle against their own departments, their own councillors, and even national policies, and do so in alliance with the working class communities and clients they serve.

Forming alliances with clients has, however, never proved to be that easy. The clients are not organised into a powerful collective organisation – they are often individuals or families in vulnerable and difficult circumstances. This was certainly the case in the Tower Hamlets dispute over homeless families. In practice such an 'alliance' is a one-sided relationship of patronage.

The need for alliances with other NALGO members has often been underestimated by social work activists. This was especially the case in relation to industrial action. This does not mean that the activists do not attempt to relate to other NALGO members, but it does mean that on occasion they do not see the need for the assistance and 'extra muscle' of other NALGO members.

We can begin to approach this question of alliances by looking at the different perceptions of national officials and rank-and-file activists in social work on the special conjuncture which faced NALGO in the late 1970s. Both agreed that NALGO was in an important phase of development. The social worker rank-and-filist view, however, was that up to this time NALGO had not been a 'proper' union. Its membership had been seen as snobbish and lacking in the sentiments of union solidarity with other workers. The development of shop stewards (and active, functioning departmental representatives' committees, to a lesser extent) was a part of the 'break' which was occurring. Calling NALGO representatives 'shop stewards', seeing the defects in Whitleyism and moving towards a more industrial (that is, local) form of bargaining were all seen as requiring NALGO members to face up to the 'fact' of trade unionism. As we shall see, this view contains a very idealistic idea of trade union struggle: NALGO would become a proper trade union, pursuing proper trade union goals, when members chose where it would go and chose to avoid the ambiguous, middle path that the union had been pursuing so far. The leadership of NALGO, so the argument goes, was seen as not wanting real trade unionism but desiring a docile, impotent form of trade unionism. NALGO was to move towards proper trade unionism by dragging the reluctant leadership behind it.

The relationship between the social worker activists and other NALGO members was a part of this whole view of NALGO's critical position in a development towards proper trade unionism. The activism and militancy of social services trade unionists, their willingness to by-pass the Whitley procedures, and their pursuit of working class goals of social justice, were to act as an example to the more backward groups in NALGO. Their successes were to provide the basis for confidence by others that something could be done despite the apparent immovability of the vast bureaucratic structures of the employers, of NALGO, and of Whitleyism.

This tendency towards political elitism began to give way to a perception that alliances were necessary because the rest of NALGO had power resources which social services needed to call on to win their own struggles. Their trade union practice was, therefore, modified by their experiences. They nevertheless continued to argue that this was a make-or-break time for NALGO: a time when the union could choose decisively in favour of 'real' trade unionism.

This task of creating a proper union through militancy and 'trade union action' is one that is still perceived as the main issue by some militants. The movements of the late 1970s, by NALGO members and structures alike, did not create a union which was 'real' in the way in which a rank-and-filist image of trade unionism would see it. Consequently, there is a continuing struggle to the present day between those who see that transformation as their major political task and those they see as 'the reactionary leadership'.

In our opinion this opposition is wrong. Indeed, it is interesting to look at the views of the union leadership, which were, certainly by the mid-1970s, by no means conservative or reactionary. In January 1975 an article by NALGO's General Secretary appeared in a local NALGO branch magazine. The General Secretary, Geoffrey Drain, was concerned to explain to a branch renowned for its militancy and activism that the leadership had a difficult task in maximising the rate of progress of NALGO because of the very uneven development of the various sections of the membership. He was arguing against the view that NALGO's leadership was reactionary and was being dragged forward against its will.

The inference which could be drawn from his statement was that the political skills of leadership were more complex than rank-and-file activists realised. He told the branch:

> I want to say something about NALGO's problems as a trade union at this important stage in its development. Although clearly the rate of progress disappoints some of your members, we shall undervalue ourselves if we do not recognise the changes in outlook and attitude which are taking place and the way in which these are reflected in action at both branch and national level. Militancy and facing up to political issues is part of this picture; so also is greater participation by branches and the membership in determining policy and fighting out local issues. The difficulty is not in acknowledging these gains but in maximising them throughout a union as complex in its make-up as NALGO, with reactions which differ from branch to branch, and from one membership group to the other. Concepts and actions which are straightforward in a first generation union with a relatively homogeneous membership in occupational terms and a background of working-class solidarity are less easily achievable in our circumstances, and it is not defeatism but realism to recognise this in looking ahead, and to plan accordingly. (Drain, 1975, p. 5)

So while the rank-and-filists, inside and outside social services, deny the existence of a middle path and insist that the membership should choose 'real' trade unionism, the leadership concentrates on maintaining the unity of the union while making progress.

In the late 1970s, the price of strengthening social work alliances with other NALGO members, and exploiting the various services and benefits of union membership, was the need to de-emphasise the very specific concerns with the nature of social services provided. NALGO's social services membership was a relatively small proportion of the entire membership and, to gain support from NALGO, social work trade unionism found itself concentrating on traditional trade union goals which are concerned with the financial rewards to workers and other service conditions issues. These after all are what 'proper' trade unionism is all about. In this respect it should be noted that the major dispute of the second phase of development of social work trade unionism was a stoppage over a demand to negotiate pay and grading at local level in 1978–9. Ostensibly, this had little to do with concerns – political or professional – over the quality of service provided.

Some might regard the price too high for social work activists; that is, if the search for allies requires a shift of focus away from concerns about the nature of the service offered to clients then they should have continued with the older strategy of 'going it alone'. In answer, it must be said that alliances have to be negotiated, that they inevitably place constraints on what can be pursued, and inevitably require some sort of pay-off for their formation. It is unrealistic to expect that an alliance will deliver to a group everything it wants even though social workers often expected this.

Equally though, the nature of alliances must be a function of the way in which these activists viewed their potential allies. With the view of 'proper trade unionism' dominated by a nineteenth-century skilled-manual trade unionism model, it is very likely that fellow NALGO members could be approached around the issues and problems that constructed these organisations. Thus 'terms and conditions' – the glue that held the new model unions of the 1860s together – becomes the single issue. Calling each other 'sister' and 'brother' becomes the necessary language. All issues which appear to separate out 'professional social work' must either be reinterpreted in the language of 'proper trade unionism' in order to communicate it to their potential colleagues, or it must be dropped as 'élitist'.

THE 'FIRST' ALLIES – OTHER SOCIAL WORKERS

Social work trade unionism, however, has also to build alliances within social services, and uneven development took place here too. In nearly every case of an early flowering of activism and militancy in social services, the activists were to be found concentrated disproportionately amongst field workers. In some branches, field workers were well aware of the need to draw other social services staff into the new social work trade unionism. Initially though, field worker activists were not able fully to appreciate the gulf between themselves and others, such as residential workers. Indeed, in some cases these other groups were much closer than field workers to the position of NALGO members in general.

While field workers were often quite sensitive to, and aware of, the different situations of residential workers, residential workers often reciprocated by seeing a divide between themselves and field workers. One residential worker, a shop steward, said in 1977 that he thought the branch listened more to residential workers than they did to field workers:

> They listen more because we're not classed as long-haired pseudo-intellectuals come doing their bit in the East End and then going off and getting nice jobs somewhere else. (Who is classed like that?) Well, field workers are, basically. And also because views coming from residential are more moderate and are therefore more nearer the branch. Although I think residential workers are well left to the majority of the branch, we're not as far left as what field work are.

Arguably, it was necessary to distinguish between residential workers' attitudes to trade unionism and their attitude to strike action in order to appreciate the difference between them and field workers, and between them and 'traditional' NALGO members.

At this time, though, residential workers were often regarded as less trade union minded than, say, field workers. This was, however, an unfair and crude assessment. Firstly, residential workers faced much greater material barriers to being active due to shift systems and the more isolated and dispersed work situations that predominated. Secondly, residential workers frequently expressed support for trade unionism in principle but found difficulty in participating directly in militancy. Participation in industrial action was regarded as inappropriate by residential social workers. The residential social worker quoted above said:

> It's just obviously people and strike action, its something completely out of the question. But they've been really good when it comes to supporting other people, like when we've had whip-rounds for other people that have been on strike or petitions or things like that.

In many ways, these very different aspects of the labour process can be too easily overlooked. Indeed, residential workers seem to be just as much supporters of trade unionism, in principle, as are field workers. This support in principle by residential workers is less likely to translate into activism, however, because of barriers associated with working patterns and location, and less likely to translate into militancy, because of barriers to strike action directly concerned with their labour-process.

What is the nature of the greater barriers to strike action? Residential workers are seen as less political, more respectful of managerial authority, and more concerned about the immediately damaging effects of industrial action on clients. The last of these seem to be the most plausible of the putative causes of the pacific nature of residential workers' trade unionism.

To understand the concern felt by residential workers about the effects of militancy on clients, we need to take account of the specific character of their relationship with the client, which is a relationship at the very core of their labour-process. This relationship is strongly defined by the fact that residential workers spend a large proportion of their time with a small number of clients. Indeed, it is still frequently the case that residential workers and clients share the same home. The residential workers, then, generally have very close working and living relationships with clients and, in consequence, they often get to know them very well on an individual and personal basis.

Moreover, the simple fact that the workplaces of residential workers are also the homes of clients creates additional ambivalences for them when taking industrial action. There is not only the obvious problem that they are bringing chaos to the homes of their clients, they are also introducing chaos, in many cases, into their own homes. And whilst the strike may be expressing suppressed conflicts and tensions already existing within the organisation of residential services, it is expressing them in a disturbing way which may be seen as hard to reconcile with caring.

The residential workers' relationship with clients is, therefore, different from the fieldworkers' relationship with their clients. And the closeness and sensitivity of residential workers to the much greater effects of strike action on clients makes it very difficult for them to contemplate subjecting clients even to short-term upset by such action. As a result, they are less persuaded by the strike rationale that short-term disruption is justified by the resultant improvements in the service which would be in the long-term interest of clients.

These differences between residential workers and fieldworkers are long-standing ones and can be seen reflected in the past attitudes of their respective professional bodies. So the RCA, then the professional body of residential workers, rejected strike action at its 1977 conference and subsequently reaffirmed this policy on a number of occasions. In contrast, BASW, in 1977, and for some time afterwards, considered becoming a trade union or helping to establish a trade union.

What are the implications for the development of trade unionism in social work? The continuing growth of trade unionism requires a recognition of the different forms of union consciousness that arise within social work. It also requires a practice that seeks to develop unity on the basis of differences. This means that fieldworkers need to accept that although residential workers have a different approach to trade unionism, they are, none the less, genuinely trade-union-minded. Therefore, alliances with them need to be built and continually rebuilt. The different forms of trade union consciousness are reflected in the fact that not all social workers will automatically see strikes equivalently. Thus some social workers will be prepared to strike because they see the strike as a means of improving the long-term situation of clients. For many of these social workers, striking is an act of caring, albeit a collective, radical act of caring. For others, caring prohibits the use of the strike. Similarly, the development of shop steward systems may have different meanings to social workers, and, consequently, it would be a mistake for field social workers to see the growth of shop stewards amongst residential workers, where this occurs, as necessarily evidence of a growing militancy. It may be an emergence of a form of trade union activism which does not involve a willingness to take industrial action. There is no doubt that many field workers are conscious of the different character of trade unionism in residential services, but only occasionally is this awareness accompanied by the necessary respect for the totally different labour-process of residential workers. For it should be stressed that the different trade union practices in social work have arisen not only because of different ideologies of caring, but also because trade unionism is affected by the different labour-processes within social work.

PRESSURES ON WHITLEYISM

The Whitley system of industrial relations in local government, with its authoritative national agreements, shapes the types of internal conflict which are latent in NALGO. The essence of the situation can be summed up by saying that the national union officials are the main negotiating agents, and rank-and-file members, in consequence, depend on them to negotiate on their behalf. As a result, there are at least three major issues around which internal union conflict can develop. Firstly, some rank-and-file members may feel dissatisfied with the level of success of the union negotiators and accuse them of incompetence, lack of determination, or even duplicity. Secondly, some rank-and-file members may form a different view from the national officials on the appropriate methods and tactics to be used in negotiations. And thirdly, some rank-and-file members may decide that they would prefer negotiations not to be carried out by national officials at all. This last type of issue, of course, concerns the basic framework of Whitleyism itself.

In the 1970s it was apparent at the annual conferences of

the union, and at the local government group meetings which
formed part of the conferences, that there was increasing
discontent amongst some branches with the Whitley system.
In 1972, for example, the NALGO conference refused to
accept a report on the union's structure by the National
Executive Council, apparently because it was complacent
about branch dissatisfactions with links to national negotiations and because it had not considered an increased bargaining role for branches.

By the late 1970s, Whitleyism had come to be seen by
substantial numbers of rank-and-filists in the union as an
unresponsive and remote bureaucratic structure over which
ordinary members of the union had little influence. This
critique of Whitleyism was tied to the issue of democracy in
the union. Rank-and-filists objected to the official union support for Whitleyism, they condemned the union leadership as
conservative and unaccountable, and, in effect, saw attacking
Whitleyism as necessary in the process of democratising the
union.

This challenge to Whitleyism still exists today in some parts
of the union. There are still rank-and-file members who would
like to see local bargaining by shop stewards. The ideal model
for them is provided by the private manufacturing sector,
where shop stewards in 'real' manual trade unions negotiate
factory or company agreements directly with management
and where full-time officials are less important. For many of
these rank-and-file members, the Whitley structure is a 'con',
an obstruction put in the way of the membership. It deludes
the rank-and-file into thinking their demands are being taken
up, but all it does is to trap the union into meaningless,
time-wasting talk.

In the 1970s there were also pressures on Whitleyism from
another direction; successive government pay policies during
the 1960s and 1970s placed severe constraints on the freedom
of national negotiators to determine for themselves the rates of
pay that were to apply. In other words, Whitleyism was not
just a system of centralised and formalised pay agreements –
it was also free collective bargaining by employers and trade
unions unfettered by the state. To what extent Whitleyism ever approached complete freedom from governmental

restraint is a matter of conjecture but governmental pay policies brought a more overtly tripartite system of pay determination. Whether employers resented or welcomed government pressure to hold down pay we can not know for sure, but it certainly helped to encourage the militancy of NALGO members. To some extent this militancy was a response from a non-party political membership that resented the harm done to the interests of NALGO members by 'political' government. It should be remembered that many of the pay policies in the 1960s and 1970s allowed exceptional increases for the low paid or had flat-rate elements which favoured the low paid. Many local government officers felt that they were losing ground, especially because they were unable to get the pay settlements which they believed were achieved by workers in the private sector and which were in excess of the pay policies. In other words, there was a belief that they were being discriminated against. Throughout the 1960s and 1970s, NALGO had a tendency to argue against pay policy inside the TUC, although where there was general support in the trade union movement for a pay policy then NALGO usually adjusted its stance sufficiently to accommodate this fact.

The pay policy of the social contract period was no different in this respect and it generated major disputes in 1978–79 amongst a wide range of local authority workers. The London Weighting dispute in 1974 appears to have been much exacerbated by the statutory pay policy begun under Edward Heath's Conservative administration (1970–74). In the winter of 1973–74 the claim for a £400 increase in London Weighting was presented to local government employers but it was turned down by the employers because of the statutory pay policy. The return of a Labour government in 1974 did not end the matter, because it insisted on maintaining the policy. Pressure was brought to bear on the union to end the dispute by the TUC but NALGO, due to the determination of members in the metropolitan district council, and a decision by NALGO conference, continued the action. The employers continued to refuse the demand right through the first half of 1974, despite full-scale action by the Islington branch and selective strike action in a number of other branches, which added up to a cost to NALGO in strike pay of three quarters of a million pounds up to the end of June. It took an intervention by the TUC, which secured governmental co-operation, to make it possible for the employers and trade unions to achieve an agreement by the late summer of 1974.

Arguably, the effects of successive government pay policies was to disillusion the mass of NALGO members with the Whitley system, thereby creating a favourable union climate for rank-and-filists who also wanted to see an end of Whitleyism for more doctrinaire reasons. In any event, NALGO's 1977 conference instructed the NEC to prepare a report considering 'the abandonment of Whitleyism and its replacement with a more advantageous system of bargaining similar to those used by the more advanced section of industrial workers'. The attraction of systems similar to those used by industrial workers (that is, more decentralised bargaining) was obvious at such a time for ordinary NALGO members. Local bargaining was less easily monitored by central government and pay increases exceeding those likely to be achieved by national negotiations were hoped for. This strategy was adopted by a range of unions, not only NALGO.

At the 1978 Conference an NEC report on Whitleyism was turned down and the NEC was instructed to explore, through the report, an alternative system of bargaining, setting out the benefits and disadvantages. It was clear that the NEC did not consider that feasible alternatives to Whitleyism existed. The rejection of the report demonstrated that the 1977 conference instruction to the NEC was not an aberration and that, for the time being, the mood of a significant section of the membership was against Whitleyism. This mood of criticism was tied up with the support for an extension of shop steward systems, which was officially supported by NALGO as a result of a 1977 conference decision – but it would be wrong to think that steward systems had been widely introduced, even by 1979. And so the criticism of Whitleyism was, to some extent, anticipating the structural developments in NALGO that would enable vigorous local bargaining. In fact, the field workers' strike of 1978–79 provided a test of the realism behind the aspiration to move away from national negotiations. In very few instances were local branches able to force employers to negotiate properly over the social workers' claim. The dispute provided very little evidence indeed that local bargaining was ready to provide a satisfactory alternative to national negotiations.

It seems that some of those who opposed the move away from Whitleyism were concerned not to see a return to the pre-Whitley days when many local authorities were able to unilaterally dictate terms and conditions of service because branch organisations were very weak. Only a small number of large, well-organised and militant branches existed and it might only be these that were able to benefit from the ending of Whitleyism. In other words, the gains of a small number of branches would be more than offset by the deterioration in the position of many others. This was the same as Drain's argument that to maximise the gains of NALGO members, the union leadership had to take account of the complexity of the membership and could not afford to move at the speed of the most progressive section. In effect, the General Secretary had argued that he had a clearer understanding of the 'alliance' that is NALGO.

The 1979 conference revealed that the membership mood had shifted yet again on Whitleyism. The NEC continued its defence of Whitleyism and, this time, the conference accepted its arguments, thereby ending the official challenge to Whitleyism.

Undoubtedly, there were a lot of NALGO members from outside the social services who considered that the 1978–79 dispute by field workers had been too costly and should not have been allowed to become such a protracted trial of strength. Perhaps if the field workers had been more successful in the dispute, the attack on Whitleyism inside NALGO would not have ended as it did in 1979. For in the views of both the militant and the more traditional trade union member, militant industrial action becomes tied to attacking Whitleyism. A tide in the direction of one will, therefore, inevitably mean a tide in the direction of the other. However, if, as in this case, the industrial action is problematic, then not only does that form of activity get a bad name, so also do those who attack Whitleyism.

The attack on Whitleyism, which started at the 1977 conference and ended two years later, tells us much about the mood of challenge within NALGO. We must now also look at the growth of steward systems, another important background factor in this period.

THE EMERGENCE OF STEWARD SYSTEMS

In 1973, a NEC report, which was accepted by the conference, recommended that branches should identify members to fill the role of shop steward. The report, which was entitled *NALGO in the 70s*, argued that such a move would enable branches to obtain facilities under the recently published Code of Industrial Relations. This new code, despite being introduced by the notorious Industrial Relations Act of 1971, helped to create a favourable climate for workplace representation. Subsequent health and safety law was to provide an even stronger boost to steward organisation throughout British workplaces in the late 1970s.

In 1976, the next official landmark in the development of steward systems inside NALGO occurred – the Sheffield branch complained to the conference that shop steward systems had not been widely introduced. It was decided to refer the complaint to the NEC because the union already had a working party studying communications within the union.

The working party submitted its report to the NEC in November 1976 and the report came out strongly in favour of the introduction of shop stewards in NALGO: 'The Working Party accepts absolutely that a concept of a steward system is of crucial importance to the effectiveness of NALGO both now and in the future' (NALGO, 1976, para. 68).

Various arguments were presented to justify this conclusion: new legislation required the identification of representatives, the dispersion of membership caused isolated pockets of members, the reorganisation of local government had increased the size of branches and led to an overloading of negotiating work on branch officers, and there was a need to strengthen the involvement of members, increase meaningful communication, and make direct links with the management structure. It should also be noted that the NALGO Action Group (NAG) had been urging the introduction of steward systems and that many rank-and-filists welcomed the report because it legitimated local pressures to move towards a steward system.

The move away from the traditional organisation of the branch was clearly envisaged by the report. The change was presented in crystal clear terms in the area of negotiations:

> In most branches virtually all negotiations have been done by branch officers and the resultant burden is now becoming evident in the growing dearth of people willing to accept Branch office. (NALGO, 1976, para. 66)

> The vital element in the duties of the steward will be that of negotiation, and it is this role which will distinguish him from the traditional role of the departmental representative. (para. 70)

The Working Party argued that steward systems would add to the effectiveness of branches but warned against stewards usurping branch policy-making and joint consultation functions. In other words, stewards were to be integrated into the branch and not be a structure separate from the branch organisation. The fears that stewards might act independently of branches were not fanciful, as we saw in the previous chapter, but it seems likely that the extreme weakness of stewards acting independently generally helped to contain the threats to branch integration.

The Working Party recommendations swiftly became official union policy. The NEC put forward a motion at the 1977 conference which recommended that branches adopt steward systems. The action which was passed included the following recommendation on the nature of the steward system:

> That each elected representative shall be responsible to and for a particular group of members and shall negotiate on behalf of his group and individuals within his group. (NALGO, 1977)

Whatever the official justifications of the move towards steward systems, rank-and-filists in NALGO harboured great hopes of change in the local union structure. Moreover, as discussed earlier, this was tied up with the attack on Whitley-ism. Some evidence suggesting that this was part of the hidden agenda of the change to steward systems is to be found in the letter from Geoffrey Drain, the General Secretary, to sec-retaries of district councils and branches, which was sent in October 1977 along with the NEC guidelines on the introduc-tion of steward systems. The letter says at one point:

> The NEC was aware that the recommendation to set up steward systems arose from the general findings of the Communications Working Party concerning the need for better communications between the policy making bodies of the Association at District and National level (and even within Branches) and the average member. It was con-cerned to emphasise that the motivation to introduce stew-ard systems arose primarily from this need and *not* from any feeling that there should be a general move away from the present arrangements for consultation and negotiation to something more like the plant bargaining of some of our industrial colleagues. (NALGO, 1977, letter)

Just as it would be wrong to see the growing militancy in NALGO in exclusively radical terms because of the rise in militancy of a large section of NALGO members (who appear to have remained wedded to party political neutrality), it is also wrong to see the growth of steward systems as exclusively the work of rank-and-filists. The NALGO leadership, for example, appear to have been in favour of steward systems as well. The difference between rank-and-filists and the leader-ship, however, concerned the role to be played by stewards within NALGO. We see yet again how the circumstances of the 1970s helped to make rank-and-filist goals realisable within NALGO. Legislation giving rights to workplace rep-resentatives (the Code of Practice under the 1971 Act and the Employment Protection Act, 1975), the effects of the 1974 reorganisation on internal union communications, and the support of the NALGO leadership for steward systems all helped to make the introduction of steward systems more likely.

The Communications Working Party had believed that steward systems could not be put in immediately and that there would be a transition period while departmental representative structures were absorbed within new forms of organisation. The NEC guidelines envisaged that the transition could take a variety of forms: in some branches departmental representatives could be renamed stewards and be given responsibilities in the negotiation area, in other branches a departmental representative system might be retained alongside a steward system, and in yet other branches variations on these approaches might be tried. An assessment of the post-1977 situation must take account of the voluntary nature of the recommendation to adopt steward systems and the General Secretary's hope, expressed in his letter, 'that Branches will select titles [for their representatives] that members themselves feel have real meaning to them in their own particular circumstances'. In other words, a branch might have a departmental representative system because it had chosen not to follow the recommendation or because it had added negotiating responsibilities to the departmental representative's role while keeping the old title.

There were reports that branch officers sometimes opposed change because they associated militancy with the introduction of steward systems, and by the end of the 1970s most branches still had departmental representative systems.

In 1982, we carried out interviews in sixty NALGO branches in English local government and this gave us the opportunity to look at how well steward systems had taken root in NALGO. We picked these branches to give us a sample which included a reasonable number based on non-metropolitan authorities, metropolitan authorities and London boroughs, which had a range of branch sizes for each category of local authority, and which, overall, had a rough balance of Conservative and Labour controlled councils.

We found that the penetration of what branches called steward systems was strongly dependent on the type of local authority on which the branch was based. Amongst the sixteen branches based on London boroughs, three quarters had shop stewards; for branches based on non-metropolitan counties, metropolitan counties and metropolitan districts, between a third and a half had shop stewards; and amongst our ten branches based on non-metropolitan districts only one had shop stewards. It can be suggested, using these figures that in 1982 only about one fifth of NALGO's local authority branches in England had shop stewards.

A very different picture emerged when we took account of the fact that in some branches departmental representatives were taking up issues with management and thus fulfilling a shop steward function. In only six of our branches was there the traditional system of representation, consisting exclusively of a system of departmental representatives who did not take up issues with management. Our sample suggests that in 1982 some three quarters of all branches in England and Wales had 'shop stewards', although they were often still called departmental representatives.

Rationally, it may not matter what posts are called. What is interesting is the response of one departmental representative from social services, who said, 'It's important that they are called shop stewards because then members have to face up to the fact that they are in a trade union.' The belief that people can be raised to a different kind of consciousness by a simple change in label is idealistic.

In many cases we found that a shop steward system was operating alongside a departmental representative system. In the London branches the most common situation was what we called a dual system: this was where there were both stewards and departmental representatives and both took up issues with management; that is, the departmental representatives were not the traditional departmental representatives who had no negotiating function.

These dual systems, when examined more closely, seemed to have a special relationship with social services departments. We had nine branches with dual systems. In two cases stewards were only in the social services department; in four cases they were in social services and some other departments; and in three cases they were in all, or nearly all, departments. It seemed that, in London branches, social services departments provided a very fertile ground for shop steward organisation even where departmental representatives were carrying out a negotiating role with respect to management. Moreover, the spread of steward systems in these nine branches also appeared to lead to an enriching of representation in the sense that the total number of stewards and departmental representatives increased the wider the coverage of stewards. Branches with a total of less than seventy-five stewards and departmental representatives were branches where stewards were only to be found in the social services department or in social services and some other departments. Branches where the total exceeded a hundred included two where stewards were in all (or nearly all) departments and one where stewards were in social services and some other departments. Overall, it seems likely that social services departments were an influential factor in the variation of representational arrangements, but not the only factor. All these results tend to underline the complex make-up of NALGO, demonstrating, as Geoffrey Drain said, how reactions differ from branch to branch.

The birth of what branches called steward systems amongst our sample seemed to have peaked in 1978 and 1979. Only two of the branches had shop stewards before 1974 and over the next four years, between 1974 and 1977, another eight branches had set up steward systems. In 1978 and 1979 ten of these branches set up steward systems, which was slightly better than the years 1980 to 1982, during which another seven branches joined the ranks of those with steward systems. The years 1978–79 were more or less the years when Whitleyism was under attack at the NALGO conference, and the years when social workers mounted their large-scale industrial action.

It is not surprising to those familiar with trade union history that all these things should have coincided. Developments in union organisation very often occur during periods of heightened militancy and changes in structures of collective bargaining. But a degree of realism is important in assessing the significance of such events and in realising that, up to 1979, rank-and-filism in NALGO and in social services departments was swimming with the tide in its favour. After 1979 the tide began to turn fiercely the other way. Consequently an appreciation of the field workers dispute in 1978–79 is essential for any wider understanding.

THE FIELD WORKERS' STRIKE

The field workers' strike began officially on 14 August 1978 and ended on 8 June 1979. It lasted over forty-two weeks and involved 2520 social workers. Its cause was recorded by the Department of Employment as a demand to negotiate pay and grading at local level.

It is interesting to ponder the significance of these bare facts before going on to look at the dispute in more detail. Firstly, what made this a big stoppage by British standards was its duration, not the numbers of social workers involved. In 1979 there were around 100 000 non-manual social services employees in the local authorities of England and Wales and so the field workers on strike represented a small fraction of this section of the membership. Secondly, if the length of this dispute was a tribute to the militancy of the field workers, it was also a reflection of the determination of the employers not to concede the demand. Thirdly, the demand was not directly and immediately related to the service provided to the clients, and thus not a 'radical social work demand', but was a demand in respect of 'service conditions', and therefore was more correctly seen as a militant action over economic objectives. Fourthly, as an attack on Whitleyism, the action had a rather contradictory reality. It was a local demand to negotiate over social worker gradings, or rather a series of local demands to negotiate social worker gradings, and was seen by some as an attack on Whitleyism. What spoiled this particular characterisation of the dispute was the fact that most other local government officers were in jobs which were the subject of local negotiations over gradings. Social workers were one of a small number of anomalous classes. Thus if the demand succeeded and the grading of social workers' jobs was subject to local negotiations they would merely be brought into line with everybody else, and this could hardly be described as bringing an end to Whitleyism. The element of truth in the claim that it was an attack on Whitleyism was that local demands were being used to try and bring about the new situation. The alternative, a *national* union demand that employers accept the right of branches to bargain over local gradings, would have been the correct way to effect the change under Whitleyism since that would have preserved the central authority of unions and employers in fixing the framework for local negotiations and consultations. In other words, it was an attack on Whitleyism because of the method used to articulate and press the demand; that is, the use of local action, rather than because of the nature of the demand itself.

The field workers' dispute was, therefore, an action involving a very small section of social services non-manual employees; which lasted for a long time due to the employer's determination not to concede; which did not involve radical union demands; and which challenged Whitleyism because it was an attempt to make a small change in the structure of collective bargaining by local rather than national bargaining. These points should be kept in mind as we review the dispute.

The steps towards industrial action began in the summer of 1977. At the local government group meeting, held as part of NALGO's conference, the question of social workers' grading was discussed. The Lambeth branch proposed that the national scale for social workers be abolished so that it would be easier to negotiate upgradings through the local collective bargaining machinery. Despite some objections that it was mainly the strong London branches that would be able to take advantage of the ending of special national grades, it was decided by the group meeting that the Lambeth proposal would be pursued.

The objections to the ending of national grades returns attention to the complexity of NALGO and the uneven rate of development amongst NALGO branches. It has to be said that those who were critical of the bureaucratic and centralised nature of NALGO, often gave the impression of overlooking the dilemma that attended a shift of power towards stewards. This dilemma is well expressed by Tony Lane (1982) when surveying British trade unionism as a whole:

> Some years ago, when but recently retired from the general secretaryship of the National Union of Mineworkers, Will Paynter expressed reservations about the shift of power within the trade union movement toward shop stewards. Paynter's anxieties had nothing to do with an erosion of 'bureaucratic centralism' or with a personal loss of power.

What concerned him was that such developments might give full rein to activity narrowly based on localised sectional interest. Looking at the problem as a socialist, Paynter was pondering the classic dilemma: while short run economic gains might be made through vigorous bargaining at plant level, gains made there would make it increasingly difficult for unions operating across a range of industries to devise national policies with progressive import. (p. 13)

These sentiments are at the very core of our analysis. In the case of social workers the danger of strong, vigorous bargaining was not only that it would leave less militant NALGO members outside social services departments behind; it was not only that it would leave other social services staffs in day centres, residential homes and elsewhere behind; it was also that it would leave other social workers in less developed branches behind.

The apparent (and misnamed) radicalism of this militant action tends to obscure the role of shortages of social workers in undermining the national gradings. Inner cities, both in London and the provinces, suffered in the early 1970s from extremely high staff turnover and understaffing. As we saw in the previous chapter, unfilled vacancies led to pressures from social workers to upgrade social work posts to attract applicants and these pressures were resisted by the local employers on the basis that they were not negotiable locally. Since the turnover and unfilled vacancies were greater problems for inner city social services departments, it was to be expected that social workers in such areas would be more determined to end national gradings. Thus the incidence of pressure on the national grades for social workers occurred in the branches that also had a reputation of militant trade unionism.

In July 1977, a circular from NALGO's General Secretary, Geoffrey Drain, recommended local negotiations by branches over the gradings of social workers. In the spring of 1978, local claims were presented to councils, especially in London. Amongst the branches involved were Tower Hamlets, where in April 1978 the staff side demanded upgradings for social workers because of increased responsibilities. The council's response was delivered at the local joint committee meeting of 5 July. The claim was rejected and the council stated that it was unable to discuss the pay scales of social workers, which, it said, should be negotiated at national or regional level.

Staff side representatives reported back to the NALGO branch at Tower Hamlets and the convener of the Social Services Shop Stewards' Committee (SSSSC) informed branch officials that social workers would back their claim by industrial action. On 18 July, NALGO members in social services held a departmental meeting and voted to go through the union's procedure to obtain official backing for strike action. This decision was subsequently approved by a branch meeting.

On 31 July, Tower Hamlets NALGO was one of three branches which made applications to the NEC Emergency Committee for authority to take industrial action. The others were Southwark and Newcastle. In accordance with NALGO rules, the district office carried out a secret ballot of social workers in the branch. Eighty-four per cent voted in favour of strike action with strike pay and 78 per cent voted in favour even without strike pay. The Emergency Committee declared an official strike, which began on 21 August, one week after similar strikes started in Southwark and Newcastle.

The lead-up to strike action contained signs of the rank-and-filist challenge to NALGO's national leadership. Thus, at the NALGO conference in 1978 the local government group meeting had referred back a section of the report which dealt with the absence of a formal national claim to end social workers' national grades. This was interpreted by rank-and-filists as an affirmation for the 1977 decision to abolish the grades, since a reference back can be seen as an act of censure on the NEC. Moreover, in the run-up to industrial action in August 1978, discussions appear to have been taking place between social services activists in the London branches which were noted for their militancy. This alliance of London social services activists realised itself in the organisation of a regional body known as the All-London Social Workers' Action Group (ALSWAG).

The decision of the NEC Emergency Committee to authorise strike action meant that the first official strike action began only days after the employers at national level refused to end

the national grades for social workers. An early event in the
Southwark dispute suggests that for local activists the principle of local negotiations was crucial. Southwark council
offered social workers the improved grades already obtained
by social workers in Lambeth; but the offer was refused
because they were not being offered negotiations at local level.

The early months of the dispute were ones in which much of
the focus remained in London as picketing was used to bring
large-scale disruption to local authorities and a National
Strike Operations Committee was established. Payments from
NALGO's Special Reserve Fund to branches involved in
industrial action showed that the base of the strike was in
London during August and September, followed later by the
rest of the country. In those early months, most of the money
in the social workers' dispute was paid out to social workers in
two London boroughs.

TABLE 3.1   Payments from NALGO's special reserve fund

Type of branch	1 Apr–30 Sept 1978 £	1 Oct–31 Dec 1978 £
London borough branches	111 743	347 874
Other local government branches	73 879	597 525
Gas, health, etc., branches	203 725	–
	389 347	945 399

SOURCE: Adapted from Newman, 1982, pp. 448 and 453.

THE STRIKE IN TOWER HAMLETS

In analysing the strike we thought it would be useful to look at
the experience in one borough as well as attempting an
overview. This methodology allows us to make most clearly
our preferred point about the uneven development of the
Union across the country.

A strike committee was set up which included social service shop stewards, two branch officials and one staff side

representative. The strike committee was an official committee of the NALGO branch executive and, by virtue of its composition, was intended to ensure good lines of communication.

The weapon of the social workers was not so much striking as picketing. Initially they picketed their area offices, thereby preventing the delivery of mail, and it was then decided to picket a number of the town halls and other buildings where administrative work was carried out. The first picketing of the town halls began on 20 September and soon the borough's administration was in severe difficulties. When postmen refused to cross picket lines, the flow of income, including rates, to the council ceased. On 26 September drivers of oil tankers agreed not to cross picket lines and accusations by the council appeared in the local press suggesting that the strikers were making old people suffer. In fact, the heating system for one of the town halls also heated flats for old people in an adjacent building and the council declined a union offer to allow deliveries of oil if the town hall boiler was used only for these flats. Picketing was extended to other council buildings on 2 October.

During all this picketing other NALGO members continued to report for duty even though the stoppage of mail meant there was less and less for them to do. They were still, however, being paid normally. A staff side representative explained the intentions of the striking social workers as follows:

> They felt that they should not involve any other member of staff, be they manual or officer, any more than they could possibly help. So they designed every bit of industrial action they took to that end. They arranged for the stopping of any form of servicing from the post office, either on the telecommunications or postal side, which effectively paralysed the council's administration but did not preclude the staff from receiving their pay. Frankly, this had been the motive all along.

These tactics not only meant that other NALGO members were increasingly being paid for doing nothing, it also maintained branch goodwill towards the dispute.

Less success was achieved when the social workers attempted to spread the disruption to the council's refuse service. They decided to try to immobilise the dustcarts by picketing the borough's garages, thereby cutting the supply of petrol and diesel on which the dustcarts depended. Picketing began on 7 October but the action led to an inter-union row. What they had overlooked was the consequential effects for bonus earnings of the manual workers. A member of staff side said:

They would only be paid their basic of £40 per week and they would lose – I don't know the figure, I've heard £12 mentioned as an average figure, but I believe it to be much higher than that, something like £20 per week – bonus. So wrongly or rightly, and many of us feel wrongly, the manual workers decided that they would avail themselves of another source of supply of petrol or diesel. They went up to a garage which the council uses in emergencies and agreed to obtain their diesel fuel there. But they asked in return the council pay them £4 a week to the drivers, £4 a week to the leading hands and £2 to everybody else involved.

A NUPE branch secretary told the strike committee that his members were going to use the garage anyway, because they weren't prepared to be on flat money, and so the stewards thought they could help the strike by making management pay for it. The TGWU branch censored its own stewards who had been involved and threatened to withdraw their cards. Relations between NALGO and the manual unions were a bit strained for some time after this incident.

What was the effect of all this pressure on the council? It was showing no signs of capitulation. Indeed, the minutes of a staff side meeting in early October recorded the results of a recent joint committee meeting as follows:

Outcome of meeting with council again was in nature of a pantomine. Offer was ludicrous. It said they would not negotiate locally on grades that are negotiated nationally and others on strike would be dealt with under Review System. All this was rejected and we were careful not to break off negotiations and we have asked to submit a paper giving what we were prepared to negotiate on.

In other words, after six weeks of strike action the council had not shifted its position in the slightest. The industrial action was having massive effects but the council remained implacable.

With hindsight, we can say that a massive strike in local government is not the formidable weapon it can be in some private sector settings. If the work of a local authority is disrupted, as it was in Tower Hamlets, the union is not inflicting financial losses. The services of the council are not sold in a competitive market situation and there is no threat that rival competitors will win the business and the council be unable to win back the service (although a council might use the industrial action as a pretext for privatisation, but this is a political decision). There might be local community pressure on a council to restore services but to be effective this would require councillors to fear being voted out of office. According to trade union activists, such fears were not common amongst councillors in the 1970s.

The pressures on councillors and local authority managers are primarily to stay within budgets – not to provide services. One of the major material points that we make throughout this book is made obvious in this context. A local authority strike does not threaten budgets, it threatens services. Indeed, a strike in local government, and elsewhere in the public services, can improve the budgetary position of the employer as a result of savings on salary costs. Thus the whole original aim of the strike weapon – to attack employer's profits – is not only useless but the strike will even have the very opposite effect to the one intended.

THE NATIONAL LEVEL

Other branches joined the dispute rather slowly. In October, Liverpool social workers became the fourth group to become involved in the action. Their strike, which lasted nearly six months and ended in March 1979, seems to have been well supported by over three hundred social workers: 'Eighty-nine per cent voted in favour of the strike and all through the strike we had no blacklegs or anyone returning to work' (Walker, 1981, p. 18). Lewisham social workers also joined the dispute in October 1978.

Still in October, there were moves towards more social services departments being drawn into the dispute, but there were also signs of preparations for a national agreement. Ballots took place in nine branches to see if strike action on local regrading claims was to be authorised. But on 25 October, the NJC representatives met and decided to form a joint working party to negotiate a national framework agreement.

Rank-and-filist criticisms of the national handling of the dispute were a feature of the dispute at all stages. NALGO was criticised for the lack of co-ordination, for the lack of publicity, and for lack of support for rank-and-filist initiatives. In London, ALSWAG called a London demonstration for 21 August, which was supported by social workers from Tower Hamlets, Southwark, Newcastle and Ealing. At a rally about the demonstration, it called for a stoppage in all London boroughs on 27 September, and while this was supported by the union's metropolitan district committee, the NEC refused to give its support.

Additional evidence of friction was provided by the disagreements which occurred in connection with NALGO's National Strike Operations Committee which was set up in August to co-ordinate local activities. At the committee's first meeting, representatives from branches were invited. Their representatives were dissatisfied with their lack of involvement in the deliberations of the committee at its first meeting and their exclusion from subsequent meetings. The reaction to this situation was to form the Standing Conference of Strike Committees.

Fears of rank-and-filists in social services in November centred on the actions of the NALGO leadership. Demonstrations were held by social workers to pressurise the national local government committee and the NEC. Chris Jones (1983), in his book on social workers, reports:

During that dispute many social worker activists were worried that they would be deserted by their union. Indeed, such was their anxiety that in November 1978, 600 social workers occupied their union headquarters in London for the purposes of preventing the union leadership from securing a 'solution' that did not meet their demands. This was just one of the many incidents which demonstrated fundamental differences between sections of the union leadership and striking social workers. . . . (pp. 140–1)

In November, eight branches were involved in strike action, three of which were on indefinite strike, and a further six branches were being balloted. NALGO was, however, spending considerable sums of money and local negotiations were showing few signs of being fruitful. What was happening at local level?

TOWER HAMLETS IN NOVEMBER AND DECEMBER

In Tower Hamlets there were fears about a 'sell out' by NALGO's national officials, and this danger arose from NALGO's financial position. Staff side's secretary gave this assessment of the situation in November:

The estimate I have heard is that the NALGO strike fund will run out early in the New Year. The rates before Greenwich came out on strike were something like half a million pounds per month, that's pretty high. This is over the country – including Newcastle, Liverpool, and so on. Given the strike's been going on in some places for over three months, obviously money is really tight!

The action had disrupted the services of the council and picket lines were operating at town halls, council depots and other buildings. Was the council being forced to consider the local claim for regrading? Was council resistance crumbling in the face of such determined, full scale and militant action? The answer to both questions is no. It was said that the council were aware of NALGO's financial situation. The secretary of staff side thought the council, a Labour one, was getting more aggressive:

> I think it's already affected the way they are conducting the strike . . . They are quite aware (of the union's financial situation) . . . we hear rumours of councillors saying to our members on picket lines: 'You're going to be out till Christmas – we're going to grind NALGO into the ground financially'.

It appeared that the councillors were saying that they did not care how long the social workers stayed out on strike. The council seemed not to 'care about the extension of the strike. . . . when I say care, I mean as an industrial weapon'. The attitudes of Labour councillors during this dispute, however shocking they seemed to striking social workers and their NALGO colleagues, require more than an emotional reaction. A careful, analytical response is also needed: why did the successful stoppage of much of the council's services over such a long period not put pressure on the council? How many private sector employers would have been willing to withstand this pressure for so long? The very need to pose these questions underlines the importance of public service workers considering what modifications they need to make to their tactics when pursuing the militant methods that appear to work in the 'industrial' sector.

At this stage in the dispute, when it had become clear that the councillors were being very tough and they showed no signs of backing down, the social workers had two major options: they could start making concessions and seek a compromise solution, or they could escalate.

The path of seeking compromises was bound to be unattractive in the circumstances that existed after two to three months of full-scale industrial action. The strike was for the principle of rank-and-filist democracy and it was, therefore, against Whitleyism. Compromising on principles, 'splitting the difference', is intrinsically more difficult than compromising on a demand for more money. What could the council concede that would be presented as a partial gain by the social workers if the principle of Whitleyism was the issue at stake?

This obviously made ending the strike difficult. Not surprisingly, the striking social workers went for escalation: the principle of Whitleyism was going to be decided by the balance of power. But which was the weaker party?

The strike committee called on the members of the Tower Hamlets branch, at a branch meeting held at the end of October, only to cross picket lines at their own place of work. It was pointed out by the strike committee that the payment of salaries would not be affected by the action. The branch meeting, attended by about a thousand members, which was an exceptional turn-out, voted in favour of the strike committee's motion.

Up to this point the pickets had been effective in stopping mail, income and supplies; they had not been intended to stop NALGO members. The borough's non-manual staff worked in a multitude of sites and many meetings to co-ordinate and plan work required trips to other sites. If staff observed the picket lines at other places of work the already-disrupted work of the council would be further hit.

What effect did escalation have on the council? The council responded by becoming more aggressive. On 22 November, four NALGO members were suspended without pay, and two more were suspended, for refusing to cross picket lines. Where this would have led eventually is not known but 700 NALGO members went on strike and the suspensions were withdrawn. On 28 November, at a joint committee meeting, the council refused to continue the meeting while a striking social worker was amongst the staff side representatives in attendance. The meeting was not continued and it took action by the provincial joint council, the Greater London Whitley Council, to resolve the impasse.

NATIONAL COMPROMISES

Towards the end of November, at the NJC joint working party (which had been set up a month earlier), an offer was presented by the employers' representatives. This offer proposed that the salary structure of social workers be based on three levels. NALGO's National Local Government Committee obtained the approval of the NEC for a special local government group meeting towards the end of January at which the offer would be considered.

The offer was recommended to delegates at the special group meeting by national officers as being a move towards local negotiations. The offer, which was accepted by the delegates, was described as a national grading framework within which local negotiations could take place. But was it that? This is a matter on which opinions can vary but, arguably, it did build in some scope for local bargaining. It widened the salary range for the main body of social workers, chopped up the main grade into three separate scales, and thus produced some headroom for local bargaining. At the very least this seemed likely to buy time for Whitleyism as local bargaining pressures might be absorbed in the process of negotiating the regrading of social workers on to higher levels for a few years.

ENDING THE DISPUTE

By late January, 1979 there were fourteen branches on strike and the cost of strike pay had reached £1.6 million. It was reported that another five branches were taking industrial action other than strikes. Now that the national framework agreement had been accepted, the union had the job of ending the local actions in some semblance of order.

Most of the striking social workers were able to reach some sort of settlement with their local authorities but in three cases terminating the strike proved difficult. At Tower Hamlets, Gateshead and Knowsley the strike continued despite returns to work in the other branches.

The strike at Tower Hamlets was the last to finish. It finally came to an end in June 1979, some nine and a half months after its start, and thus the longest of the strikes in this dispute. It ended because of pressure put on the council by the employers' bodies in the Whitley structure to accept the January national settlement. The employers remained aggressive and unwilling to compromise right to the bitter end. It was said that councillors were motivated by a desire to show the social workers who was boss and to teach them a lesson. The union side to the agreement included staff side representatives, the NALGO district official and two members of the strike committee.

Many of the union side agreed that negotiations had resulted in generous pay increases and that there had been some move towards local negotiations. On the other hand, there were fears about the effects of a proposal to reorganise social services and there were those who wondered whether improvements in pay would solve the problems of social work vacancies.

AN ASSESSMENT OF THE FIELD WORKERS' DISPUTE

Various characterisations of the dispute were offered at the time and have been offered since, and rarely have they done justice to the complexity of the issues concerned. We will look briefly at a few of these characterisations.

Firstly, some observers saw the social workers as the instrument of NALGO policy to bring about local negotiations. The policies and actions of NALGO in this period were to a substantial extent the results of opposing forces within NALGO: doubts and uncertainties were widely held at national level. It was the rank-and-filists amongst social workers that fought for policy changes on local bargaining and saw the field workers' dispute as a challenge to Whitleyism.

Another view of the dispute saw the militant social workers as using their strength to gain advantages for themselves at the expense of weaker sections of membership. This critical evaluation saw in their action, therefore, sectional self-interest which was undermining the policy of national negotiations, a policy valued by many for the greater equity it brought to pay structures. The problem with this view is that it ignores the fact that social workers were paid according to a nationally prescribed scale which placed them under greater restrictions than most other staff and meant that they had less scope for locally agreed improvements based on upgradings.

A third assessment of the dispute was that it had occurred because of a deep sense of grievance amongst social workers that they were being underpaid. There is much validity in this view but by itself it is not adequate. There is no doubt that many of the leading activists were also deeply concerned about what they regarded as fundamental principles of union democracy, which tied in with the rank-and-filist critique of Whitleyism. Time and time again, social work activists insisted that a scrupulous concern for clients could authentically coexist with a belief in the legitimacy of strike action. The long-term welfare of the clients, they argued, was not damaged by militancy.

There is a fourth view of the strike, which is sometimes expressed: that the strength of feeling in favour of local negotiations became stronger amongst social workers because of the way in which NALGO's national officials handled the dispute. It is sometimes said that the national leaders used the Whitley machinery to engineer a national agreement to end the dispute. It has also been said that national officials held out for a national settlement. Variations on these themes include the judgement, just after the dispute, that the national leadership would have to be recommitted to the policy of local negotiations and, alternatively, the argument that the rank-and-filists could now see that they had to demand the power to negotiate from the union leadership.

The problems with this overall position are not the implications that NALGO's leadership 'sold out' or that it was trying to undermine the rank-and-filist movement in the social workers' dispute. Whether these implications are true or not, the difficulty with this assessment is that it sidetracks the analysis and takes it up a dead end. Firstly, the history of rank-and-filism in NALGO plainly shows that feelings against Whitleyism had been very strong long before the field workers' dispute. Indeed, it was the rank-and-filist feelings against Whitleyism that helped to define the leaderships' actions as selling out. Secondly, even if it is assumed that the union leaders had been totally behind the aspiration to decentralise collective bargaining, would they not still have had to intervene to find a compromise settlement? How far were union leaders to go in backing this very small section of the membership? In 1978, NALGO's membership stood at 729 405. Its membership involved in the field workers' strikes was, according to union figures, 2600, which was not even half of one per cent of the entire membership! At one point the strike was costing nearly £500 000 per month and, at that rate, the strike fund would have been exhausted in the spring of 1979. It is true that special measures could have been taken to boost the fund, but what evidence was there that local negotiations could be forced by continuing industrial action?

The dissatisfaction of those who see the actions by NALGO's union leadership, the union 'bureaucrats', in negotiating the compromise national settlement as contriving a sell-out, is based on a reluctance to see any justification in compromises. To some rank-and-filists a compromise is inevitably a betrayal.

The complaint that the national leadership 'held out' for a national agreement is a nonsensical one. The whole point about the local claims was that they would obviate the necessity of a national agreement. If the national leadership had intervened sooner and made a national agreement, the complaints about 'selling out' would have been made earlier than they were. Likewise, complaints of inadequate national publicity and national co-ordination by rank-and-filists is illogical given that the point was to demonstrate the superiority of local bargaining. That such complaints were made, especially the complaint that the national leadership 'held out' for a national agreement, only draws attention to the weak power position of the striking social workers and their lack of realism in thinking that 'plant bargaining' similar to that found in private manufacturing industry would make national agreements no longer necessary. Bluntly, national leaders could only hold out for a national agreement if striking social workers were too weak to force their councils to make local agreements on regrading.

Finally, those who have argued that the social workers as a result of their experiences during the dispute, became more and more committed to *demanding* local negotiations so that power would be shifted away from union leaders, obviously underestimated the extent to which that had been one of the original motives for the dispute. More to the point, however, is the implicit misunderstanding of how bargaining structures change. If rank-and-filists had held a more powerful position they would not have been demanding local negotiations – they would have got on and negotiated. In other words, a shift in power was the prerequisite for local negotiations, not something that depended on local negotiations. Moreover, these critical views of the union leaders concentrates on the distribution of power in the union and ignores what was critical in this dispute – the balance of forces between social workers and their councils. It was the weakness of social workers *vis-à-vis* their councils that was the real stumbling block to their seizure of the chance for local negotiations.

We turn to one final view of the dispute. In this case, the focus is kept entirely on the social work occupation and the dispute is viewed as a critical test of its development towards trade union consciousness. The occupation is divided into those who passed the test, who went on strike, who saw the strike as a legitimate trade union action which was in the long-term interests of clients, and those who failed the test, who were too concerned with professional issues of short-term impact on clients, and who refused to take part in the strike action. For some the major reason for the prolonged nature of the strike and the failure to secure proper local negotiations was the strength of professionalism amongst many social workers. This view recognises that while the determination of a small number of branches was considerable, the problem was the limited support it achieved amongst field workers. If more had joined the strike, and joined it early on, the argument goes, we would have had better results. Either the small number of militant branches that had taken the lead did not think they needed the rest or they were not sufficiently realistic about the uneven development of social workers in terms of trade union consciousness and organisation.

The dispute may have fallen short of the hopes that some of the social work activists had entertained but the dispute and the settlement was of great significance. Most immediately, it left many in NALGO more rather than less convinced of the need for the 'safety net' provided by national agreements. It also changed the grading of social workers creating more scope for local bargaining and for local competition for upgrading to the professional status associated with the Level 3 social work scale. This obviously potentially had contradictory effects on local rank-and-filism. Formally speaking, Level 3 provided for a role with professional discretion and individual's career ambitions could thus become focused on promotion to that level.

UNION LEADERS AND RANK AND FILISTS

So far in this chapter we have explored the difficulties of creating alliances within NALGO for militant social work trade unionists. We have characterised these difficulties as stemming from two linked sources. On the one hand, NALGO is intrinsically a union of very varied workers with very varied labour processes and ideologies. Therefore materially the union is extremely likely to develop in different ways according to both locality and labour process. These differences will take a myriad forms, with different groups of members experiencing different rationales for belonging to the union. One significant material difference in this analysis has been around the issue of militancy.

In a union such as NALGO there will always *materially* be one group or section more militant than another who will feel that the rest of the union membership doesn't really understand its position. It will, therefore, enter any dispute with some real, experiential separation from its fellow members. It is the work of the national leadership of such a varied union to struggle to maintain the overall approach of the organisation. It is inevitable therefore that the national leadership must represent these different experiences of militancy back to each section of the union. It is further inevitable that in a dispute involving only a part of the membership these different sections will tend to feel either 'pushed into action' or 'sold out' by this national role. This produces, in consequence, a feeling that the leadership is out of synchronisation with 'us', in this case field social workers. The leadership *is*, in fact, out of synchronisation because it has members who are themselves – because of their different localities, different labour processes and different levels of work – embracing very different attitudes towards this particular dispute.

As a union with well over 700 000 members, if NALGO

wants to maintain itself as an organisation, the leadership must act in this way. This in turn will lead militant social worker trade unionists to try and appeal around the leadership direct to other members who they feel will (or at the very least should) support the strike. These appeals are sometimes successful, sometimes not, but if they are made on the assumption that all members of NALGO are in some way essentially the same, then they are more then likely to fail. This happens because the appeal fails to recognise these material differences of experience.

However, whilst we have characterised the leadership of unions such as NALGO as inevitably having to represent different aspects of its membership to each other, this can only occur within a union where democracy is clear and in perfect working order. We recognise that NALGO, alongside all other trade unions, is not in this happy position!

There are a wealth of reasons why there are serious dislocations between the hopes and aspirations of ordinary members and the values and actions of a national leadership. The most significant of these is the very limited proportion of members who are ever involved in the activity of trade unions. We believe the crucial 'gap' is not between union leadership and the activists, but much more so between these two groups and the vast mass of membership. In Chapter 6 we outline our appreciation of this issue.

Secondly, as a problem for alliance building within the union, the ideology of rank-and-filism will see this form of union leadership – that represents different sections of the union one to another – as a bureaucratic structure which has at its core the necessity to 'clamp down' on militant action. When social workers are the group involved in the action, rank-and-filist ideology will be able to demonstrate that the leadership is carrying out this role. How? Militants involved in action almost totally experience the rest of the union through their national leadership. They may also occasionally meet other groups of militant shop stewards to discuss the action, although this would further our point. They do not, nor could they, meet the vast bulk of the real rank-and-file membership with the varied material experiences we outlined above. They only experience them through the mediation of the national leadership, and experience that in contrast to the other militants that they meet.

Therefore, they can truthfully represent the leadership as 'not really understanding us'. Less certainly, though, could they claim that 'the rest of the union membership wants to support us', but since they usually speak through the collective leadership, this rank-and-filist supposition of a 'hidden militancy amongst ordinary members' is only tested through the mediation of national leadership.

Thus, in struggle, a union leadership can be experienced as hesitant and holding back on its own behalf rather than as representing a varied membership. In this dispute the leadership, and the rest of the union, contributed £1.6 million in strike pay to the action. For every social worker on strike this represents an average of £700. Undoubtedly for those workers on strike the longest this average would triple in cost. Simply in financial terms, then, it is likely that the most militant branches were supported by the union to the tune of about one hundred years of personal financial cost of membership. Against that background the experience of being 'sold out' is, we believe, an unusual representation.

4

Trade Unionism and the Struggle for Municipal Socialism – Progressive Practice in Reactionary Times

INTRODUCTION

Experienced trade union activists amongst social workers found the early 1980s to be a more difficult period than the preceding decade. They looked back on the 1970s as a period in which they had enjoyed early success and in which they had been able to make a major impact on NALGO. They had built much of the early trade union activity on the enthusiasm and commitment of field social workers and had used union militancy to turn the glare of publicity on to their employers. Making sense of social work trade unionism under Thatcherism, however, means that two points about the historical legacy of the 1970s must be understood. Firstly, the social workers did have a major impact on NALGO and the union was changed permanently as a result. The effects of this impact will be seen when we look at the residential workers' dispute which occurred in 1982. NALGO had not been known for its militancy, but its increased involvement in strike activity in the 1970s, in which social workers took a prominent role, led to a different attitude to industrial action on the part of the union leadership. Secondly, the experienced activists in social services learned lessons from the disputes of the 1970s which led them to reappraise the strategy of sectional militancy.

The move away from rank-and-filism, however, has also spelt, for the time being, a move away from the 'one best way'

135

view of trade unionism. Social work activists now assess the mood of the membership, which is cautious and worried, and the state of the relationship between stewards and members, which is more fragile and tentative than before. The increased awareness and sensitivity of the social work activists has resulted in experiments with new forms of organisation and strategy to deal with the new political climate.

In this chapter we bring out some of the diversity in the trade union experience of social workers in the 1980s, some of the cautious experimentation in organisation and strategy, and some of the movement towards a refashioned social work trade unionism. We will also be emphasising the importance of very specific local conditions in the development of social work trade unionism and the new relationship between NALGO's national leadership and social services activists. First, however, we must start with the political developments which add up to Thatcherism and which provided the context for trade union struggles and developments in social services recently.

THATCHERISM

If social work activists are asked about the nature of social work practice under Thatcherism, the answers which come back are generally similar. The field social workers say that there have been increased demands on personal social services, due in part to demographic changes which have meant an increased proportion of elderly people in the population, but due mainly to the growing numbers of social casualties of the recession. The field social workers feel that they are, to quote one of them, 'picking up the tab'. Unemployment, bad housing and poverty have become widespread and social workers are the people left with the job of trying to solve the problems.

The residential workers have a different experience of Thatcherism, and it is, if anything, worse. The growth of anti-institutional ideologies amongst policy makers, administrators and professional groups has led to a devaluing of the work carried out by residential workers and a consequent disparagement of them as workers. The new policy of the

1980s was community care, a policy dedicated to obviating the need for hospitals and residential homes. In many areas the residential workers felt, rightly or wrongly, that they were 'living on borrowed time': they felt there was no future in residential work.

The rising demands on field social workers and the threats to residential services were combined with increased attempts by the state – in the shape of the Thatcher government – to control public spending. For field social workers, the attempts to control public spending meant pressure on them to cope with rising demands but without concomitant increases in resources. In the residential area, public spending controls aggravated fears about the future; lack of money being seen as giving a pecuniary reason for speeding up the move to a community care policy done on the cheap.

What is Thatcherism? It has been characterised as an experiment in monetarism, and this approach to defining Thatcherism puts the emphasis on the government's commitment to reducing inflation by decreasing the growth of the money stock. Accordingly, other aspects of the government's actions, such as attempts to reduce public expenditure and to cut out 'bureaucratic waste' in the public services, are seen as subordinated to the overall aim of monetary control.

There are some grounds for rejecting this particular characterisation of Thatcherism, however. An examination of budget statements in the 1980s suggests that the Government's policy of monetary control has been a shambles. Monetary targets were exceeded in 1980–81, 1981–82 and 1983–84; and in 1985–86 the Government's target was exceeded in the case of the 'broad' money measure, although the growth of 'narrow' money was well within the target range. There may, then, be doubts about the credentials of Margaret Thatcher's government as agents of monetarism. There can be little doubt about the determination with which Thatcherism has attacked public sector forms of social production (that is, nationalised industries and public services), the welfare state and the organisation and strength of trade unionism.

The Thatcher government has been openly pursuing a policy to strengthen the private enterprise nature of the economy and one aspect of this has been the privatisation programme. In the years following the 1979 General Election, stock market flotations were used to create major private sector companies out of bits of the public sector. In the process some 400 000 workers were transferred from the public sector to the private sector. Privatisation has taken other forms as well. Contracting-out of services has been pushed by the government in respect of the civil service, the National Health Service and local government. In the case of local government, the Thatcher government's Local Government Planning and Land Act 1980 created a legal requirement to put building and maintenance work out to competitive tender.

'VOLUNTARY CARE'

The state welfare services have also been victims of the government's attack on state forms of social production. 'Rolling back the state' has meant the encouragement of the private health sector and support for charitable giving. In their 1979 Manifesto, the Conservative Party said that more must be done to help people to help themselves, to help families to look after their own, and to encourage the voluntary sector. In November 1980, Patrick Jenkin announced on behalf of the Conservative Government, 'A great encouragement of voluntary and community effort will now be a central thrust of our policy towards the Personal Social Services' (Webb and Wistow, 1982, p. 34).

In the context of these attitudes, it was inevitable that government approval of community care policy aroused widespread fears that it was to be done on the cheap. While there was a lot of support for closing down hospitals and residential homes and bringing people who were elderly, mentally ill or handicapped, as well as children, out of these institutions and 'back into the community', social workers were concerned that the support structures did not exist in the community on the requisite scale.

Government support for charitable work, which had mainly taken the form of developing the system of tax reliefs, was part of the intervention to reduce the state sector. Since charities also operate in the area of social welfare, the tax changes were directly undermining the position of state welfare services.

TRADE UNIONISM

The Thatcher government's hostility to trade unionism is well known. Trade unions were condemned in speech after speech for their lack of restraint in wage demands, for their restrictive practices which blocked efficiency, and for their irresponsible attitude to modernisation. These speeches seemed to accord well with the public mood, which opinion polls indicated strongly favoured legal reform of trade union power. The Conservative government passed the Employment Acts of 1980 and 1982, and the Trade Union Act of 1984, legislation aimed at reducing the power of the trade unions and at making the unions more democratic. As a result of this the government expected more moderate pay demands and more flexible working practices. In the same way that it claimed the credit for the fall in inflation as a result of its monetary policy, it attributed the marked drop in strike frequency to the trade union legislation it had imposed.

BOLSTERING PRIVATE ENTERPRISE

On the whole, there can be little doubt that Thatcherism was fundamentally an attempt to bolster the private enterprise form of social production and only superficially was it an experiment in monetarism. Tory ideologues of the right saw this in terms of a struggle between the enfeebled capitalist sector and the 'unnaturally' vigorous public sector. Sir Keith Joseph expressed it like this:

In simplest terms, the burden of the state sector became too heavy for the economy to bear without strain. Even 40 per cent is very high, perhaps too high, when it means that the private wealth-producing sector is milked in order to support increasing legions of deficitary activities. These included not only state non-profit making services, national and local, but also rail, coal and other industries of which the nationalisation was calculated to keep more people in jobs than were needed for their economic function.

As the ratio between wealth-producing private and wealth-consuming state sector changed in favour of the latter, the private sector became increasingly anaemic and sluggish. (Hutber, 1978, p. 102)

But the Thatcher struggle to revitalise the private enterprise sector required not only that it be enlarged by taking bits out of the public sector, it also meant attempting to shift the balance of forces in the private sector. Both the privatisation of the welfare state and the weakening of trade unionism might be expected to have the effect, if not the intention, of strengthening the power of employers in the private sector.

According to public spending figures, the extent of the Conservative cuts in public spending has been modest (see Table 4.1). Indeed, public expenditure, as a percentage of GDP, rose every year in the first three years of the Conservative government and was still higher in 1984–85 than it had been under the Labour administration in 1978–79. This failure, however, was due to the rising cost of pensions, unemployment benefit, debt interest and other items.

Some headway was made in the attack on public sector forms of social production. Between 1979 and 1983 over half a million public-sector jobs were lost, many of them due to redundancies in the British Steel Corporation, British Leyland, British Rail and other public enterprises. But at the same time, private industry lost 1.4 million jobs (Rose, 1985, p. 90).

PROBLEMS FOR TRADE UNIONISM

These Conservative governments made it clear from the out- set that they wanted to see cuts in local government expendi- ture and cuts in jobs in public services. This was evident from the assumptions about pay increases that were built into cash limits by central government. In the early 1980s the cash

TABLE 4.1 Public expenditure planning totals

	Total at 1980 survey prices	Total using 1984–85 as base year	Chain index showing rate of change
	£ billion[1]	£ billion[2]	
1975–76	81.3	–	–
1976–77	79.2	–	97.4
1977–78	74.4	–	93.9
1978–79	78.0	(117.4)	104.8
1979–80	77.8	(118.5)	99.8(100.9)
1980–81	–	119.2	100.6
1981–82	–	121.5	101.9
1982–83	–	123.6	101.7
1983–84	–	125.7	101.7
1984–85	–	129.6	103.1

SOURCES: [1] *Economic Progress Report*, (Treasury, 1981) no. 131, March.
          [2] *Economic Progress Report*, (Treasury, 1986) no. 182, January–February.

limits were set at levels below the rate of inflation, although some freedom of manoeuvre was available to local authorities by virtue of their control over the level of rate income. The freedom was also there for local government employers to finance pay increases by means of staffing cuts.

An effective union response in these circumstances was not easy. It wasn't just the existence of a hostile Conservative government; the mood of the members was a major factor. Obviously the picture varied from one branch to another, but a field social worker in London expressed the problem in this way:

The hold we have, if you want to call it that, over our members, is very tentative and there have been times in the last year or so when I have been extremely worried about lines that we have been taking and the way we have been directing our minds to that. Because in a way it's a very fragile relationship and it's the whole political climate – it affects everybody. And people feel downtrodden and scared. Even local government is coming much more in the firing line so I think caution is the watchword of local government trade unionism at the moment.

As we have argued above, Thatcherism has been an attack on public sector forms of social production. But is was easier for the state to attack some forms of social production inside the public sector than others. The really massive job losses occurred in the nationalised industries – British Steel, British Leyland, British Rail, and British Coal. The state found more obstacles in the way of attacks on services inside local government. In this respect it is interesting to contrast the different outcomes of two disputes in the public sector which were both of long duration: the coal miners' dispute of 1984–85 and the teachers' dispute of 1985–86. The state's relationship to the two different forms of social production is distinctly different. The nationalised industries have been run as state-operated public corporations over which government ministers have considerable direct control. The welfare services in local government are under the direct control of elected members, although the central state has some *de facto* power in the operation of these services, while also providing a substantial proportion of the finance for them out of national taxation.

The complex relationship between the central and local state is illustrated by the ambiguity of the relevant government minister's position on cuts in personal social services in the early years of the Thatcher government. According to Webb and Wistow (1982) the Secretary of State

has placed considerable emphasis on the indicative nature of the White Paper's guidelines for individual services within the tightly drawn limits for local authority spending. However, it must be noted that this approach aroused, rather than cooled, passions among some LA personnel. What was seen as a 'nod and a wink' to ignore the government's working assumption that PSS would be cut was experienced as an act of hyprocrisy rather than as a reprieve. (p. 51)

Given the hostility of Thatcherism to public sector forms of social production, this complexity did not halt the attack on local government, but did impede it. The early attempts to cut council spending by reducing the level of central government grants failed to have the desired effect because many councils chose to increase rates. The government then attempted to control actual spending by withdrawing grant if councils 'overspent'. Finally, in 1984 the government brought in rate-capping legislation to try to deal with the assertion of independence by those elected councils which had continued to ignore the state's wish to cut back public spending. These councils were Labour controlled.

What options did social work trade unionism have? All-out national strike action? Local strike action led by more militant social services shop steward committees? Joint action with other unions? Alliances with 'progressive' Labour councils against the central state? Should the social workers strike in an attempt to put pressure on central government? Or was industrial action best directed at the employers – the council?

All-out strike action had been supported by only a small number of social services shop steward committees in 1978–79 when unemployment was lower and there was a Labour government. What prospect could all-out action have against the Thatcher government in the very different conditions of the 1980s? Alliances with progressive Labour councils could not be a universal strategy since not all councils fitted this description, and in any case, many of the social work activists distrusted Labour politicians.

NALGO CHANGES

The 1978–79 dispute marked a turning point as far as the role of social work activists in NALGO was concerned. This was due partly to an increasing tendency for social workers to be drawn into, or move into, leadership positions in NALGO branches and at higher levels of the union and there were several reasons for this. Firstly, the trade union activity in social services became more acceptable to other NALGO members in local government. In some places this was tied up with the blurring of the distinction between the old type of local government officers, and social workers as a new type of local government officer, or as a social services convener put it, 'There's much less the feeling that social workers are not really local government officers'.

Secondly, there may have been, in some places, an element of left-wing annoyance with the behaviour of NALGO in the 1978–79 dispute. A northern social worker said of the strike:

> Naturally I think it had a major impact because a lot of social workers were extremely disillusioned with NALGO and actually took the option of staying in and campaigning. And when you go to national conference now the number of social workers who are in branch positions, the number of social workers on the national executive committee, you know there's three or four on the national committee now. . . .

Thirdly, and not to be underestimated, is the fact that social workers became a repository of trade union experience which was a valuable asset. A London NALGO branch secretary, who had previously been a convener of a social services shop stewards' committee, agreed that social workers had moved into the mainstream work of NALGO at branch and higher levels:

> Really, I suppose, because a lot of social workers have been around for a long time, have actually been involved in quite a lot of trade union activity, which can't necessarily be said for all sections. And it really is quite important when running a medium to large sized branch that you have somebody who has had some personal experience.

In the years that followed the dispute of 1978–79 the social workers began to appear more frequently on NALGO's district and national level bodies. Indeed, whereas sometimes the impression had been given that NALGO had regarded the activism of social services as a problem, after the dispute it appeared more and more that social workers were seen as a section of active and committed members who were much appreciated for the work they carried out at various levels of

the union. Dennis Reed, a NALGO national officer, said of
field social workers in 1985:

> We have problems with steward systems in NALGO
> branches. It is difficult to get the stewards in a lot of the
> departments like architects and treasurers and so on. But
> normally if there is one section of the local authority where
> the steward system is functioning it's going to be in social
> services. Also their organisation in terms of the impact on
> the branch is very high. You often get field social workers or
> people with field social worker backgrounds as branch
> officers.

While social work activists were moving increasingly into
the mainstream of NALGO, this did not mean that the
development of steward organisation in the workplace was no
longer a priority. National pressure to extend and consolidate
steward systems continued and further progress was made in
November 1982 when more guidelines were issued by
NALGO. These guidelines stated that branch rules were
acceptable which restricted the nomination of departmental
representatives on the branch executive to stewards or workplace representatives. In 1983, the NALGO conference passed
a motion instructing the National Executive Council to set up
a campaign committee and to mount a campaign encouraging
all branches to adopt a shop stewards' organisation with shop
stewards elected by, and from, 'shops' and with a branch
executive consisting of branch officers and of stewards elected
from steward committees.

The significance of these developments should not be overlooked. In the mid-1970s rank-and-filist social workers saw in
shop steward systems a means of by-passing the local Whitley
structure. Their tactics in disputes initially reflected their
desire to create rank-and-file organisations in and against
NALGO. In the years that followed the 1978–79 field workers' dispute, militant social workers ended up reconstructing
NALGO along more rank-and-filist lines. What resulted partially reflected their rank-and-filist principles but the unity
and the integration of NALGO, originally threatened by
rank-and-filism, was preserved.

THE RESIDENTIAL WORKERS' DISPUTE

If the continued building of steward systems under NALGO represented a continuity with the 1970s, the residential workers' dispute of 1983 was a mixture of continuity and discontinuity. On the surface, it was a continuation of the militancy of the social workers but its underlying nature was quite different from that of the 1978–79 dispute.

The dispute started on 12 September 1983 as an admissions ban and an overtime ban. It was soon realised, however, that local support from residential workers was patchy. The employers held firm throughout the dispute, showing a firmness which surprised the union, and NALGO, in effect, conceded defeat when normal working was resumed in late December. In the light of such a disappointing conclusion the inevitable question is: what went wrong?

Two important ingredients for successful action were undoubtedly present: the residential workers were a reasonably trade-union-minded group of workers and most people recognised that for many years they had been discriminated against in terms of pay and other conditions of service. But these ingredients by themselves were not enough.

We have argued earlier that residential workers hold positive attitudes towards trade union membership. There is certainly only circumstantial evidence that their loyalty as trade unionists is not as great as that of, say, field workers. Moreover, this circumstantial evidence tends to show either a lack of activism, which is impeded by shift-working patterns, geographical dispersion and isolation, or a lack of militancy, which is not the same as loyalty to trade unionism.

The case for an improvement in the pay and conditions of residential workers was given a public airing in 1978. At the local government group meeting, which took place at the annual conference of NALGO that year, the supporters of the 'Residential Workers' Charter' were in action and the resolutions discussed included one on residential workers. The demands of the Charter included parity with social workers, a 35-hour week, no split shifts and an allowance for unsocial hours. The pay of residential workers at this time was generally regarded as low and a common view of them was that the poor pay and working conditions was due not only to their dispersion as a workforce but also to their indifference to trade unionism. It is true that residential workers have not had such a high union membership density as field workers (estimated by NALGO in 1985 to be 65 per cent and 75 per cent respectively) but this difference is not at all substantial when the greater difficulties for the union of organising the more scattered residential workforce are taken into account.

One view of the residential workers' dispute advances a 'contagion' theory of militancy: the residential workers were emulating the 'successful' action of the field workers in 1978–79:

> The eventual success of that action was bound to influence other groups – residential workers, for example, who have inferior conditions of service in hours and unsocial working patterns than most other groups of local government staff. Industrial action could have been avoided had serious attention been paid to their grievances and negotiations been initiated by employers.

The implicit assumption in the view that the 1978–79 dispute influenced the residential workers is that the 1983 dispute was also rank-and-filist, or, less strongly, that the initiative came from the membership. The subsequent, and more detailed, official view from NALGO came in a report by the National Local Government Committee to the 1985 Local Government Group annual meeting. The events described there emphasise that the locus of control of the dispute was national rather than local.

The events that made up the dispute can be described in their bare outline as follows. In January 1982, a national claim was submitted by NALGO to the employers. The claim was for a reduced working week (residential workers had a basic working week of 39 hours which was more than that of other non-manual workers in local government) and premium payments for unsocial working hours. The employers rejected the claim on 10 February 1983. At a residential workers' delegate meeting on 13 April 1983 NALGO's National Committee argued for an overtime ban, but the delegate meeting recommended an admissions ban as well as an overtime ban if negotiations failed again. At that same delegate meeting a motion proposing an all-out strike was rejected. While the delegate meeting had gone beyond the National Committee's original proposal, the National Committee subsequently identified itself with the decision to recommend an admissions ban by endorsing the recommendation of the meeting.

In early June the employers again rejected the union claim and a ballot on taking industrial action was carried out in August 1983. Despite concern at the low response rate to the ballot, the large majority in favour of strike action led the National Committee to recommend the initiation of bans on overtime and admissions from 12 September 1983.

During the early weeks of the dispute there seem to have been contradictory signals arriving at union headquarters. There were few requests for advice from branches but, on the other hand, positive reports were received from Strathclyde and Lambeth (branches with well organised residential workers) about the effectiveness of the action.

In late September the employers again turned down the union's claim. Back in April, when tactics had been decided by the union, no contingency plans had been made to deal with the event of industrial action failing to force concessions from the employers, so in the face of continued employer resistance to the claim branches were encouraged to escalate the action. It was agreed by the delegate meeting on 11 October that locally determined escalation would occur if the employers still held firm at the next joint meeting on 17th October. It was also decided that a day of action should be timed to allow a lobby of this meeting on 17th October, but the employers continued to stand firm.

Strikes in Cleveland and Salford had begun early in the dispute, and around the time of the NJC meeting on 17 October, the number of residential workers on indefinite strike had reached about five hundred. This was to rise to about 1500 by the time the decision to return to normal working was taken. NALGO's view, was that the strikes were mainly the result of employer provocation. It is very important to note, however, that branches 'allowed themselves' to be provoked.

Reports were received from NALGO's officials at district

level that escalatory action was low and that overtime and admissions bans 'continued to be patchy'. A third delegate meeting was held on 17 November, at which the National Committee recommended a ballot on an unsocial hours ban. The ballot was held and the vote went against a ban. The fourth and final delegate meeting, held on 22 December, brought the end of the dispute. A joint inquiry was accepted by the union and there was a return to normal working.

So much for the events that made up the dispute. What do they show? Firstly, the key decisions in this dispute were plainly taken by both the National Committee and the delegates who attended the delegate meetings. Consequently, the field workers' dispute of 1978–79 and the residential workers' dispute were quite different in terms of the locus of control. The former began with a rank-and-filist leadership and ended with the national leadership in control. In the 1983 dispute the leadership was a combination of national and local trade unionists at all key stages. So there is little benefit to be gained in accusing the leadership of bureaucratic conservatism or the rank and file of irresponsible militancy. Whatever error was made in choice of tactics or in judging the mood of the membership, it could not be adequately explained in terms of the old dichotomy of bureaucratic leaders and rank-and-file militants.

Secondly, the union leadership had either misread the militancy of the residential workers, or the toughness of the employers, or both. According to the union's official report on the dispute:

It has to be said that the major reason for the failure of the dispute was the reluctance of residential workers to take the necessary action for its success. (NALGO, 1985)

This judgement can only be partially correct. The trade union leadership was responsible for tactics and if residential workers were reluctant to take the necessary action then the leadership should not have chosen tactics which required the membership to act. Of course, it is a precondition of the choice of correct tactics that a leadership accurately judges the willingness of the membership to act. If the real problem was that the union leadership were over-optimistic about the willingness of the members to act, then the major reason for the failure of the dispute was the failure of NALGO's formal democratic machinery to enable the reluctance of residential workers to be fully expressed prior to the commitment of NALGO to industrial action.

The validity of this argument may not have been fully conceded by NALGO's national committee, but it was acknowledged. The report states:

> Every effort should be made to ensure that the recommendations made by delegate meetings are representative of the views of the wider membership . . . Furthermore, the Committee's recommendations on industrial action to a delegate meeting should only be made following extensive consultation and honest assessment of likely membership support. (NALGO, 1985)

The fact is that the residential workers did not support the call for industrial action as much as was believed. Dennis Reed, NALGO's National Officer responsible for social workers, suggests that there was very little pressure put on the employers:

> It became quite clear early on that the action short of strike – the overtime ban, the admissions ban – were not actually going to be sufficient to change the employers' views . . . it was a very patchy position. Some branches abided by the letter of the bans but found quite a few ways to mitigate the effects of it. So there wasn't really that much pressure being put on the employers. They were finding all sorts of ways round it. In the areas where we'd got really good organisations of residential workers, like Strathclyde for instance, where there is a superb organisation of residential workers, and Lambeth, places like that, there were immediate impacts, homes were closing, lots of publicity and so on. But in other areas we were a bit worried that it wasn't having a major impact. In every branch some members implemented the action but there were pockets of people who refused to have anything to do with it.

The accounts of the residential dispute that are given by social workers vary enormously from branch to branch. In some branches nothing at all seems to have happened, while in others quite determined action was taken by some of the residential workers. In Durham, for example, there seems to have been very little organised action. A social services departmental representative told us, 'you were told you could have the day off with the blessing of the union but there was nothing organised. We had a few talking of demonstrations outside Country Hall'. In Cambridgeshire there were forty-five residential workers on strike. The NALGO branch organiser said:

> There were plenty of people who weren't effectively taking the action or we were having to whip on a daily basis, you know to keep them in line. And there were those homes that effectively didn't take any part in it at all. But maybe they were never affected anyway. There were those homes who don't get admissions on that kind of basis – they might only get a couple of admissions in a year, sort of thing. Whereas the ones who get the short stay, observation and assessment, where the problems come to a head earlier. We did finish up getting people out . . . The object of the exercise wasn't to get people out. But that's the way it went. Management effectively forced our hands.

Interestingly, the main support for the action was in the children's homes, but there was very little in homes for the elderly. In Cambridgeshire attempts were made to prepare for the dispute but these were hampered by the 'absence of any effective residential stewards' and by the attitudes of residential workers: 'we hadn't really achieved a great deal in terms of preparation. One reason because, I suppose, most of the residential workers were hoping it wouldn't come to it'. This hope that action would not be needed seems to have been shared by the union leaders and may explain why no contingency plans were laid in the event of the initial industrial action failing to extract concessions. Dennis Reed again:

> We would say that there was general support for the justice

of the claim, everyone could see it was unfair that they should be working weekends and not getting any extra money for it, but it was translating that feeling of injustice into taking industrial action. . . .

The organisational problems didn't help, well obviously, we would have to spend far more time on organisational development before we launched into industrial action again. But I think the main problem was, yes, the clients. I mean if you're actually living in an extended family, which most homes are now and a fairly limited number of clients, its a bit much to actually want to walk out. And the employers were very, very tough about it. We thought, erroneously, we thought that once we got residential workers to vote for industrial action the effects would be seen as so horrific that the employers would start negotiating with us, which they didn't do. They were quite willing to accept adverse effects on clients in order to win the dispute. And they very much put the blame on our people. They said 'How can these people walk out of homes in the middle of the night and leave their clients?'

Why didn't the vote do the trick? David Townsend, the director of social services in the London Borough of Haringey, argued that the union claim would cost employers £120 million, which was a 50 per cent increase on the current cost of residential care and would put something like a 5 per cent increase on the social services budget for an average London borough (Townsend, 1983, p. 17). This was an expensive claim, especially in the context of government penalties for 'overspenders'.

The union side also underestimated the toughness of the employers. The unexpected toughness and the expense of a settlement on NALGO's terms meant that the union's expectations were completely wrong. Dennis Reed again:

We were surprised by how hard they were in the residential workers' dispute. They didn't seem to care two hoots what the effects were. They were going to stand firm on their position.

This is precisely what field workers found with some local authorities in 1978–79. In Tower Hamlets in 1979 pressure had to be applied by national organisation on the local employers to bring the dispute to an end – Labour councillors had seemed not to care how much disruption had occurred or for how long it went on.

What happens when councillors are not shocked into making concessions? What power do residential workers really have? The scattered and isolated nature of residential workers means that picketing has real limitations. Dennis Reed could see this as he visited places where industrial action was occurring:

> I used to go round touring the homes where action was taking place. And you go to some places where there is a home right in the middle of the country and all round are fields and little country roads. And there's a picket line there. They just had to stop the odd postman or somebody coming in, milk supplies or something like that, inside are their kids who are being looked after by management.

While the union leaders may have made errors of judgement about the lack of enthusiasm of residential workers for the dispute, the toughness of the employers and the realism of the claim, these tactical errors may prevent a more fundamental question being asked about the wisdom of the strategy. That question is: how much power did the bans and strike action give the residential workers? Most of the strikes in the 1983 dispute were, according to the union, provoked by the employers. If the strike is the weapon of the trade union, why did the opposition provoke them into striking? The long-protracted disputes of 1978–79 and 1983 suggest the need for a careful analysis of union power in social services. Arguably, that analysis has yet to be carried out but is imperative if social work trade unionism is to achieve a greater strategic maturity.

The failure of the 1983 dispute seems not to have left any major scars on social work trade unionism. It's true that the joint inquiry, which lasted a year and ended in January 1985, was disappointing from NALGO's point of view. Some concessions were made by the employers but the chief aspects of the union claim in respect of conditions of service were not satisfactorily agreed. On the other hand, NALGO gained some members amongst residential workers and improved workplace organisation. Moreover, the credibility of NALGO with its membership seems not to have suffered. There is a considerable degree of pragmatism expressed by field social workers and branch officials. They say that everyone knew it was going to be difficult to get residential workers to take industrial action because of their concern for the clients. Some people within NALGO have said that the union had little choice when the ballot showed a clear majority in favour of action – even though there was a low response to the ballot: the militant, well-organised branches in the inner cities and in the big cities would have criticised NALGO for doing nothing when there was a majority in favour of action.

The product of the attempt by NALGO to learn the lessons of the 1983 dispute is a frank and self-critical report. It remains to be seen whether, and how, the union can respond to the verdict of its Strike Operations Committee:

> The fundamental message is that national industrial action will only be successful if steps are taken to ensure that it has the overwhelming and committed support of the members involved. (NALGO, 1985, p. 28)

LOCAL STRUGGLES IN THE 1980s

The experience of the 1978–79 dispute affected social workers in various ways. In some cases, the dispute showed them that they were right to see trade unionism as a way to help the advancement of the social work occupation. In other cases, there was a development towards a synthesis of trade union and professional concerns. At an individual level there were undoubtedly those, especially among team leaders, senior social workers and area managers, who reacted to the dispute by distancing themselves from involvement in trade unionism – although nominally they often remained union members.

On top of the effects of the dispute came the depressing conditions of the early 1980s. In local government, as everywhere else, trade union members were cautious and worried. The trade union activists in social services departments certainly did not give up because of the difficult conditions, but mobilising the membership was difficult and required a lot of thought and a lot of effort. Now developments were heavily conditioned by local factors, producing considerable diversity in union practice. Three examples below illustrate this diversity.

Tower Hamlets in the 1980s

The 1978–79 strike left social services battle-weary. As the former social services convener, and the current branch secretary in 1985, put it:

> And although the structure of the shop stewards' committee continued as ever, and met with the same amount of frequency, I think it's fair to say that it was a bit of a struggle. I mean the idea that one comes out of that action feeling invigorated and game for more, that may be so for people like myself. I feel that we learnt an awful lot out of it. I am interested and committed anyway in this particular sphere. I think its true to say for the average member it was slightly depressing.

It seemed to him that for a couple of years or so after the 1978–79 dispute, probably until 1983, the branch itself was in the doldrums and there was a loss of confidence in the unity and effectiveness of the branch organisation.

The changing level of official financial support for strike action by NALGO was seen to be an important factor in the response of the branch membership to calls for industrial action. In the 1978–79 dispute, social workers had not lost out financially because of the level of NALGO strike pay. In the 1980s, strike pay was first brought down to 60 per cent of take home pay and then in most cases to £40 per week. The former convener was very conscious of the significance of the very generous strike pay in the 1978–79 strike at Tower Hamlets:

With the lot of money that NALGO was prepared to spend on it, to be quite honest, we were in a fairly unique position. And inevitably, although it was far from trouble-free, we didn't have the financial problems, obviously, that the majority of strikers have on disputes that last that length of time.

Thus the reductions in NALGO strike pay was bound to make taking industrial action more difficult. The branch responded to the reductions in NALGO's strike pay by setting up, in 1982, a branch industrial action fund, maintained from membership contributions.

Another factor making the union position more difficult in the early 1980s was the peculiar state of local party politics. The leading Labour councillors, who had been dominant figures on council committees for over ten years, were losing their grip on the local council. The relations between them and the local Labour groups appeared to have become strained and the overall position of Labour in the borough was being challenged by a highly effective Liberal Party machine. The hopelessness of their position was believed to have made the Labour councillors indifferent to the point of view of the council trade unions, although there were NALGO members who had long suspected some councillors of being hostile to the NALGO branch and its social workers.

Prior to the 1986 council elections in London, there was much speculation amongst NALGO activists in Tower Hamlets about the possibility of a Liberal victory. For people familiar with the political history of the area, such speculations had to seem almost unbelievable, but the Liberals had begun to make headway as early as 1978, when they won seven of the fifty council seats. And since then they had put in intensive work at ward level and consolidated their bridge-head continuously throughout the 1980s. Tower Hamlets had always belonged to Labour as far back as anybody could remember. It was in the deprived and run-down East End of London, the East End of militant dock workers and, further back, of George Lansbury and 'Poplarism'. But the evidence was there. The Liberals looked set to replace the Labour Party in Tower Hamlets, and they did.

But shouldn't that have made the Labour Party leadership in the council more eager to have the support of the unions to fend off the Liberal challenge? And shouldn't this have given the unions more influence with the council leadership? In fact, the possibility of a Liberal victory did not give NALGO any leverage. A Liberal victory did not bother leading Labour councillors: 'It has not bothered the council leadership very much because a lot of them seem to be either resigning as councillors or not being selected or know that they will get beaten. And so, basically, they don't care.'

Not all changes since the 1978–79 strike had been for the worse. Firstly, trade union activity in the social services department had become more acceptable to the rest of the NALGO branch and the blatant hostility that had originally been directed at social workers by other NALGO members had abated. Secondly, lessons had been learnt about working with the manual and craft unions. Social services activists realised, as a result of the problems which occurred in the 1978–79 dispute, that inter-union relationships needed to be improved. Efforts had subsequently been made to give real support to manual and craft trade unionists. Financial support had been given by the NALGO branch to the manual unions, and manual union picket lines had been observed in a dispute between the council and caretakers. As a result of these and other efforts, the relationship with the leadership of the manual and craft unions had improved slightly and inter-union solidarity in the mid-1980s stood at a higher level than it had ever done.

In the early 1980s, social work activists in Tower Hamlets continued, despite the difficulties, to build steward organisations. A major effort was made in respect of nursery nurses, a lot of whom were not even union members:

And the first task was always to get them into NALGO and get some stewards elected and to have meetings. And to build up. That ended up with them being offered a pretty good interpretation of the national agreement, virtually days before some serious industrial action was being contemplated and would, I am sure have been taken by the nursery workers. They had already turned parents away . . . That, in a sense, quite surprised and made us realise that with a reasonable organisation and basic ground work, which is absolutely crucial, we can still get or encourage a whole load of workers, who were totally unfamiliar and disinterested really in trade unions, to actually do something.

But there had been difficulties in maintaining union organisation amongst the nursery nurses, and a hard lesson had been learnt about the instrumentalism and limited capacity for action orientated towards solidarity amongst these workers. The stewards initially elected to represent the nursery nurses appear to have lost interest and stopped attending the social services shop stewards' committee:

As soon as their campaign was over, there wasn't the interest in the individuals who had been stewards during that campaign [to get a good interpretation of the national agreement], to come into the shop stewards' committee and perhaps listen to a meeting where nursery nurses may not even be mentioned. There wasn't the sort of sufficient commitment.

Interest in trade unionism amongst the nursery nurses membership began to fall back and there were no stewards to foster or maintain the level of interest amongst them. In 1983, during a strike of the whole branch, only a third of the nursery nurses were prepared to come out on strike. Indeed, many of them left NALGO over this – they felt that unreasonable pressure had been put on them to take strike action.

There had been a miscalculation here. Having created a union presence in the nursery nurses area, the social services activists had misunderstood the nature of the union allegiance created – especially its limits and durability. The lessons had, however, not been ignored. Whilst the former social services convener acknowledged that the nature of nursery work had something to do with the reluctance to take strike action in support of other workers, he described the main lesson as follows:

That demonstrated you can never assume that because you get a bunch of workers to do something for themselves, and for the trade union, one day, that that is necessarily going to follow that they are going to continue their interest or support the union the next day. Bacause it doesn't follow at all.

Despite the difficult conditions, industrial action continued to be a method used by the Tower Hamlets branch – although social services has not been the main arena for it. In the summer of 1983 there was a stoppage of the whole branch for four and a half weeks when management stopped the pay of NALGO members in the libraries department who were protesting against planned library closures by refusing to collect fines on books. The branch leadership had been uncertain about the likely membership response in this dispute. According to the branch secretary, a social worker, 'When the library workers walked out, we had really been biting our nails thinking: "God, what's going to happen now?" In fact, the response was very good. . . .'

The dispute ended, not with total victory for the NALGO branch, but, despite several years of demoralisation and Thatcherism, the union machinery was clearly still in working order:

It became apparent that the structures we had, when it came to the crunch, actually [still] worked. We actually ran a very, very well-organised strike and I think we decided to call it off just at the right moment. That resulted in a climb-down by the council – not a complete one of course – but instead of closing libraries, they agreed to review it and keep them open.

If the library dispute of 1983 brought a restoration of union confidence, this is not to say that the way was then clear for escalating militancy. The branch leadership handled a subsequent case of discrimination against two branch officers very cautiously. When reviews of the departments they worked in were carried out, the council rejected the tripartite

recommendations by the trade unions, the personnel department and management for an upgrading in one case and a pay
increase in the other:

> And basically the council never turns over tripartite recom-
> mendations and then suddenly within three weeks they've
> turned over two which happen to be recommendations
> relating to those two people . . . Now, we dubbed it a case of
> blatant victimisation.

Realising that there would not be a willingness on the part of
members to take all-out strike action, the grievance was
pursued through constitutional channels: 'We went through
all the right procedures. Right up to Joint Committee level.
And so on and so forth, in applications to the leader of the
council.' But this did not get anywhere. Subsequently, the
branch decided not to process council members' enquiries –
which are usually mainly on housing matters – and the
council retaliated by stopping the pay of twenty-five people in
the housing department: 'I suppose in years gone by the
immediate reaction would have been: 'Right, its a walk-out' . . .
[but] what we did was we told our members to continue
working. . . .' The branch used its industrial action fund to
top up NALGO strike pay and the twenty-five continued to
work without loss of money. This went on for five weeks and
then the action was called off by the branch in return for the
council agreeing to go to the Greater London Whitley Council's dispute committee. The matter wasn't resolved at this
committee but the council resumed paying the housing workers
because they were back to full duties.

Social services members have been involved and have supported these branch actions. Whilst social service activists
have, it could be said, submerged their 'separatist' identity in
favour of branch unity, this branch unity is not based on total
industrial pacificism. And although the 1980s have not produced in social services 'heroic' struggles similar to those of
the 1970s, this reflects tactical thinking rather than a disabling
incorporation into official structures and procedures. This last
point can be seen in respect of the union response to planned
spending cuts in 1985 which threatened to severely damage

social services. The union tactics to block the cuts are vividly described by the branch secretary, and former social services convener:

> What happened here was that, like some other councils, the council did not set a rate . . . It didn't set a rate because the council leadership found itself in a minority in the council chamber in terms of actually getting the budget through. Because their proposed cuts was so swingeing as to be unacceptable to the majority of councillors, Liberal and left-Labour . . .
>
> Social services was the budget which was going to be chopped most. And again, one has to ask oneself, why was it social services budgets that was in for the chop? I mean, there were some terrible things being proposed.
>
> But what we did there was very much try and influence the political process by personal contact with officers of the local Labour Party, sympathetic councillors on the left of the Labour Party, we had several meetings with the leader of the Liberals and other Liberal councillors, all attempting to bring factions on the left-Labour and the Liberals together to actually agree on a budget, which was a bit of a nightmare as you can imagine, because they both hate each other's guts. And we didn't actually succeed [in getting an agreement on a budget] in the end. But what we did succeed in doing was [getting them to meet] . . . I really do think it was our initiatives that started the two sides meeting and ended up putting sufficient pressure on the council leader for him to be able to put in a compromise which was eventually appropriate for the Liberals to say that they would actually vote for it. And although it involved cuts in social services, there weren't nearly so swingeing cuts.

It seems that the social services director had been considering various options to implement cuts in social services, including 'abolishing the Homeless Families Section, the Youth Workers, decimating IT, and so on'. As a result of the union tactics of intervening in the political process – overt meetings with groups in the council, writing letters, sending circulars, telephoning – the cuts were ameliorated. But over and above this, there was a coincidental improvement in the position of social services:

> In fact, since the budget we've had a notable upturn in the number of vacancies that have been filled in social services. For about two years we have been operating at about 40 or 50 per cent under strength in the social work department. Now, in this office, for example, we find ourselves with only a handful of vacancies and promises that these jobs will be filled.

If we recall from earlier chapters the issues and disputes which Tower Hamlets social services membership have taken up, and if we think back to the different strategies which have informed the actions of the social services activists there, we can't help but be struck by the changes. The attempts to 'go it alone' and shock and embarrass councillors by means of industrial action which characterised past disputes can be contrasted with the integral place in the branch held by social services and by the reliance on political methods to counter cuts in social services. The vanguardism of the earlier days has given way to a more refined tactical repertoire in the mid-1980s.

The movement in trade union organisation and strategy which characterises Tower Hamlets social services, stands in marked contrast to the relative backwardness of social work practice in the borough. This raises a question about the nature of trade unionism in this setting: why hasn't social work trade unionism improved the quality of service provided? Partly the answer must be that the council social services committee and senior management in the department had never encouraged social work activists to think that the union had any role in determining the nature and quality of the service. But there may also be an unwillingness on the part of union activists to see the union function as including a pro-active role in service development. Union activists were happy, as we have seen, to attack aspects of the service which they considered inadequate (for example, the homeless families dispute). And they had taken up, with little success, the recruitment of black social workers. They had also attempted

to defend the services from public spending cuts. This sometimes involved the defence of services at the same time as
taking up service conditions issues:

> We have been plugging away at our new local agreement
> for day centre workers and one of the reasons we have been
> doing that, is not only because they are appallingly paid,
> but because we are aware that day centre workers have
> been saying to us, 'Because of our low pay we can't get staff,
> there are hundreds of people on our waiting list, the service
> we can provide in the day centre is rotten' . . . We were able
> to talk in professional terms about service to the public, at
> the same time as we were talking about getting a decent rate
> for the job.

In fact, as far as this line of thinking is concerned, *all* service
conditions issues have a professional or service aspect. But in
the face of a backward social services committee and social
services management, attempts to influence the service have
been reactive and indirect.

So, to sum up, the integration of the social services stewards' committee into the NALGO branch did not lead to the
emasculation of the spirit of struggle. Instead the picture in
the 1980s is one of a cautious tactical approach, but still
taking action and still organising. Moreover, the movement
into action in the political sphere, to try to form an alliance
between left-Labour and Liberal councillors against the cuts,
shows the activists in social services transcending the syndi-
calist strait jacket of rank-and-filism.

Leeds and the Social Workers' Action Group

Leeds city council is much bigger than the Tower Hamlets
borough council, employing well over 30 000 people in the
1980s, which is something like six times the number in Tower
Hamlets. But it also covers an urban area and its field social
workers have a long involvement in the development of shop
steward systems and a reputation for left-wing radicalism.
Leeds social workers, like those in Tower Hamlets, took strike
action in the 1978–79 dispute, but despite these similarities,

the trade union experiences of social workers in Leeds have been very different in the 1980s from those of their London colleagues. What were these different experiences and why were there the differences?

The most important developments in trade union terms were, firstly, the activities of Leeds Social Workers' Action Group (SWAG) which occurred in the years from 1979 to 1983. Secondly, there was the lapsing of the local Whitley machinery. And thirdly, there was the persistence of intra-branch conflict over the role of staff side. These three developments, each of which was an important aspect of the Leeds situation, appear to have also had some interconnections.

The Social Workers' Action Group was formed during the 1978–9 strike at Leeds. In the course of this dispute, the anger felt by social workers at poor levels of service was able to find expression in an unusually articulate form through the formation of SWAG. The social workers involved in SWAG have provided their own account of its formation:

> The Leeds strike commenced in November 1978, and about 80 per cent of fieldworkers employed by Leeds City Council came out on a strike that was to last for four and a half months . . . In Leeds there had emerged . . . a general concern about the poor standard of social services in the City . . . In January 1979 a member of the fieldworkers' stewards' committee examined published figures which made it possible to compare expenditure and staffing in Leeds with other local authorities . . . Leeds compared very badly . . . The social workers' representatives who discussed the figures at a stewards' committee meeting were unanimous in deciding that some action should be taken to publicise these figures. It was agreed that the findings should be discussed at the next mass meeting of those on strike and a working party was established to publicise the figures. Some 30 people came forward to help produce a duplicated report based on the comparative statistics. (Jordan and Parton, 1985, p. 189)

So SWAG began as an organic development of the striking social workers and the stewards' committee. Initially it had no constitutional relationship to the NALGO branch in Leeds City but a formal role within the branch was later sought as pressures to incorporate SWAG came initially from the social services director and later from the new Labour council. This formalisation of the union base for SWAG was seen as necessary, therefore, to counter incorporation:

> There have been two main occasions when the group has been made offers where incorporation was a danger. The first was when the Director of social services suggested that external production of reports was damaging to the department and therefore we should provide reports for internal consideration only. The second was when the leader of the Labour group offered workers seats on internal consultative machinery in exchange for a commitment not to publish reports. (Jordan and Parton, 1985, p. 196)

SWAG produced three reports: the first was based on comparative statistics, the second focused on services for the mentally handicapped, and the third examined services for the physically handicapped. A feature of the two later reports was the lengthy consultative process involved in their production so that they 'became the collective produce of a union branch'. Also important was the fact that SWAG held conferences to launch the two later reports with the aim of attracting handicapped people, their relatives, pressure groups and professionals.

The activities of the Leeds SWAG aroused some interest in the social work field generally because of its novelty. What was the essence of this novelty? It was clearly an attempt to intervene in the political process of determining the development of services within Leeds, but rather than seeking to do this in alliance with a political party which enjoyed power in the local state, the social workers were seeking to exert pressure on the holders of political power (that is, the councillors). That the SWAG initiative should have come out of a dispute which was over the right to negotiate social work gradings locally is more comprehensible in the light of the special local characteristics of the Leeds strike. A Leeds social worker told us in 1985:

Certainly part of the period when we were on strike in the late 70s, part of that anger was about the lack of provisions at the service level, apart from our remuneration, and our career prospects. And there was a lot of anger about then and I think a lot of our motivation at that time was to try and improve the services and to expose the lack of service in Leeds.

The poor level of service was put down to the Conservative administration that ran Leeds City council in the 1970s. In May 1979 the Labour Party, which had previously held only 40 per cent of the ninety-six council seats, came to power in Leeds, at the same time as, nationally, the Conservative Party under Mrs Thatcher was triumphant. Arguably, therefore, the Conservative control of Leeds City Council, with its under-funding of social services, caused the 1978–79 strike in Leeds to be more concerned than the other social worker strikes with poor standards of service. Nevertheless, like many other social work struggles we have examined in this book, the stratagem of issuing reports was based on making the facts public. The reports, in other words, were meant to bring pressure by means of publicity: hence the concern of SWAG members not to give up the right to issue reports in return for involvement in the internal processes by the social services director or the council.

But why did SWAG cease to operate after 1983? In the opinion of one Leeds social worker, there were two reasons for the 'collapse' of SWAG:

One, the expansion of services . . . which actually takes the edge off some of the anger. When we did the original research and Leeds was bottom of the league on meals on wheels, bottom of the league on the number of social workers per thousand population . . . it couldn't have been worse if it was a conspiracy. And people were really angry then. And there was also, with the Labour Party being in power, there's a hell of a lot of Leeds social workers who are active in the local Labour Party and are raising policy issues in social services and on welfare issues in general through their [Labour Party] branches. We've got two social workers on the district Labour Party working group on social services. So there are a lot of different avenues.

Expenditure (see Table 4.2) and employment data (see Table 4.3) on Leeds City suggest that there was no massive surge in services generally after the election of 1979.

TABLE 4.2   Net current expenditure at Leeds City Council (January 1974 prices)

Year	£ (000s)	Percentage increase
1978–79	60 064	–
1979–80	61 551	2.5
1980–81	62 302	1.2
1981–82	64 951	4.3
1982–83	61 842	– 4.8

SOURCE: Department of Environment. Expenditure figures deflated by index of retail prices.

TABLE 4.3   Number of staff at Leeds City Council

	Full-time	Part-time
1978	21 103	12 050
1979	20 893	12 094
1980	20 787	12 415
1981	19 990	12 644
1982	20 162	13 083
1983	20 101	13 528

SOURCE: Joint Manpower Watch, December returns.

In fact, around 1982–83, there was a serious dispute between the City Council and the NALGO branch over the restructuring of services, merging of departments and job losses. Full-time jobs with the council decreased slightly after that – but there was an increase on the part-time side. By December 1985 there were just under 20 000 full-time jobs and just under 14 000 part-time jobs.

In Leeds City social services, growth has occurred in a piecemeal and opportunistic manner, with the council making use of joint funding, community programmes, Section 11 money, and so on, to finance new areas of work. One Leeds social worker summed up the council style in this matter as follows: 'They pull off deals to get money, to create something because they want the money rather than because they actually think its a good idea and they are committed to it.'

Amongst Leeds social workers we found a lack of agreement and certainty about the effect of the Labour council on social services expenditure, but one view was that, whilst generic social workers still predominated, there had been a substantial expansion of specialist social workers:

What they've done – and the Director says it's not a strategic device on his part – is to create lots of specialist jobs. So what the Director says is that he can go to the leader of the council and say, 'We have a specific need with mentally handicapped people, or mentally ill people, or the elderly, and we need more social workers'. Six years ago every office had its teams of intake or long-term or whatever. Now, you've got your teams and loads of specialists – mentally ill, mentally handicapped, children in trouble, fostering, child minders, you name it.

Assuming that SWAG did collapse because of the improvement in social services and the growth of new avenues of influence via the local Labour Party branch and a Labour Party district working group, was the attempt to build a trade union base for the pursuit of professional concerns a mistake? Was it bound to be shortlived? And were the members of SWAG correct to be so worried about incorporation? The crucial question here concerns the relationship of social work trade unionism to the Labour Party when it is in power in local government and the attitude of social workers to this relationship. Both these matters enter into our discussion of the two other important developments in Leeds City Council in the 1980s: the fading away of the local Whitley machinery and the persistent intra-branch conflict over the role of staff side.

There was no local Whitley committee in Leeds City Council in 1985; in fact there were no formal regular meetings of
any description between the council and representatives of the
NALGO branch. Where union representatives encountered
difficulties in sorting matters out in a directorate, the only way
of proceeding, very often, seems to have been a direct and
informal approach to the leader of the council. A field worker
stressed that the pattern of centralised informality which
characterised industrial relations had developed only under
Labour control of the council:

> Under the Tories there used to be the regular monthly
> official negotiating meetings that the staff side went in and
> they sent in the personnel, the chair of the personnel com-
> mittee, and a few advisers and so on. That used to happen.
> Since the Labour administration took over that has more
> and more fallen into disrepute. [The] leader of the council
> – [and] people in the branch leadership who have been
> politically sympathetic to him have tended to do things
> on a 'come on, let's sort something out here'. And that's
> been successful in some instances and in others it hasn't.
> But . . . that first-name-terms negotiating, in the toilets, or
> in the corridor, or whatever, has replaced official negotiat-
> ing machinery in the branch. And I think to the detriment
> of the branch and the membership.

This informal bargaining relationship apparently had not
been there from the start of the Labour administration at
Leeds; initially the Labour council had been anti-white-collar
worker in their attitude. But this had changed abruptly at the
time there was a serious dispute between the council and
NALGO over the restructuring of services in the 1982–3
period. A Leeds social worker argued that it was the NALGO
stance on restructuring that brought about the change:

> But we actually moved the council leadership through that
> dispute from a very anti-white-collar worker stance to this
> sort of cosy relationship with NALGO which was quite a
> dramatic transformation. I think it was the NALGO line on
> restructuring that brought about the transformation.

While some social workers may still have felt that the preju-
dice against NALGO as a 'bosses' union was still around, the
dispute over restructuring appears to have been a turning
point.

The creation of this cosy and informal bargaining relationship seems contradictory – in moving together the two sides
have given up a formally recognised joint institution. Surely
Labour councils are better supporters of proper collective
bargaining arrangements than Conservative councils? There
is no doubt that Labour councils are generally perceived to be
in favour of trade unionism by NALGO branches whereas
Conservative councils are more likely to be seen as neutral in
attitude or, even worse, against trade unionism. In Leeds in
the early 1980s, the Labour council, in common with many
others, seems to have regarded white-collar unions as not part
of real trade unionism – until the restructuring dispute.
Presumably, after this, NALGO was perceived as part and
parcel of the trade union movement and thus as allies of the
Labour Party. Between allies the formal structure of bargaining may seem inappropriate – formality makes give and take
more difficult and makes problem-solving seem out of place.
Therefore, a tendency towards informality may have developed out of the Labour Party's abrupt redefinition of the
NALGO branch.

That would not have been enough, however, to account for
the decay of the local Whitley machinery. Alliances between
Labour councils and trade union branches are commonplace
in local government in the 1980s, but this has not produced
wholesale abandonment of local bargaining and consultative
machinery. There must have been another factor in the Leeds
case. That factor could well have been the existence of a major
conflict inside the NALGO branch over the role of staff side.

In the mid-1980s, the NALGO branch's staff side consisted
of four people elected by the branch executive, which itself
consisted of stewards elected by the departmental stewards'
committees. A field worker explained the work of stewards'
committees and staff side as follows:

Since we've had the steward system, the theory of it is that
stewards' committees are responsible for the negotiations

with their own managements on their local issues. The staff side is responsible for negotiations on branch wide issues and they would be guided by a committee in the branch which consists of the senior steward from each stewards' committee, called the salaries and services [committee], who meet once every six weeks to give general guidance to the four staff side people, who actually go in and negotiate or attempt to negotiate, with the central personnel, the industrial relations heavy, and, on occasion, the elected members.

But this was the theory . . .

In practice the better stewards' committees, the stewards' committees that are better organised and more competent, rarely use their staff side rep. And if they do it's very much on their terms, 'We want you to come but we're in charge of the negotiations'. The poorer stewards' committees have fallen into the trap of just phoning him up every time they've got a problem and the stewards' committees never get involved in negotiations.

Another field worker argued that the existence of staff side was preventing some of the poorer stewards' committees developing, and indicated that its role was under attack as a result: 'And so we have this sort of strategy of trying to do away with it. And concentrated on opposing it rather than try and affect the people who actually get on it.'

Not all social work activists at Leeds were opposed to staff side:

I think if it was abolished then you'd have a lot of undeveloped stewards' committees which would cease to function completely and you'd have whole areas unrepresented. Whereas [other social worker stewards] would say it would be a stimulus to them to go on and organise. That makes it sound as if its a very small difference but really the roots of it all go right back to the issues of rank-and-filism and all the traditional debates on the left.

One field worker, who was actively involved in the fight for stewards' committees in the Leeds branch prior to the 1978–79 strike, provided a useful historical background to the conflict in the branch over staff side:

> The history of it is that when the broad left were in the branch in the mid 1970s were successfully arguing for the creation of stewards' committees, in the transition period it was felt that you needed something. You couldn't just stop, you had to have something transitional. So it was agreed that for a six month period there would be a continuation of the staff side, to allow six months for the steward committees to get established and take over. It was then decided that wasn't long enough, it needed to be a year. Then that coincided with the left in the branch taking over from the old guard right wingers. And the people on the staff side were no longer the right wing reactionaries. They happened to be the progressive left wingers. And therefore the staff side became in the eyes of some people in the branch OK now because we've got the right people there. And certainly it looked a lot better with left-wing people there than right-wing old-guarders. But it still had that fundamental problem. So it's a throw back.

A throw-back. A survival from the old bureaucratic structure of Whitleyism. And while it survived, it prevented stewards' committees from developing fully.

In reconstructing the trade union developments in Leeds it is important to stress that the factional struggle in the mid-1970s had been between the right wing and a broad left alliance of different types of socialist activists. Some of these activists were committed, and full-blown, rank-and-filists; others were not. The conflicts in the 1980s are now between the rank-and-filists – especially those in social services – and other left-wingers in the branch and they appear to have become stalemated, despite the skirmishes that are fought over the role of staff side. For example, in a recent dispute over home help organisers, there were complaints that a staff side representative approved a scheme despite a vote by the social services' shop stewards committee against giving it approval.

The intra-branch conflict has not led to a rupture between the rank-and-filists and the other left-wingers in the branch. The situation appears to have been stabilised by the adoption of the centralised and informal relationship between the council and the NALGO branch. The rank-and-file activists have an anomaly to live with: 'One of the anomalies is we've got a staff side and its not a staff side of anything because we don't have a local Whitley council'. As a compromise it seems to work. But for how much longer?

It is clear from the foregoing, that, in Leeds, social work trade unionism had fought hard for many years to structure its relationship with councils, including the Labour ones of the 1980s, according to the principles implicit in their support for stewards' committees. This meant an opposition to strong, formalised bipartite arrangements between the council and the union centralised at branch level. Stewards' committees had to be paramount.

The attitudes of social work activists appear to have strongly reflected this stalemate situation. Their own stands were seen to be more principled by comparison to other groups in NALGO. In consequence, one field worker thought that social workers were seen as 'holier than thou':

I think sometimes we may be seen as being a bit holier than thou with other sections. And with haranguing about what is the correct way to do things. And it is seen as those sorts of social workers.

Another attributed the hostility felt towards social workers by the rest of the branch to their tendency to take principled stands:

I think at times I've felt that our stewards' committee has pursued things too ruthlessly, which have probably been correct in principle but haven't been pursued very well. And I think that's why there's been a lot of anti-social work feeling which is then reflected in the elections – particularly the last just gone.

This principled trade unionism was implicitly seen as inform-
ing NALGO's trade unionism locally and thus differentiating
NALGO from the other unions:

> See, I think NALGO . . . has better policy of standing up to
> the worst elements of the Labour Party's policies, Labour
> councillors policies in Leeds. YTS, for example, community
> programme. I mean the other unions are really just door
> mats for the Labour group. NALGO has some vestiges of
> opposition to it and that opposition is rubbished by: 'Ah,
> you're white collar, you're bosses' union'. Its actually a
> better policy, a much more socialist stance, much more
> principled stance, that NALGO I think, amongst the local
> authority unions, has tended to adopt better, more prin-
> cipled positions.

The rank-and-filists still, however, have the anti-social
worker hostility to live with. How is this conflict understood?

> If you're consistent and keep it up you'll win. So that the
> stewards' system, in arguing about that we were smashed
> year after year after year after year. And eventually we won
> it . . . Support for flat rate pay claims was something that
> was heresy . . . Field work stewards, amongst others in the
> branch, argued year after year after year for them . . . But
> eventually that's now branch policy . . . So I don't mind
> being unpopular because the experience is that if you are
> consistent enough you will win.

So the message is that rank-and-filists have to be prepared for
a long, hard struggle, but if they stand by their principles –
socialist principles – others will eventually come round. It is
also evident that having staked a claim to the high moral
ground, they have to stick to their guns and oppose the
policies of the Labour Party. Compromise is abandoning
opposition and abandoning principles.
 Understanding the relationships inside the left-wing alliance is clearly tied up with understanding the different
approaches to a proper union relationship to the council and
the different attitudes to that relationship. It now becomes

apparent that the centralised, informal relations between the council leader and the leadership of the NALGO branch is, at the very least, made more enduring because of the rank-and-filist position. Furthermore, it is striking that the collapse of SWAG (which was an external political pressure strategy) was not succeeded by a centralised, formal union involvement in the (political) process of determining services but by a back door – informal involvement based on individual membership of the local Labour Party. The collective bargaining relationships were reflected, in other words, in the political relationships between the council and trade unionism. None of this is to deny that the Labour Party locally may also prefer centralised informality. It might also be added that the material reality of the political alliance between the Labour Party and the unions, even though expressed in an informal, 'back door' way, was obviously stronger than the oppositional stance implied in the SWAG initiative, with its careful emphasis on not being incorporated.

In summing up the trade union experience at Leeds, several points can be usefully made. Firstly, SWAG showed that professional concerns could be taken up within a trade union base. Secondly, SWAG underlined the need to involve clients and the local community in the development of social services policy and indicated that ways could be found of realising this involvement. But there were also negative lessons. Professional concerns could be taken up within a trade union base but the long-term prospects for such a fusion of professionalism and trade unionism depended on getting the relationship between the trade union and employer right. Oppositional, pressure group tactics as used by SWAG, were difficult to reproduce when the employer became interested in a genuine political alliance. The question remains, however, of whether a formalised involvement for the union in developing services is bound to lead to incorporation? If this formalised involvement can be created on the basis of at least partial union autonomy, then desirable alternative ways forward may exist for developing professionalism within a trade union base. Another lesson from the Leeds experience was that, however deficient the formal democratic accountability of Leeds City Council, the sporadic involvement of clients and community groups in the SWAG experiment represented only slight popular interventions in local democracy. The social workers in SWAG were right to argue for the need to open up greater possibilities of democratic accountability, but 'workers' reports' – even workers' plans – do not provide an adequate vehicle for greater democracy for consumers of social services. As the Lucas workers' corporate plan in the 1970s showed, such rank-and-filist initiatives have many positive consequences but they are not powerful enough to determine corporate strategies.

Cambridgeshire County Council

The experiences of trade union activists in the social services department of Cambridgeshire County Council in the 1980s bear few resemblances to those of their counterparts in Tower Hamlets and Leeds. The social workers here are not known for militancy and political radicalism – the more usual adjectives used to describe their trade unionism are reactive and apathetic. They did not take strike action in the 1978–79 dispute, and, whilst they have a shop steward system, in the mid-1980s the steward body consisted of about nine to ten individuals. This is not, however, the complete picture of the social workers in Cambridgeshire. A steward from social services felt that they, the union, did not have a high profile, and yet many people 'actually do see us as quite powerful, although, God knows why – we ain't got any bloody power'. And the picture of low-key trade unionism was also belied by the determined action taken by residential workers in the 1983 dispute.

In developing an understanding of their experiences in the 1980s, the single most important factor to appreciate was the introduction of corporate management into the running of Cambridgeshire social services. In tandem with corporate management came much talk of 'value for money' and community care, significant moves towards decentralisation of budgets and harder managerial control. This produced more work for the social services' stewards and contributed ultimately to the strike action in the residential workers' dispute. As one shop steward said:

I came back in '79 just when the Tories had just got elected and the difference was noticeable. You know, the emphasis on management. I mean, previously they weren't so much called team leaders as seniors . . . It was bloody obvious that the emphasis was different. Now what that was all about I really don't know . . . But by the time I came back the emphasis was on good management rather than on good social work practice.

The new team leaders were not like the old seniors:

Before, seniors were people you went to and said: 'Here, Jesus Christ, I'm having a bad time with blah blah'. 'Oh are you mate? Hang on. I'll make a cup of tea and let's talk about it'. Seniors then had become team leaders. Supervision was clearer.

The new emphasis on management was felt in more formal ways later on, in the early 1980s, when social services management started making great use of the formal disciplinary procedure – although it seems the deputy Director denied that the procedure was being used more in social services than elsewhere.

Whilst the social services stewards were having to deal with the problems created by corporate management, the senior managers in the social services department were better placed to see the causes of the changes in management practice. An analysis was provided by one manager; he explained the policies that had been pursued under the right-wing Conservative council:

The overriding objective was to manage within cash limits. So a fiscal view very much within the minds of the elected members. And to put it at its most, you might say they didn't give a damn what you eventually did as long as you didn't spend any more than they had voted for it . . . it was often a difficult job that I had to convey to field workers that members were actually interested in what they were doing and understood about it. Because I very much often feel myself that they didn't – which I suppose one would expect from a fairly right wing Thatcherite County Council who were under cash limits and those sort of pressures themselves.

The Conservative county councillors were under pressure. In fact, the council was into the first level of government penalties in 1985 for overspending and senior officers in the council had been telling them that more resources were needed if the council was to meet its various statutory responsibilities.

It seems that, in the 1980s, the county council had been increasing the social services' share of the budget. According to one manager, the increase had not been enough:

> The department started from a very low baseline. We were in the bottom half dozen of expenditure per head. I think we are well up on day-care for the elderly but that is about all. Most client groups and services are well down in the second half of the league table. And . . . the county council has proportionally allocated a much larger slice of the cake over the years to social services. So presented in that way you could say they've been very generous to social services. What it hasn't done, of course, is kept anywhere near in line with the demand. We're the fastest growing shire county in the country.

Certainly a comparison with both Tower Hamlets and Leeds indicates that Cambridgeshire spent a comparatively small amount on its personal social services and that spending in this area was a smaller proportion of its rate income. Public service unions, including NALGO, have been concerned that community care should not be seen as a cheap option or as a cost-cutting exercise. Cambridgeshire County Council were keen devotees of both cost-cutting and community care:

> In terms of their objectives, I think it would be true to say that they were, apart from their usual value-for-money, cost effective, and all those sort of things that spill easily from the tongue, they were pursuing non-residential methods of care. Community Initiatives. Very much trying to develop work in the voluntary sector.

TABLE 4.4   Expenditure on Personal Social Services, 1983–84

Local authority	PSS expenditure per head of population £	Total rate per head of population £	PSS spending as a percentage of total rate %
Tower Hamlets	137.40	621.62	22.1
Leeds	48.34	205.00	23.6
Cambridgeshire	31.35	184.46	17.0

SOURCE: CIPFA, *Finance and General Statistics 1938–84* (The Chartered Institute of Public Finance and Accountancy, May 1983).

Along with the 'Thatcherite' interest in value-for-money went a determined strategy of creating a strong managerial structure. The well-known Hay–MSL firm of management consultants was brought in and their influence in the 1980s was all-pervasive. The result was, in social services, to produce a management which was much more self-consciously concerned with managerial control issues and 'sold' on a corporate management approach to developing policies and implementing them. The manager, who was in favour of 'corporateness' but worried about the quasi-business approach of the consultants, assessed their significance as follows:

The work the management consultants were doing . . . is very much quasi-business. I mean, this is why elected members at the time were so attracted to it . . . Hay–MSL are pretty big . . . What they were advocating was a system which very much strengthened the line of management, including discipline in this department. Which emphasised the importance of managerial skills and the need for training. On the corporate [dimension], across departments as well as within departments [co-ordination was stressed]. I mean, if one is looking at that sort of model, Cambridge is probably the most advanced in the country.

In structural terms, this meant the development of a social services management team; this was still new in 1985:

There are certain objectives which the [social services] committee will lay down, we hope. At their first meeting next week [after the local election]. And then the management team has a corporate job to implement those policies and pursue those objectives.

The social services management team had created a number of sub-committees and what were called 'policy and practice groups', which reported to the management sub-committees. Divisional directors of the social services department (known in the pre-consultant days as divisional officers) chaired the policy and practice groups, which involved carefully-selected workers to represent different types of social work and the different territorial divisions of the county. This brought a wide spectrum of staff into the process of managerial policy-making.

Another structural consequence was a decentralisation of control to the divisions: 'There is more budgetary control in divisions . . . This year, for the first time, major chunks of the budget are being decentralised and expressed in divisional terms.' This should not be confused with the decentralisation of a range of local authority services into mini town halls which has occurred in a number of progressive councils. The decentralisation in Cambridgeshire was part of a control strategy to increase control by management at a local level.

Another important change resulting from the work of the consultants was that senior managers were taken out of the local government conditions of service and salary structure. Arising from this was the formation of a new organisation called the Senior Staff Society, which was seen as necessary because NALGO appeared not to be in a position to represent these senior managers. Informal discussions were, however, in process in 1985 to see if the Society could become a special interest group within NALGO. Irrespective of the outcome of these informal discussions, the fact was that the emergence of this new organisation had caused considerable concern in local NALGO circles.

Inevitably, all these changes had consequences for the climate of industrial relations. Around 1983 there was a crop of formal disciplinary cases. The social services' senior steward described one of them:

> There was one bloke who was very interested in community-based things. So he'd get the clients active. [Management] didn't like that. [They] didn't like that at all. 'Can't do that sort of thing'. It seemed to me that they were much more interested in a kind of social control than anything . . . it was alright if you did case work and kept your files up to date and all that sort of business. And there was a nice tidy management line.

It seemed to the stewards in social services that a new, rigid managerial style was emanating from the very top of the social services department:

> You'd get the Divisional Officer [Director] who tended to wave with the wind, and then a fairly rigid senior. And somebody, at the bottom who actually wanted to do something for the client . . . They would try and put the pressure on. Then the Divisional Officer would be called in and he'd have to support the senior as all part of the management. And when he was looking for support and wondering what he'd got to do, he got this rigid order: 'crush them'.

The senior manager from social services thought that the surge in the number of disciplinary cases, a surge which had passed by 1985, was to do with a 'covert or overt policy or attitude of management'. He said:

> I just think that at the time there was a view that one way, one legitimate way, of influencing organisational behaviour was the disciplinary code. And that these were procedures which were a tool of management.

He saw it as being partly a product of the work of the management consultants, which had changed the structure and practice of management. But these changes also evoked a response within certain sections of the social services management:

> It was also to do, I think, and this is a very subjective comment, I think it was to do with some people seeing the need for senior management to be more macho. Demonstrate to the elected members that: 'We'll sort them out, you know'.

So, social services management had started to make use of the disciplinary procedures and it was clear to social services' stewards that this tough approach was being backed by the deputy director.

The move towards a more self-consciously managerial approach did not provoke wholesale resistance. But then again the union was not completely ineffective: it raised the awareness of its members as to what was going on and it was able to mobilise the membership sufficiently to achieve a bargaining position. And it did, for example, extract guarantees about no redundancies from the management.

The more hard-nosed managerial approach, in the opinion of some, also resulted in Cambridgeshire suffering the worst action in the residential workers' dispute in the region. The social services' stewards had offered to set up special arrangements for emergency admission to residential homes during the dispute, but the social services management refused the offer and tried to force some admissions. This provocative action had triggered walk-outs by residential staff and the action had looked very solid. Looking back, management had been surprised by the extent of unrest in Cambridgeshire and were surprised when it was called off.

The events in Cambridgeshire in the 1980s stand in marked contrast to those in Tower Hamlets and Leeds. In this case we see that community care and decentralisation have been developed in the context of inadequate funding and a shift to stronger managerial control. The result has been to undermine NALGO's organisation amongst senior managers and to cause rigid and authoritarian managerial practices to flourish. Less obviously, it has meant that professional concerns have not been articulated within a trade union base but have been constrained to expression through channels constructed in the new corporate management structure of sub-committees and policy and practice groups.

A PROVISIONAL ASSESSMENT

In 1985 NALGO's estimated membership amongst social workers consisted of 20 000 fieldworkers and 25 000 residential workers in England, Scotland and Wales (NALGO does not recruit in Northern Ireland). On the basis of these figures the union headquarters has tentatively estimated that NALGO's strength in the local government sector was moderately strong with a union density in fieldwork of about 75 per cent and in residential work of about 65 per cent. It is unfortunately impossible to present good estimates of the strength of NALGO amongst education welfare officers, staff in Adult Training Centres, and so on. One guess was that NALGO had 35 000 other social services staff.

The membership of BASW in late 1984 was approaching 9000. Thus, collective organisation in social work is primarily on a trade union basis. Indeed, BASW seems to have become more representative of middle management within social services: that is, team leaders, senior social workers and area managers. It has failed to recruit substantial numbers of 'first-time' qualified social workers; these workers have instead been more interested in representation through NALGO. In Cambridgeshire, for example, where BASW was very well represented in the middle and higher levels of the social services department, we were told by a senior shop steward in social services that 'People see BASW as more beneficial if they're going to go for careers'.

There is no doubt, therefore, that trade unionism is strongly established in local government social services. But even a provisional assessment of social work trade unionism must also look at:

(i) the state of union organisation;
(ii) the effectiveness of trade union action on pay and job security; and

(iii) the effectiveness of trade union action on the quality of
service.

Social work activists in the 1980s have continued to build up
steward systems and they have argued and pressed for
changes in branch organisation. The picture, in terms of local
organisation, is a very complex one. Some of this complexity
has been shown in our detailed studies of Tower Hamlets,
Leeds and Cambridgeshire in the 1980s. In some of the
London boroughs and some metropolitan districts the shop
stewards' movement has been recognised alongside well-
developed departmental representative systems. In these
cases departmental representatives have continued, often, to
play an important role in leading local union organisation.
These NALGO branches have become large and elaborate
union structures, with very dense representation systems, and
they have had more than their share of intra-branch conflict
where branch officials continue to be the most important local
negotiators. But, it should be noted, the shop stewards' movement has made little progress in many other branches.

General impressions in NALGO are remarkably consistent
on the nature of stewards' committees in social services. Field
workers are seen as having the most effective stewards'
committees. Indeed, as we saw in the case of the Tower
Hamlets branch, for a long time the only effectively functioning stewards' committee in a branch is likely to be in the social
services department. Field workers are increasingly carrying
the load of branch work and are seen to be active at higher
levels of the union. Nevertheless, there are still many places
where progress is still being made in establishing workplace
representation. For example, the Durham County Council
social services department still did not have a shop steward
system in the mid-1980s. Nor, for that matter, had the social
workers ever taken any industrial action, apart from once
when they 'withdrew their cars'. Since 1983, however, the
effectiveness of their representational system has improved:
there were, in 1985, sixteen departmental representatives,
who were regarded as the most vociferous in the NALGO
branch. According to one of the representatives, 'the social
services reps have been a credit to the social services depart-

ment'. Whilst there are no scheduled meetings of social services representatives, they do meet frequently, they do take up
issues, and they carry out an important role in 'trying to link
up the members with the branch exec'. There was no sign that
this branch would be moving in the near future to a shop
stewards' system: 'NALGO here follows the line of strictly
non-political [action] so it feels that we shouldn't have shop
stewards.' In a union with such a diverse membership it is not
surprising that social services' activists are moving at widely
differing speeds. But the Durham case illustrates the need to
recognise the on-going developments within the traditional
departmental representative form of organisation.

Developments on the pay front have aroused considerable
controversy amongst social work activists. The settlement of
the 1978–79 field workers' dispute, in particular, with its
introduction of three levels of social worker, has evoked a
range of strong reactions. A Leeds social worker saw the
outcome of the dispute as good in cash terms but had other
reservations about the settlement:

> In terms of the setting of these goddam levels, that's like a
> major problem area, in terms of it's given management a
> sword. It's given management a tool for dealing with people
> – divide and rule. And because the levels stop – it hasn't
> addressed the issue of what happens [to social workers] who
> are getting very long in the tooth, want to stay at the
> coal-face, don't want to go into management, but now
> getting to the tops of our ladders. We don't get any more
> money.

Up to 1979, social workers were on a single national salary
scale which ran, in terms of the National Joint Council's
Scheme of Conditions of Service, from Spinal Column 14 to
Point 25 (with a qualification bar between Points 20 and 21).
The 1979 agreement on social workers' pay replaced the single
scale by three scales; Level 1 was from point 19 to 25; Level 2
was from 24 to 29; and Level 3 from 28 to 33.

In fact, the situation on pay only becomes clear when the
effect of inflation has been taken into account. Table 4.5 shows
the money and real salaries of social workers at the bottom

TABLE 4.5   Money and real salaries of social workers, 1970–85

| Year (July) | Money salaries | | Real salaries[1] | | Salary |
	Bottom of the range £	Top of the range £	Bottom of the range £	Top of the range £	Gap (Real)[2] £
1970	1 038	1 776	1 309	2 240	931
1971	1 395	2 055	1 607	2 368	760
1972	1 530	2 232	1 647	2 403	756
1973	1 644	2 373	1 620	2 338	718
1974	1 866	2 694	1 720	2 483	763
1975	2 529	3 474	1 876	2 577	701
1976	2 841	3 786	1 808	2 410	602
1977	2 983	3 975	1 639	2 184	545
1978	3 279	4 368	1 664	2 216	553
1979	4 080	6 090	1 826	2 725	899
1980	5 178	7 998	1 964	3 033	1 069
1981	5 652	8 733	1 916	2 960	1 044
1982	5 973	9 231	1 864	2 881	1 017
1983	6 264	9 660	1 869	2 883	1 013
1984	6 555	10 107	1 863	2 872	1 009
1985	6 900	10 638	1 833	2 826	993

[1]   The money salary figures were deflated using the retail price index (15 January 1974 = 100).
[2]   These figures have been rounded.

SOURCE: Pay scales data provided by the Employers' Secretary of National Joint Council for Local Authorities (Administrative, Professional, Technical and Clerical Services), September 1985.

and top of the range for the years 1970 to 1985. It can be seen that whilst the money salaries of social workers at the bottom and top of the range appeared to move up sharply in 1979, the trends in real salaries were more complex. The picture which now emerges for the bottom of the range is one of real improvement up to, and including, the year 1975, followed by three years of decline, and then a restoration of real pay levels in 1979. The top of the range also tended to enjoy a rise in real salaries up to, and including, the year 1975. In this case, however, the 1979 settlement led to a shift in real salary to a level above that achieved in 1975. The combined effect of these movements was to produce a salary gap between the top and bottom which was increasingly compressed in the years 1970–77. The 1979 settlement put an end to this tendency and the real salary gap in the 1980s was greater than it had ever been in the 1970s.

It could be argued that the post-1979 salary structure created more scope for local bargaining. The wider range of real salaries created, theoretically, more 'headroom' for local bargaining over social worker pay. In addition, the definition of the different levels of social worker in the national agreement was so abstract that there was plenty to argue about at local level. Take, for example, the agreement's definition of a Level 3 social worker:

> With access to advice and within normal arrangements for professional accountability are expected to accept full responsibility for managing a caseload which will include the more vulnerable clients or those with particularly complex problems in situations where personal liberty or safety is at stake. Such officers are expected to contribute to the development of other social workers. They may be expected to concentrate on specific areas of work requiring more developed skills. They may be expected to contribute to the development of new forms of work or service. (Scheme of Conditions of Service, 1979, p. 37)

Social workers who had aspirations to professional status welcomed the settlement because they saw in Level 3 a recognition of the professional nature of the social work role. Others, like the Leeds social worker quoted earlier, saw in the new pay structure the creation of a 'job ladder' which management could use to divide the rank and file. This sinister aspect of the settlement has been described as follows:

> Professionally qualified social workers are aware that for some there is now a real possibility of being able to engage in the type of social work practice that is taught on the professional courses. But to reach this goal they also know that they will have to satisfy the social service management that they are loyal and capable workers trustworthy enough

to be given the 'professional' freedoms that go with Level 3 work. (Jones, 1983, p. 137)

These contradictory perceptions of the 1979 settlement – professional recognition, 'headroom' for local bargaining, and management-controlled job ladder – in themselves give voice to the interacting forces within the social work field that we have been tracking throughout this history. In fact, the significance of the 1979 settlement has depended on local conditions. In some authorities there is automatic progression to Level 3 and so it has not functioned either to demarcate a professional elite in social work or to bring about managerial control via a job ladder. In others, quotas were initially set up to regulate the proportion of social workers on Level 3 but 'informal' pressures have led to a disregard of the quotas. As usual, the final result has depended on the balance of forces and union determination to overcome barriers to pay improvements in each locale.

The bargaining headroom provided by the three-level structure has been reducing in the 1980s as social workers have started to bunch on the higher levels. This is shown in Table 4.6. It can be seen that the proportion of social workers on Level 3 went up substantially over the period. To some extent this was the result of union activities. But possibly more important were the increasing workloads and the increasing numbers of vulnerable clients who were casualties of the

TABLE 4.6   National distribution of social workers on pay scales,
1980–84 (England and Wales)

Social worker level	1980	1981	1982	1983	1984
1	2 941	2 875	2 483	2 057	2 146
2	5 811	5 795	5 695	5 673	5 234
3	4 831	5 806	6 282	6 765	7 530
Other[1]	3 752	3 588	3 766	3 781	4 729
	17 342	18 064	18 226	18 276	19 637

[1]   Mostly linked grades – often in level ⅔ range.

SOURCE: NALGO Headquarters, 1985.

recession. In 1985, social workers submitted, through NALGO, a claim for an upgrading of scales by three incremental points because of the increased demands on social workers. A national claim would have in all probability been made sooner than 1985 if the 1979 settlement had not provided for a three-level structure.

We saw in the detailed studies of Tower Hamlets and Leeds that social workers have been busy defending the social services and their jobs against cuts. Sometimes they have done this in the context of a Labour council that has been politically committed to defending public services. In other cases they have been faced by councillors demanding 'value for money' and rationalisations. It is difficult, practically impossible, in fact, to accurately estimate the effectiveness of trade union struggles in defending jobs because services have also been defended by the elected members in many councils. It is doubtful, however, that social services staffing would have fared anywhere near as well as it has if social work activists had not been taking defensive action. In fact, staffing in social services increased between late 1979 and early 1984, whereas employment in local government generally declined (see Table 4.7).

TABLE 4.7   Local government and social services staffing in England and Wales, 1979–84

| | Numbers employed | | Percentage change |
	Dec. 1979	March 1984	
Social Services			
Full-time	136 961	144 394	+5.4
Part-time	166 747	181 326	+8.7
General Services			
Full-time	1 560 853	1 471 856	−5.7
Part-time	924 414	913 140	−1.2

Note: Staffing numbers include manual and non-manual workers. General services includes all staff with the exception of law and order staff and agency staff.

SOURCE: Joint Manpower Watch. The December 1979 return was published in the form of a press release by the Department of the Environment in March 1980. The March 1984 return was issued in June 1984 by the Local Authorities' Conditions of Service Advisory Board.

Social workers in NALGO have, as trade unionists, been prone to concentrate on pay and conditions. But in the 1980s NALGO has been moving, nationally and locally, into an area usually regarded as the province of the professional bodies – the development of a good quality service. At national level NALGO became more involved in the professional concerns of social workers when it made a response to the Barclay Report, and in 1984 published a lengthy report (*The Personal Social Services*) spelling out its own views on the role and functions of social workers.

In these national contributions to the development of social work practice, NALGO has articulated a very progressive position. It has supported the development of community social work and has been prepared to criticise existing institutional care (for example, hospitals and residential homes). It has argued that 'it may be that NALGO should press for collective provision within the community' (NALGO, 1984) and, of course, it has attacked privatisation and argued for the provision of social services in the public sector. Moreover, its support for a community approach is conditional on it being 'carefully planned and executed, with sufficient resources and agreed jointly by unions and employers'.

At local level the movement of social work trade unionism towards developing a concern for professional issues is very uneven. In some places there has been a conscious search for a trade union base to professional action. In others, the concern with the quality of service is seen as being an indivisible aspect of the trade union struggle and the professional question has not received much in-depth consideration. In yet other places trade unionism and professionalism are organised in the separate bodies of NALGO and BASW and exist in a state of some rivalry. A NALGO branch organiser in a shire county, for example, told us, 'Most of our activists spit at the mention of the name of BASW but I think a lot of that is a bit of a laugh. I don't think it's that serious.'

In the future, developments in social work practice will be crucially important for the way in which these matters are resolved. Growing numbers of specialists and approved social workers have caused concern amongst social work activists regarding sharpening conflicts over élitism within the social work occupation. Specialisation is seen by some social work activists as fracturing the trade union unity that was rooted in the solidaristic orientation of generic social workers in area teams. On the other hand, progressively inspired moves towards decentralised services in mini town halls could foster amongst social workers a stronger perception of common cause with other local government officers.

At the national level there has been a restoration of formal relations between NALGO and BASW. In January 1985, BASW applied to NALGO for readmission to its joint consultative committee and on 1 April 1985, NALGO's National Local Government Committee agreed to let BASW rejoin.

The impact of NALGO's social workers on the quality of social service provision is the area which is most difficult to assess. Furthermore, the possible end result of these moves into the professional area is presently very difficult to predict. But it is the aspect of social work trade unionism that promises to be the most innovative in the next decade.

Part III
Theory, Politics and Programme

5
Making Sense of History

One of the main troubles with 'theory' is the way many people are introduced to it. It is always portrayed as in some way special and separate from practice. In both social work and trade union politics, people tend to talk about it as external to their day-to-day lives, something that has to be 'dealt' with as the precursor to the real activity of practice.

Our primary motive in this study has been to try and inform the social worker and the trade unionist that their specific situation can only be understood and changed through a clear understanding of its very specificity. How can theory assist this process of understanding then, when we know that theory is in some way an overarching, non-empirical part of the world, yet our basic belief is in the necessity of specificity rather than the simple application of blanket principle? This chapter will demonstrate the way in which theory can relate both as a guide to approach and as a way of understanding the specificity of every situation we approach.

CLASS STRUGGLE

Class as a category is in constant use both in trade union practice and in social work. We couldn't have written a word so far without an understanding of class, and we will explain more exactly what we mean by 'working class' in a few pages; here we must start with a different idea. For us class as a category of understanding is useless, however it is defined, if it is static. Classes are not born, do not exist, nor do they

195

disappear in isolation. They only exist in relation to other classes; they make and are made by other classes struggling with each other. They cannot be defined, understood, let alone worked with, as 'things' in isolation from other classes. Most importantly for us, the British working class only develops and acts in close relationship to the bourgeoisie and the petit bourgeoisie. Historically, people will only work in factories, only engage in wage labour if there is a factory or an employer and these people, usually peasants, are turned into a labour force and as such into a working class, in close relationship with other classes.

Having been so constructed, and having played a considerable role in their own construction, working class people and people from other classes continue to struggle for their own interests. They do not do this abstractly, following a set of ideas laid down by historical directives or rules laid down by Karl Marx and Friedrich Engels; they struggle in specific situations with whatever there is to hand. This struggle only takes place in real historical situations and never in the pamphlets and through the guidelines laid down by left-wing groups. Such a distinction is important to make because the phrase 'class struggle' has come to mean something really very limited; that is, revolutionary class struggle.

For us, class struggle is endemic, it is everywhere. As a concept it represents a way of looking at the whole history of British society, and most significantly for us, the history of the trade union movement and welfare in Britain. Working people have organised and struggled in a very wide variety of forms; on occasion they have been successful and on occasion they have failed; but the criteria for failure or success must properly be found within their own aims, and not against a set of criteria that have been abstractly worked out. As far as we are concerned it is disappointing that only a small section of the working class have struggled with any consistency for socialism. It's a pity, but that in no way detracts from the historical reality that they have been struggling, and that struggle has brought gains for them which can only have been won at the expense of other classes, or as we shall see, 'fractions' of classes. Throughout, we see trade unionism as a form of class struggle; it may be primarily 'economic', it may be 'reformist';

it may be unconcerned with large sections of that class, but it still represents one of the formidable ways in which the British working class have engaged in struggle. Similarly, we believe that much of the struggle around the welfare state also represents a form of class struggle. Struggle sometimes through the ballot box, sometimes through pressure groups and sometimes through trade unionism; but struggle there has been.

Historically, it is unfortunate that the left in Britain has seen only a small section of class struggle; in carrying out their analysis they have misinterpreted the day-to-day imagination of the way in which working-class people will use whatever is to hand to further their interests.

Our last point in this section would be to say that not all forms of 'class struggle' are progressive. Only a very moral 'left-wing' person who wrongly idealises working class people as paragons of political and social virtue would expect that all class experience of working-class people is progressive. The actual class experience of working-class people is, as we shall show, one of day-to-day insecurities and fears. Under these circumstances, forging politics that defend them from the very worst excesses of the ruling class means they will often use a range of tactics and strategies that are far from progressive. As an extreme we must remember the millions of working-class Germans and Italians who helped the struggle for Fascism; the many millions of British working-class people who express their struggle through racism and imperialism; the many trade unionists who attack all forms of change at work because they defend the organisation that they know; the people who live on council estates and refuse to have a home for people with mental handicap in their area. Most class struggle is defensive and may not appear, to any of us, as very 'nice'. It is still class struggle, however.

CLASS FRACTIONS

Whilst we believe that classes struggle with each other and we use the idea to help our analysis 'move', we also think it imperative to claim that each class is itself made up of 'fractions'. These are bits of classes which definitely have the same overall interests as their fellow class members, but also have different interests over a range of specific issues. Whilst this insight is obviously necessary for any analysis of contemporary politics, it's startling how very often classes are written about as if every experience within them had to be all the *same*; the same form of work, the same culture, the same fears: all exactly the same.

This preoccupation with every working-class person being exactly the same as every other one always leaves left-wing analysis wide open to the very simplest attack. For its obvious that the skilled engineer does live a different life from the miner, from the home help, from the local government officer, from the old-age pensioner, from the unemployed person, and so on. These people are self-evidently different, and as such any class analysis which fails to describe and encompass that difference within an overall unity are quickly revealed as useless.

The importance of class fractions goes deeper than this however. For example, the last twenty years has seen the important resurgence of the women's movement. Within both the world of welfare work and the trade union movement, feminism has engaged in detailed struggle for change, and it has had to do so in a way which has been aggressive towards other working-class people, most commonly men. It was obvious that men were working-class, and therefore had interests in common with oppressed working-class women, but it became obvious that working-class men maintained an oppressive relationship both individually and collectively with working class women – both things are true at once.

We believe that these differences are of vital significance in understanding class struggle in Britain. It is now a manifest nonsense to say that the position of working-class women is in some way 'the same' as the position of working-class men; it is not, it's plainly different. However, we also believe that there *is* a similarity, which springs from the experience of being in the same class and that this is important in understanding the lives and behaviour of both men and women of the working class.

Just as importantly, within trade unionism and welfare has been the development of the black movement and the movement of different ethnic groups. Analytically we believe that it is an important truth to describe most black people in Britain as working-class; yet again they are not only different, but have themselves experienced a detailed oppression by working-class white people. Their 'specificity' has been underlined by the experience of attack and discrimination from another section of the working class – as well as capital.

So the working class is greatly differentiated; and, more importantly, it also plays a significant role in its own differentiation of one section from another; also, whilst the British labour movement is unified by its single trade union centre, it consists too of unions which differentiate themselves sharply from one another. Indeed, that is how the trade union movement started and has developed: skilled separated from unskilled; public sector from private; different grades of civil service from one other. This separation plays an important role in the history of the working class. It is inevitable that as the class is reproduced generation after generation, its *own* organisation plays a significant role in reproducing divisions and fractions.

We primarily use the concept of fractions in order to show the variety of experience and organisation within the working class itself. It does, however, assist us in making two other points. Firstly, the nature of the fractions within the working class are themselves not static: they change and move over history. The examples that spring most noticeably from this book show the way in which the working class today has a totally different occupational structure from that of thirty years ago. Equally, those members of the working class who are in paid employment have a very different gender division from that of thirty years ago. People do different work now; and women do more paid work, therefore to simply assume that the working class stays the same over generations is itself very wrong – it is quite the reverse. It is also certain that these fractions will change in relationship to each other in the future; some will grow and others will diminish. At the core of our analysis is the realisation that here and now there are over three times as many trade unionist teachers as there are miners and there are now very more trade unionist welfare workers than there are dockers. These are climatic changes;

they will accelerate and may well be overtaken by others: the one certain thing is change in the relative size and importance of these class fractions.

The Labour Movement and the organisations of the working class do not necessarily reflect these changes; indeed, historically it is most likely to always have a cultural and organisational 'lag' behind the occurrence of the changes and much of our analysis has been based upon an understanding of this 'lag' and its effects.

Class fractions also play an important role in the way in which the working class (and other classes) are organised. For a class doesn't simply reflect all the different aspects of its reality within its organisational form. It is very much more likely that one particular section of the class will represent itself as the totality of the whole class. This representation will take place through the form of the organisation of the class itself. Within the British working class such a role has been played by the skilled, respectable, male, organised section of the labour force. This section had until very recently played a formidable leading role in the way in which the whole class organised itself and represented itself politically. In other contexts this political role has been referred to as 'hegemonic', denoting the full power of the way in which one section of a class has the power to present its own partial reality as that of the whole class.

Thus a hegemonic fraction of a class would define what was 'real working class' and what was in some way 'non-real working class' behaviour. Such representations take place not simply within ideas or arguments but, much more significantly, through the power of political and social organisation. In this way the male, skilled, respectable working class have succeeded in forming not only the whole image of the class in that one section but have also used those aspects of power within the labour movement to belittle, decry and hide any other form of class experience or class struggle. Those involved in class politics have detailed experiences of how such a form of hegemony works; for some, such struggle would be either declared irrelevant or at best a 'side show' which would be defined as not 'real class struggle' precisely because it wouldn't fit in with the predetermined image of what real class struggle is; an image which had become defined by the form and nature of struggles carried out by only a single section of that class – that section which had become 'hegemonic'.

Thus for white-collar workers in the public sector there is a previously-defined reality of what 'real' trade unionism is. NALGO, the association that they join, has been dominated by a form of organisation which was not created purely for white-collar public sector organisation in the late twentieth century. What counts as real working-class struggle had become defined by one section of that class alone, and that historically. Other forms of struggle have themselves to fight hard against an existing form of organisation in order to be recognised as 'proper' trade unionism. We have described the way in which a very specific form of experience of working class organisation, that of social workers employed by the local authority, has had to battle not to be defined as simply the 'same' as the struggle of skilled engineers. Under these circumstances it is more than likely that many of the social workers coming new into the movement would become hegemonised by the existing powerful forms of struggle, even if they are inappropriate. We have already noted that there are more unionised welfare workers today than there are unionised miners but the latter group has successfully defined what 'counts' as struggle through their historical power. In this way such power of hegemony may not necessarily reflect the contemporary balance of day-to-day power within the class or the movement; rather it will reflect a past reality.

The power of class fractions over the image of reality will also be of significance in the world of welfare. The image of the 'normal working-class family' as one which has two adults with children under 16 living with them, and where the man is the only wage earner, is a powerful hegemonic image of social reality. It is to be found not just within the media world view or that of bourgeois literature; it also exists within the way in which the working class represents itself through its organisation. Yet statistically only some 11 per cent of all households reflect that reality any more: this clearly shows how a reality does not need to have a 'simple majority' to hold hegemonic sway over the rest of the class. Within the world of welfare, such images are oppressive not simply through state structures that have been instituted by the ruling class but also through those that have been heavily influenced by the working class. In this way class fractions can have great social power over the rest of their own class, let alone the rest of the social structure.

CLASS

So far we have outlined the way in which class can only be understood as a set of movements, in situations where one class interacts and struggles with another. We have also pointed out that classes are not simple unities, with the same straightforward interests, but exist as fractions where one section comes to dominate the class and represents itself as the *whole* class. We have deliberately introduced class in this way to ensure that the reality of class as a set of movements and processes is communicated. Class is too often treated as a set of static categories, a yardstick where we can 'read off' definitions to find out whether something is 'really' working-class or not. In this section we want to discuss issues about the nature of class experience and class definition. For social workers these are especially important since their own 'class position' is continually under discussion, not just among Marxists but also within the coffee rooms and pubs. It's discussed not in an abstract way, but in direct terms of identity. For social workers and their clients being working class, or sub-working class, or middle class is an issue of identity which goes beyond cosmetics to the direction and meaning of much of their lives. It is an important issue for peoples' real life experience and is beyond a discussion of theory.

Secondly, within the trade union movement class location has always been an important point. For most industrial manual workers their location in the working class has been obvious. Individually, many of them may define themselves as 'middle class' but as a collective organisation they adhere to a working-class image; indeed, following the point we made above, they define the image for the whole of that class. This leaves the position of the rest of the trade union movement as importantly ambiguous. On many occasions within struggles, the 'blue-collar section of the class', (representing itself as *the* working class) has reacted against the white-collar section of the class, as if it were a different class. Consequently, within the actual practices of the trade union movement the question of whether people are, or are not, in the working class is something which gravely effects the day-to-day realities of trade unionism. However much traditional industrial trade unionists may politically welcome sections of the workforce into the movement, there are very many trade unionists who still see, for example, a miner as a 'real worker' and a shop worker on the perfume counter at Harrods as a snobbish member of the middle class. There are moments of solidarity but, generally, being in the 'real working class' or not is used as a sectarian hammer to attack other sections for simply being different.

Since class is such a central issue in Marxist theory and practice it is inevitable that there are very many important debates about the definition of the concept. The aim of this section is not to provide a short precis of the debates, but rather to provide the reader with a clear understanding of the way in which we ourselves define class. In doing this, we will, of course, touch upon other definitions but will not fully elaborate the important debates.

For us, social workers are members of the working class. Despite their qualifications, despite their hire-purchased cars, mortgages and different working hours, they are members of the working class. Crucially, also, as we shall see, despite what they *think* they are, they are working class by historical definition.

The context within which we make that definition obviously needs some important explanation. We believe that British society contains three important classes: the bourgeoisie, the petit-bourgeoisie and the working class. Peasants and members of the aristocracy used to be important but those classes, as indigenous parts of the British social structure, have declined in importance as other classes have expanded. It's true that there are occasions when members of the peasantry from other social structures migrate to this country, but they become assimilated into either the working class or the petit-bourgeoisie.

We define these three classes both in relation to their ownership of the means of producing wealth and in relationship to the other classes. This way of defining class must not be seen as a purely economic definition; on occasion it is attacked for a simplistic economic determinism. This is not the case for two important reasons: the ownership or non-ownership of the means of production is an issue which moves far beyond the sphere of 'economics' into that of politics, power and ideology. The means of production, and wealth itself, are not simply issues of economic importance. Owning a factory or a part of an industry involves the owner in decisions which include almost every part of society. Similarly, being responsible for the way in which wealth is created ensures that this class has a very great influence on the way in which people live their lives as a whole. For us, the nature of production within a society quite literally relates to everything. Within capitalism, it's ownership or non-ownership which affects all social relations.

Karl Marx pointed out that for most of history there had been a ruling class and therefore there had always been a subordinate class (or more usually classes). What is new about capitalism is not that there is a ruling class which runs society; what is new about capitalism is the way in which that ruling class is differentiated from other classes; that is, by their complete ownership of the means of producing wealth. This didn't happen suddenly, but occurred gradually over many centuries and needs to be continually reconstructed by the historical actions of the bourgeoisie.

Equally specific to the capitalist era, the subordinate classes who are under the bourgeoisie are not simply ruled and have less power, but are specifically defined by the way in which they experience the basis of that lack of power. Crucially, the subordinate class created under capitalism – the working class – does not own the means to produce wealth. All it owns in terms of wealth production, is its own labour. Without selling its labour, without being in the labour market, the capitalist would provide it with nothing and it would produce nothing. The members of the working class, then, within a capitalist society are reduced in circumstances precisely because they are totally dependent for their economic survival on the capitalist class. Within the pure capitalist system this dependency is total; it pervades every single aspect of their life. For the capitalist requires collectively from the labour force a continual pool of labour that would compete within itself at every level in order to reduce both its price and its power: for the role of labour is to have no alternative except to work and produce value for the capitalist. This lack of any alternative reduces both the individual and the collective power of members of the working class completely. For where alternatives exist, of any sort, then the capitalist has to try to encourage the working class to work in their factories, and this very encouragement must provide the working class with some power since they then have the bargaining position of a 'needed' group of people.

Theoretically, then, a pure capitalism would have a large number of atomised and powerless workers competing one with another in full and 'free' competition. It is important to reiterate that such a situation is not simply about economics and material wealth or poverty but is also most strongly about power and control over one's own life. The total dependency aimed at for working people within the pure capitalist mode reduces them to a set of expendable 'hands' (occasionally attached to a brain) dependent for their total existence on the power of others.

This powerlessness is further compounded by the way in which it is explained within the capitalist system. For whilst the capitalist is the person who actually has the power in the interaction over whether the worker is employed or not, the whole interaction is explained through a system called 'the market'. This system is beyond the control of human beings – it rests within the hands of the market mechanism which itself 'decides' whether a product sells or not. Thus, if a product stops selling because of the market, the workers stop working and are thrown upon the open labour market. The consequent explanation for this action is rarely to be found in any human agency at all, it's just 'the market'. Consequently, not only are members of the working class meant to be powerless within this pure model, but they are also told that their powerlessness is caused by something beyond the control of people.

Anyone who has practised social work would realise that

these material conditions described as 'normal' for the work-ing class are extremely likely to lead to some considerable psychic damage. To live in a world where we are powerless is one thing, it is an experience which causes grave and continu-ing insecurities and which in turn may hurt the individual psychically. However, for this lack of power to be constantly attributed to arbitrary and unknowable economic forces means that *anything* can happen to a person at any time and without any prospect of either foreknowledge or change. A deeply mysterious powerlessness leaves individuals with no power and no knowledge of why they have no power.

This is the material basis of working peoples' experience within a capitalist society. However, as we stressed at the very beginning of this section, within real, lived history, nothing as 'pure' as this exists. In every historical situation, working people actually think, feel and act to find ways of resisting this total, mystifying powerlessness. They use anything to hand to attempt to stop this from happening; they gain scraps of power from as wide a range of ideas and activities as possible; and they also gain knowledge which they use to undermine the mystery caused by this unknowable thing called 'the market'. This knowledge may centre around the perceived reality that some other people don't seem to 'suffer' from its bad effects. It may centre on the fact that they do see some form of human agency involved in these actions rather than a complete mystification of the 'hidden hand' called the market.

In fighting against this insecurity people do come into contact with others in similar situations. They talk to each other about what's happening, they listen, compare experi-ences, learn and teach. Yet all the time the push towards competitive individualism and insecurity exists. In different places and in different ways this is resisted; people hang on to anything which would provide even a flimsy base for security: the fact that they are 'British'; the importance of being Tyne-siders; the importance of having a 'decent' home; or of ma-terial possessions. Many, many things are adhered to in order to provide this security base.

To many of us these may be very odd. Why was it for example that in the nineteenth century poor men and women set so much store by having sufficient money put by for a 'respectable' funeral when they had nothing else? Why, when some people get small sums of money is it spent so very quickly on a range of different consumer goods to fill their homes? These activities and many more represent attempts to construct a limited form of security out of a grinding experience of insecurity. It can never be effective in any full sense since the items which create the appearance of security develop out of their experience as working-class people. The homes and consumer goods can only construct a passing security; a security that exists for only as long as the worker can control their ability to sell their labour power. Yet, as we have found, the underlying fact is precisely that they have *not* got control over their ability to sell their labour power. They can be sacked. As such the security caused by ownership of goods is only a passing event. It is not cemented in a long-term security.

What, then, of political action and trade union action? For it is obvious that the experience of this unity also leads to a wide series of activities involving other working-class people in the struggle for security. The trade union movement represents one of the most established organisational forms of increasing security around the vitally important location where labour power is sold: work. Nearly all trade union activity represents attempts to reduce the power of management to manage labour and increase the power of labour to create security in the workplace.

The collective action of trade unionism is a reflection of the way in which the individual experience of insecurity (and where workers experience conflict between themselves as one of its main forms) is reproduced. The main relevance of trade unionism, though, is to be found in the ways in which the purely individual experience and knowledge of the workplace is shared and collectivised. The organisation, in its very form, encourages a sharing of knowledge and activity within an institution – work – where the worker is both individual and separate.

Most studies of trade union action underline the ways in which workers, when involved in action, talk about their work and their colleagues entirely differently from the way they do the rest of the time. During action they talk to each other as brothers and sisters; they see the union as a living, powerful part of their work experience; and most obviously they see that institution in contradiction with their employer. This contradiction is not simply about the issue that caused the dispute (pay, conditions of work, etc.) but it represents institutional conflict based upon two different world views about work. It goes beyond a simple opposition to the very nature of the 'us' (a collective experience which will represent a move towards security for labour) and the nature of the 'them' (those who dominate work specifically in order to increase the insecurity of workers thereby allowing management to manage). People join trade unions, then, as a major attempt to reduce their insecurity: it is a *conscious* decision.

We would, however, add two points about trade unions and the struggle for security. Firstly, that working people experience trade unionism itself as a part of the move towards security; whilst this may be particularly acute during the heightened experience of struggle, it is also developed through the experience of membership itself. To stress this point, trade union leadership is usually committed through newspapers, education and the organisation itself to increasing the day-by-day experience of being a member of a trade union. In so far as they achieve this within the everyday structure of experience, then they do actually involve their membership with a struggle for security; in so far as they *fail* to involve their membership then the union itself could be experienced as either an irrelevance, or, at worst, just another institution external to the workforce and even occasionally oppressing it.

The other issue that comes through strongly reflects upon our earlier comments on the nature of class fractions. Individual trade unions do not represent the whole class: their membership is specific and fractional. Consequently, however 'successful' trade union struggle is it cannot completely destroy the grinding experience of insecurity. In so far as they are individually successful, a union may well demonstrate that, for some of their members, a passing security can be constructed for a period of time. On occasion, when trade unions are especially strong they may be able to control recruitment to the industry or occupation for some time. This limited security, however, cannot last, since the dynamics of capital ensures that production processes change, and, try as they may, individual trade unions cannot stop this for long. Their vision and their power must inevitably be fractional and partial; their capacity, therefore, to end the insecurity of the membership is limited.

In the struggle against insecurity a wide range of other forms of collectivity are used: community groups based on locality or associative experience, tenants' groups, gender groups, youth groups, and so on. A wide range of collective organisations encourage the growth of both the understanding and the struggle for security. The women's movement has highlighted the way in which such movements provide both a personal experience of collective understanding as well as political struggle for change and security. It has also demonstrated how important the specific nature of the group (women) is in determining the character of conflicts and alliances in struggling for collectivity. It is a struggle *against* as well as struggle *for* – the two opposite poles being dialectically intertwined, for on many occasions men *are* the enemy; and on other occasions the enemy – the causes of insecurity – can include political and social forces where 'men' are not so universally on the other side. Here, as with the trade union movement, the nature of the organisation represents a close understanding of and struggle against the experiences of insecurity.

We have underlined the concrete nature of these organisations without intending to criticise them from a 'pure' left position. Quite the reverse. We believe that this day-to-day attempt to increase security within a capitalist system must be termed class struggle. As we outlined at the beginning of this chapter we do not reserve the label 'class struggle' for the specific form of class struggle that takes place in a revolutionary situation: rather, we see all forms of struggle for security as representing ways in which the class, and fractions of the class, struggle and organise itself. For as long as the class struggle is dominated by small sections of the class in a sectarian way we do not believe that it can overcome the long-term insecurities caused by capitalism. It cannot achieve this 'sweeping away' because its sectional visions of the new world are based on an incomplete view of the class as a whole.

Its consciousness and therefore its politics are partial and fractional.

Such a view of class has great importance for the way in which we understand social workers within their class perspective. We have stated that we believe social workers are members of the working class because they only have their labour power to sell. Whilst we believe this gives them the same basic interests in overcoming long-term insecurity as the rest of the working class, we also would stress that this does not in any simple way make them 'the same' as every other section of workers. If we were to imply that skilled artisans were the same as an unskilled farm labourer no one would believe us. The split between skill and lack of skill in manual work is mirrored by the important differentiation between mental and manual labour. People who work mainly with their minds do different sorts of work than do people who work mainly with their hands. This does not, however, make them a different class. It will certainly affect their consciousness, just as being skilled engineering workers affects the consciousness of those workers. That is an important but separate issue to be discussed in the next section.

The white-collar worker, as mental labourers are called within the language of industrial relations, covers a very wide range of jobs, and there are very many 'clerical workers' whose rates of pay and conditions of service are worse than those of very many skilled manual workers. Similarly, there are some high-level white-collar workers who earn many, many times the wages of unskilled manual labourers. However, within this differentiation it is certain that there are groups who carry out a different kind of labour process, one over which they have more control than do unskilled factory labourers over their work. The experience of parts of their work is different: there may, to use one of our major terms in this section, be less insecurity in the experience of their work by highly qualified white-collar workers, and such differentiations are important. We must recognise that a field social worker in her car does a job different from that of many labourers; equally, though, she also does a different job from those of most residential social workers.

However, in analysing the material position of social workers in recent years we must recognise that their experience of 'autonomy' in their labour process – the caring process – has been severely limited. Indeed, this limitation provides us with one of the main rationales for the growth of trade unionism. Similarly, their material position as salaried workers, who can suffer redundancies alongside their blue-collar colleagues, has been fully experienced in recent years. In Chapter 7 of this book we will deal with some of the social work issues which have been understood as being about professionalism that have helped to mark this change. Here all we need to underline is the way in which their experience as wage labourers (apart, that is, from those who have private therapy businesses) has increasingly underlined the definition of themselves as 'working class'.

CLASS CONSCIOUSNESS

As an historical category – a category which assists us to understand the whole development of historical change – class has two distinct uses. Firstly, it helps us to see the way in which large and distinct groups of people, through their interaction as different groups, actually change the course of history. Obviously, under these circumstances, if a class analysis is used, then the way in which these groups are seen as distinct one from another is of importance in understanding the way in which social change occurs. Why peasants are peasants, why the working class is working class, etc., must be decided if we are to understand anything at all about the way in which the world moves or we can be moved. We have said something about our definitions of these matters.

Secondly, though, we must make the point that no *category* called class ever changed anything: history has been moved and changed by people acting in historically specific situations, people living and acting and in struggle against other people who are in a different class category. To take part in this historical activity in making the world, members of classes – people – act on the basis of their world view. Class, therefore, is an important analytical category but it only ever effects real historical change through the agency of people, and *that* only happens through people's consciousness. We must recognise, then, that the category of class means nothing at all if it is not in some way reflected in the way in which people think and act.

These two things are separate. We believe that peasants were peasants even if they thought they were small land-owners; we believe that working class people are working class even if they think they are petit-bourgeois. We believe then in an objective view of class as a historical category: historical actors are in one of these categories. Yet also, if they don't see themselves in that category, people obviously act differently from those that do. Therefore, the question of class conscious-ness is never one of secondary importance since only when people see themselves in the class that they objectively *are* in, will they act as that class.

In Britain this is the paramount political question of the last 150 years. Since this nation saw the first creation of industrial capitalism, we also have the longest history of any working class as a large historical bloc. Edward Thompson's brilliant book, *The Making of the English Working Class* (Thompson, 1968) covers only up to the 1830s, by which time the class is 'made'. Having such a large working class that is more than 150 years old is of unique importance for two reasons. Firstly, it means that we have not had to bother, either analytically or politically, with understanding a national peasant movement for more than a century and a half. The working class became, and has continued to be, the major subordinate class in Britain during all that time. The problem, then, has not been one of alliances between classes, rather it has been about the working class internally forming itself as a class.

Secondly, the fact that the working class in Britain is the oldest in the world, and it has a long history, means it has developed ways of organising and thinking about itself that date back a long way. We have also stressed that there are very distinct changes in the structure of class that are brought about by the changes in the nature of capitalist production. Yet the history and culture of the class may not change as quickly as the objective reality of it, thus leaving it imagining itself as it was at some period in the past. Maturity, then, has costs as well as benefits. And those costs will usually make themselves felt most strongly in the field of consciousness.

This is a book about social workers and the way in which they play a role in constructing their class position. The book could not have been written but for the fact that social workers, since 1970, have become a very active section of a trade union that is affiliated to the TUC, and this seems to represent an important shift in their consciousness as well as making it more likely that social workers will see themselves as members of the working class. They have developed what V. I. Lenin (1970) has called, in his classic work *What Is To Be Done?*, a 'trade union consciousness'. The joining of, and active participation in, a trade union which is itself linked with the major working class organisation of Britain, is obviously a large individual and collective step towards an understanding of being of the working class; but it is extremely different from actually having class consciousness; different from seeing yourself fully as a member of a class which has a wide and different set of social and economic relationships.

It is that very breadth which would demonstrate the full power of class consciousness. A realisation that an individual worker on an intake team for example, has similar interests to those of a teacher, a miner, a farm worker, an unemployed young person, and so on. That those similar interests span an enormous spread of 'difference' between all those different groups; that the differences exist and are of importance, but less so than the weight of similarity in interests.

How does this happen? What is the drift towards class consciousness? Marx noted very early on in the development of capitalism the way in which the various production processes force workers into relationship with larger and larger numbers of other workers. To produce something under capitalism, workers are brought into real, active relationship with many thousands of other workers. Producing goods under feudalism could be achieved by small groups of peasants in isolated communities, but producing, say, one Ford Escort within industrial capitalism can *only* be achieved by bringing thousands of people in relationship to one other; it is an inevitable part of the production process and cannot be dodged. This relationship inevitably brings different sorts of workers into contact with each other, too. Even if they never meet, their labour and their work only has social or productive meaning because of all the other workers they relate to. There is no sense that this magically creates class consciousness, for we have already underlined the vital importance of class fractions, and the way in which different sorts of interests exist within the working class. Anyone who understands a factory line would know that sets of workers can act in close collaboration with each other and yet disagree very strongly about their interests. But, again and again, and perhaps against their constant wishes, working people are forced into contact with one another to produce things. Equally, in their experience of subordinacy, working people of all sorts realise that they can only overcome that subordinacy and 'win' anything in the long term by struggling alongside other people collectively. Both in politics, then, as well as in work, there is an inevitable impetus towards a collective understanding of the world, an understanding which if eventually completed in such a way as to link all working-class people together, would lead to a most powerful and comprehensive world view able to create a society.

We know we are, however, far short of this, and we recognise that there are also powerful countervailing historical trends. We know that the labour market actively splits people one from another every day; we know that a society dominated by the extreme fetishism of commodities also brings people into sharp and individual competition one with another; and such experiences are powerful in undermining the move towards a collective class consciousness. For every time a person actually takes a collective stand around anything, it is also undermined by the individualism of everyday life. The most fervent striker worries deeply that she or he will be evicted, say, or perhaps have to sell their car.

We believe that these trends in consciousness are there for social workers. Caring in the 1980s can only take place if there are many hundreds, and most usually thousands, of people involved in the process. Many social workers find it inconvenient that they are not solely in charge of their whole caring process and it would, of course, be much easier if they could do the teaching of the kids at school (also providing the school dinners), if they could run the housing department, the social security office, be the home help and the district nurse and doctor, and so on. It would be nice simply to do the lot, but it is increasingly obvious that, as the whole process has developed in the 1970s and 1980s, it inevitably brings the social worker, in completing his or her task, into contact with hundreds of other people.

It is unfortunate that some social workers treat other social workers with whom they come into contact with ill-disguised contempt. We have all sat in on discussions where social workers bitterly criticise their colleagues in other caring jobs for being vicious, uncaring or thoughtless. Yet, again and again, they have to return to the social reality that these people play an intrinsic role in the caring process. They simply cannot work without them. It is this inevitable part of the contemporary caring process that pushes social workers more and more into relationship with other workers. It is not something they choose. In fact, many workers in different occupations have resisted being confronted with their total interdependence, but if one wants to practice in the main-stream of social work there is simply no choice in the matter; it just happens, inevitably.

Such a reality stops short of creating full class consciousness; this will take a much wider set of political and historical processes. But it does explain how, in the midst of their labour process of social work there is an inevitable pressure to see their work, their practice, as only being possible, as only happening because of thousands of other workers and it is this pressure that is at the core of the development of a greater collective consciousness amongst social workers.

MODES OF PRODUCTION

We have characterised British society in the late twentieth century throughout this book as 'capitalist', and we have no doubt that the dominant set of social relationships that affect us all are those of capitalism; where one major class owns the means of producing wealth in the society and where one other class, the working class, holds no direct ownership stake in those means of production. The imbalances of power and the insecurities caused by this crucial differential affects every single aspect of the society in a direct or indirect form. Equally, both trade unionism and social work have to see the market mechanism as central to capitalist social relations. In a capitalist society things are valued by being bought and sold within a market place. People are valued in direct relationship to the number of things that they can buy in that market place; the value placed upon their contribution to society is worked out through the market place of buying and selling their labour.

The Thatcher government increasingly defines as much of life as it possibly can within a very direct relationship to the market mechanism; nearly all of welfare should, as far as it is concerned, be distributed through the market. Equally important, it has been trying directly to import the notion of competition into the way in which public sector workers have their pay agreed. Consequently, in recent years, for social worker trade unionists the growth of the direct influence of the market has been a major issue.

There is, however, a conceptual point to be made in addition to the characterisation of British social structure as 'capitalist', and one that Thatcherism's attempts to extend the market has politically brought home to us all. For if it is true, as it undoubtedly is, that the government has been struggling very hard to extend the full effect of the market, then, logically, it must be trying to extend it *into* something which has social relations that are not already dominated by the market. Oddly, for us, these areas are characterised by the present Conservative government as 'socialism'; sectors of society where distribution does not take place through direct capitalist social relations.

Equally, the government has characterised certain sets of relations, for example, in the shire counties and in the professions, as old-fashioned and in need of the market mechanism to 'bring them up to date'. For Thatcherism, the market mechanism represents 'normality' and 'human nature'; it is the way in which things should be ordered and organised both in attacking the old-fashioned ideas of socialism (what we see as the future) and feudalism (what we see as the past).

Whilst we do not agree with the government's characterisation of any of our structure as 'socialism', the political direction of this debate is important and is itself reflected in a debate within socialism. For whilst all socialists would agree to call Britain a 'capitalist' society, they do differ in the completeness of that characterisation with regard to every single aspect of the society. Marx himself pointed out (Marx and Engels, 1942) two important issues within the 'Manifesto of the Communist Party': firstly, that the creation of capitalism takes place over many centuries and moves faster in some aspects of society than others. Thus there were still very significant aspects of a feudal mode of production in the middle of the nineteenth century and the new industrial bourgeoisie were competent in attempting to root all these out in order to fully create a world in their image. In the fifteenth, sixteenth, seventeenth and eighteenth centuries they had been a growing power; growing from their merchant base where capitalist social relations and wage labour had become the norm, and extending their power through ceaseless economic, political and social struggle. It took a long time and as far as Marx was concerned in 1848, it was not yet over. Therefore, we should not be surprised to find, within an established capitalist society, aspects of that society which had not been fully conquered by capitalism but remained in some form of bastardised feudal relationship.

Secondly, and even more significantly, Marx claimed that each epoch had within it the seeds of the next epoch – that within feudalism there was a movement away from feudal social relationships towards those of capitalism. Historically, this was correct as we have outlined above; logically, though, this has enormous implications for British capitalism in the late twentieth century. For if capitalism existed in bits and pieces within feudalism then it is undoubtedly true logically that socialism exists (in bits and pieces) within capitalism. It is true that the ways in which capitalist social relations emerged and survived under feudalism were different from 'capitalism' when it finally emerged triumphant, but it still existed in *some* form within that society. If this analysis of historical change means anything, then the same must be true of aspects of the British social structure now. There must be some sorts of social relationships which are themselves antagonistic to capitalism and in some fragmented and bastardised way represent the future socialism. We repeat that we are not saying that these *are* socialism, but that there are aspects of them that are so antagonistic to capitalism that, in the interests of capitalism they must be smashed.

Any analysis, then, must take fully into account the fact that within each social structure there are certain to be sets of social relationships that represent different epochs. These would all be antagonistic one with another; they would be aiming to maximise their own power and influence against the power and influence of the others' epochs. Obviously, compared to a picture of capitalism pure and simple, such an analysis creates a story with much more complexity, difference and movement. It also means that each aspect of the social structure needs very careful analysis; looking closely at the social relationships involved to uncover the different ways in which it might interact with the rest of the social structure. For example, we cannot simply assume that, within local authorities, all the social relationships can be defined by the pure capitalist model or as dominated totally by the dynamics of the market mechanism.

There can be no doubt that local government *is* restricted overall by the social relationships of a capitalist society; there is no doubt that local authorities' finance is dominated by the market mechanism that characterises capitalism, that the capital necessary for building houses can only be spent as it is raised through the capitalist capital market. And of equal importance for all contemporary left analyses of the local state, the 'increasing capitalist influence on local authorities' through corporate management and through the increased control from central government has been constantly commented on. This is an analysis of recent changes that we would agree with wholeheartedly, yet it leaves us questioning how we can understand local authorities. For if we see the last fifteen years as ones where the detailed experience of local authorities has become increasingly controlled by capitalist social relations, what were they or are they, if not capitalist?

We have already commented on the way in which classes struggle with each other for dominance in society; we have also now pointed out that each social structure contains aspects from different epochs, and that such movements and changes result from different classes and fractions within classes struggling for control. Therefore, we would expect each sector of society to reflect a different result of these different struggles as classes and fractions of classes. Even more so with different sectors of government as opposed to the economy.

Local authorities, then, cannot simply be 'the same' as the private economy. They will reflect a different power relationship between different classes; their structure, representing as it does a relationship to electoral democracy is different from both large and small capital; the way in which its income is generated is completely different; the way in which success and failure is recognised is completely different. Most importantly for our analysis in this book, the way in which social workers as employees are treated will be different from those workers who have a direct experience of the market mechanism.

If we review the points we have made in this section some vital issues emerge. Firstly, we believe that it's inevitable that some of the social relationships of a future socialist society will emerge from within the old society. Of course we are not simply claiming that 'social work' or 'the welfare state' in any way represent the way in which socialism will develop, or what it will look like in the future. We are saying that elements of this work are directly antagonistic to the simple power of the market mechanism: it gets in the way of the ideology which sees people simply as sets of hands: it gets in the way of those that can only see 'human nature' in terms of buying and selling. It's not only us that believe that, but quite obviously Thatcherism believes it and so do large sections of the left who have struggled so very hard for local government in recent years. So have the working people who have struggled for the welfare state. It's not perfect, in fact it's full of problems, but it is different.

Secondly, recent years have seen a powerful attempt to

push change upon the welfare state. John Benington (1976) and Cynthia Cockburn (1977) are only two of the writers who have demonstrated the way in which central government has attempted to introduce both the accounting system and the ideology of the market mechanism into local authority welfare. It has been a difficult task, and, it must be stressed, it is an incomplete process. Every month there are more and more attempts to introduce the market mechanism into social work, but, however it is constructed, the profit mechanism can never simply or completely construct the labour process of social workers in the same way as it has, for example, constructed car workers. The demand for their services is, in nearly every area of state social work, not backed up by the cash for buying their product. This must mean that their experience of their labour process is different. Of course, this doesn't mean that they are working 'under socialism', but it does mean that it's different from working under 'pure capitalism'.

Thirdly, this must have some effect upon the nature of trade unionism and the action that can develop from it. If all trade unionists were working within the same mode of production, a capitalist one, say, then their relationship to the market and their relationship to profit would be fairly uniform. This would structure their ability to take powerful action. As McIlroy (1984) points out, workers need to have a clear idea of times when it's better to strike (those times when order books are full and profits may be hit) and those times when it is not so useful to strike (those times when order books are empty and the employers may want to save on the wage bill): they don't always succeed in choosing the right time.

Therefore, striking under these circumstances has nearly always been an attempt through the power of a unified workforce to hurt the profits of the employers. It's this power that lies at the root of that particular form of industrial action. Of course, it may mean other things as well: it will mean an act of solidarity with fellow workers: it may reflect great rage at the employer; but, underneath these ideas and moralities, it reflects a powerful threat to the material wealth of the employer. What, however, if that mode of production, the market, the production of profit, isn't the major characteristic of your particular institution? It may characterise society, but it may not fully construct, for example, the way in which an old peoples' home is run, or the way in which child policy is formed in an area. Under these circumstances it's not that the strike is morally wrong (such categories do not concern us here), rather it will not operate in the same way on the same power differentials as if the institution was run for profit.

THE STATE

Thirty years ago, most trade unionists, in so far as they considered the matter at all, believed that the various aspects of government represented different and countervailing elements of power. Some believed this power could be won or lost in elections. Others believed the constitutional picture of a separation of powers was still the case. For the former, all political power could be decided by an electorate which held the real sway in society. For the latter, the executive, the legislature and the judiciary all represent different and counterbalancing aspects of power, none of which could be controlled by any single section of the population. The theory was a part of a belief in the plurality of power within a capitalist democracy; equally significant, the state machine and its operatives (including social workers) were neutral professionals whose practice and allegiance could be won by that section of the population who won enough votes.

It's interesting, now, though, how very few people will honestly admit to holding these views in the past. Yet this world view, when combined with the notion that the welfare aspects of government represented the 'moving frontier of the nation', did actually form part of a major social movement. Indeed, it was desperately difficult to believe anything else either to the right or to the left of such a set of social democratic beliefs. Within the caring professions, they were normal.

Beliefs have changed radically, the importance of consensus, the necessity of understanding how we have progressed, forward and upward, as a caring nation, have all become old-fashioned notions about the role of the welfare state. Two different theories emerged about state action, that have both come to influence the whole terrain of the welfare state. The most important ideology, though it is one that carries little weight amongst welfare practitioners, is the new right theory of the state. We must remember that in the late 1960s, at the time of Seebohm, there *were* people who believed that the state's involvement with welfare was undermining the individual's own responsibility for looking after themselves and their families. The new right see the state as over-involved in the day-to-day experience of peoples' lives; public expenditure not only represents a waste of money but, more significantly, that money is spent in such a way as to challenge the correct, 'natural' way in which individuals and society should interact – the market.

In detail, the market mechanism is posed against the state not simply because it is cheaper but, much more significantly, because it provides competition and choice between service providers. In later years, Margaret Thatcher was to represent this clearly through the graphic image of the corner shop. Here, the customer, however poor, experiences the reality of choice between different products and between different brands of products. Such an experience happens thousands of times a day for every person in society. When it was posed against the experience that people have of state organisations, of schools, of hospitals, doctors and social security offices, all places where there is little choice and much humiliation for people, there was an understandable reaction. Thatcherism characterised the state as deeply monolithic and bureaucratic; the characterisation made sense particularly when it was supplemented by a view of state workers as unaccountable professionals, somehow above the marketplace that the rest of us had to live in. The welfare state, then, had to be attacked and dismantled, and since 1979 that ideology has had considerable success.

The left never fully accepted the social democratic consensus image of the welfare state. In the late 1960s and 1970s, it powerfully developed a very different and, in some important ways, a completely opposite view of welfare state apparatuses. Where social democracy stresses pluralism amongst state institutions, what we term Marxist functionalism stresses a unity of purpose in these institutions; where social democracy sees the state as neutral above political struggle, a set of institutions to be 'won' by one group or another, this ideology sees the state as powerfully representing the interests of one class and one class only – the ruling class in that particular society. All the activities of the state are bent in this one direction, towards the interests of the ruling class.

In the late 1960s and through the 1970s, this approach gained some following amongst many new social workers, and some social workers still adhere to this; they may not be Marxists themselves – indeed, many of them will never have read the Communist Manifesto's edict about the modern state's representation of the interests of the industrial bourgeoisie – yet they still believe some of the aspects of this theory. Significantly, they believe that the state that they work for is controlled by a powerful, uncaring class and that they as individual workers have their practice structured by these forces. Under these circumstances there is very little that the social worker can actually do – very little chance of a successful week's caring; little chance of clients feeling that their lives have been enriched; little chance that the social worker can feel humanly enriched by the work. Indeed, on occasion, little chance that they can achieve anything at all.

This, then, has been the theory's towering strength in the late 1970s and 1980s. It explains how, despite all the hard work and care, so very little in terms of caring interventions appears to be ever achieved by social work. It explains the impotence and powerlessness by pointing to the overwhelming power of others, who are themselves unreachable. It also puts off being able to really achieve anything until those people can be swept away. Obviously, though, given the whole thrust of our history of trade unionism and social work, given the outline of democracy and the public sector below, and given the way in which we approach the difficult possibilities of the organisation of social work practice, we do not accept this theory of the welfare state.

Throughout this chapter we have stressed our belief that socialism contains a wide range of debates and nowhere is this truer than in the theories of the state. Of course, there are still those who tell trade unionists that there is only one socialist theory of the state, and that is usually approximate to what we call Marxist functionalism. We believe that the state in modern capitalist society is not run in the interests of one class, but represents the results of continuing and unremitting struggle between the classes. This is one reason why we began this chapter by looking at the importance of class struggle. We see it as the only way to make sense of what is going on in the welfare state. It is obvious to us that working people have throughout the last hundred years been very active in their struggle around welfare state provision and we cannot believe that every government and all local authority provision through-out the ten decades since the 1880s has been purely represent-ing the interests of one class, the ruling class alone. Not when the working class have been so powerfully active in their own interests; all of that has meant something. Nor can we go along with the notions of false consciousness where those trade unionists who have fought hard and long for, shall we say, a state pension scheme, are to be characterised as fighting for something, in this case pensions, that is really in the interests of their oppressors. All those working class people, for all that time, could not have been so consistently false in their con-sciousness about their own lives. To believe that puts the arrogance of the theorist above all that vital and rich experience.

What, then, is the result of this class struggle within the state? At the very least it means that every single policy, every single practice and every single state institution will reflect different sorts of movement and processes between the classes rather than any simple static class interest. It also means that we need to look at every single aspect of the state separately with a different expectation of what that aspect of state will represent in class terms. We would expect, for example, that the working class would have a greater impact on the policy and practice of the state in a location where they had consider-able strength and at a time in history when they were powerful (in Glasgow, say, with regard to housing in the post-war period) than in a situation when all those strengths were reversed (law and order in Hampshire in the 1930s for exam-ple).

In the area of interest to us in this book – social workers and trade unionism – these differences caused by class struggle in different locations and at different times are of crucial importance. The local state is the major employer and organ-iser of social work: it is a very specific sector of the state. If the 'state' is all the same, one section with another, then we would expect our experience of the social services to be 'the same' as our experience of social security; our experience of nursery education to be 'the same' as prisons. There are occasions when someone might be trying to make a nasty point, when she or he might say that the area team, or head of a home, is as authoritarian as a prison governor, but it is rarely, if ever, true. Different sectors of the state are different partly because at different times the working class has taken an organised interest in them.

The personal social services have only been at the edges of their interests. Certain localities have had some experience of long-term client groups, or political parties that have taken a keen interest; or even sections of trade unions who have taken up those sets of issues. All these influences, whether through political, trade union or client organisation can, if strong enough, make an impact upon the way in which services are considered and conducted.

Our view of the state, though, is *not* one where we see the state machinery as being constantly variable, as simply being 'up for grabs' in some voluntaristic way. Rather it's much more significant to see all those forms as structures which have emerged from a specific historical period, where this or that class had more or less power in specific and general situations. Thus, for example, if a local authority set of unions could overcome the differences between them and launch a campaign, this campaign could be constructed with the local authority itself; it could even include a large number of client groups, all of them fighting for, say, a change in the resources and democratic nature of policy for children. Such a set of alliances would be formidable. It would form a powerful part of class struggle. But given the fact that child care policy is constructed through the state form of national legislation, they may quickly come up against the power of that state form stopping them from changing their local policy and practice. This would then need the development of class alliances at a national level to change fully the nature of the state form in that instance.

All this needs two major theoretical components. Firstly, the state must be seen as a set of policies, practices and institutions which are eventually changeable; in the short term through the impact of class activity within a capitalist society and in the long term through action by the great mass of a unified working class. Secondly, both the short- and long-term changes will only happen if there are great sets of alliances *within* the working class.

HOW DO WE USE THESE APPROACHES TO THEORY?

In understanding trade unionism, we have used theory generally to explain *movement* in the social world. We have, especially, tried to explain the way in which a class only ever exists in a dynamic relationship with other classes and only ever exists with its constituent fractions being in constantly changing relationships with each other and with other classes. In contrast, class, as a theory, is often used to set up rigid and powerful boundaries about what is and what is not working-class action. This latter approach to theory is by no means confined to academic studies. Thus, white-collar workers in the 1970s had to 'prove' their class location not by any objective test of analysis or by any imaginative creation of their own experience of action, but much more by acting in the history and tradition of what counted as 'working class'. Now these tests may or may not be important: what is certain is that they are concerned not so much with the way in which the real and actual working class had developed in the real world of class history, but much more with the cultural images of what was or what was not a real part of the working class.

For us, as materialists, theory is something which we try and relate to the world, learning as much as we can from past interactions. But because theory must question itself and learn from practice, it is inevitable that it may well change in the particular application of categories. It is this interactive process that we believe Marx to mean by the 'dialectic'. Moreover, the dialectic of history can only take place when a part of theory interacts with practice in such a way as to become a part of the historical process of change itself.

A key implication of our approach is that new realities call for changes in theoretical categories, and, concomitantly, changes in the relationships between categories. For us, concerned with trade unionism in social work, the categories of class and the state have to interact with the new realities of class and the state, and they have to come to terms with the difference between what the realities once were and what they are now.

The working class, for example, has undergone major reconstruction over the last sixty years. In the 1920s, few working-class people had mortgages, qualifications in mental labour, cars, children at school after 14, or foreign holidays. So, if we simply apply the categories of the 1920s, hardly anyone is really working class in the 1980s. A dialectical understanding of class requires that we do not force the reality of the reconstructed working class into the image of the old working class.

Similarly, when we look at the state, there is a need to come to terms with new realities. It is true that the 1850s had a state formation that largely excluded the working class from executive power. That is not the case now. The working class is bigger, more experienced and different. A hundred years of male franchise and fifty years of universal franchise have not created a revolution, but they have created changes in the form and practice of different aspects of the state. Since there have been changes in the past, we believe that changes can be achieved in the present, and in the future, and that significant organisations of the working class, such as NALGO, can play an important role in bringing about these changes.

6

Democracy and the Public Sector

We ended our theoretical section by pointing out the significance of the local state as the set of specific institutions that employ state social workers. This must mean that the experience, practice and policy of social work represents a small part of what is known as 'politics', and the same is true of the trade unionism that it has constructed. Working for the public sector in general, and for social work in particular, any understanding of what can or cannot be achieved is inevitably 'political'.

In this chapter we want to discuss the various political themes that we think are essential for any politics of social work trade unionism. We do so under the general 'banner' of democracy because we see the concept and the reality of democracy at the centre of both trade union and social work politics and we will run through the different political positions in order to provide the reader with an overall framework. We should, however, provide yet a further warning about 'form' in this chapter. For it is mainly written around a core absence within our social structure. Whilst we believe in and defend those aspects of democracy which exist, we also see them as pathetic. In 1987, British people experience very little democracy indeed. In most of the institutions that control our lives, we experience being pushed around. At work, as consumers, in schools, on the buses, in our personal lives, there is very little democratic experience to build on. We are quite simply not very used to doing it. It is, therefore, against this yawning chasm of the absénce of democratic experience and democratic involvement that our politics develop. This affects everything; filling the absence with as much mass democratic

228

involvement is, we believe, of essential importance, although it does *not* exist at the moment. We do, however, start with what passes for democracy so far, the struggle for electoral success which has had such a direct impact upon the experience of the public sector.

THE CONSERVATIVE PARTY AND THE ELECTORATE

It would be easy to suggest that most of the criticism aimed at today's public sector workers is inspired by a right-wing authoritarian government and its attempt to reconstruct an ailing capitalist economy more in line with monetarist ideas and values. The systematic attacks and reductions in the size and scope of various parts of the public sector (rail, steel, coal and other public services) through closure, cuts and privatisation might lead the average member of the labour movement to conclude that it's all the fault of the Tories. It would be fruitless to deny their impact. However, if we are then led to dismiss Conservative criticism as class-based, malicious, cynical, punitive, exploitive and, therefore, not worthy of serious consideration, we would be making a grave error.

What socialists and the Labour Movement have to face up to is that the Conservative Party is the most successful party in modern British politics and it has dominated the electoral politics of the twentieth century. Some would not be surprised by this. Hyman (1975) for example, argues that electoral politics are a poor index of democracy – it amounts to the time it takes to put a cross on a form. The five minutes it takes to vote in an election is the extent of the average person's democratic involvement. Using this argument, democracy in the twentieth century amounts to multiplying five minutes by the number of elections we have had this century. If Hyman is right, it clearly does not matter if the Conservatives dominate such a meaningless, empty democratic structure. It is true that we do not have a very mature democratic system which successfully involves large numbers of the electorate in a continuous manner between elections, but a significant minority of activists in the trade unions and the Labour Party are so involved and have been sufficiently effective to make all the difference during the odd election. There again, the Labour Movement has been strong enough at times to persuade the Conservatives to implement a series of reforms or to enhance Labour Party reforms, at least until recently. In other words, the class struggle has ensured that pre-Thatcherite Conservatives have been forced to respond positively to the organised working class and this has produced thirty years of social democratic consensus in the post-war world. This consensus was an achievement for the working class and should not be lightly dismissed; however, as we shall see, it had serious weaknesses which help to explain its breakdown and the coming of the authoritarian populism of Thatcherism.

Another response to the fact that the Conservative Party has been the most successful electoral party in modern politics is to argue that the ruling class has created and controlled the 'ideological apparatuses of the state' which allow it to win elections when necessary and to dominate hegemonically when in opposition. In other words, the Conservatives can use their control of capital, both private and public, to manipulate the media and persuade a majority of the electorate in enough constituencies to vote them into power, and when the Conservatives lose elections their hegemonic control of the family, education, work, leisure and trade unions is sufficient to moderate Labour Governments.

It is true that Tories can, and do, dominate the media and have a hegemonic presence in the other institutions, but in neither case is it absolute, since counter-hegemonic practice is visible in all institutions – especially in welfare under Thatcherism. The weakness of this model is that it is undialectical and élitist. It sees no part for class struggle – other than ruling class and subordinate class relations and only the educated cogniscenti understand what's going on or can do anything about it. Those members of the Labour Movement who vote Conservative are labelled as suffering from false consciousness and, as such, they know not what they do! Far from being 'false', these working-class Conservative voters are engaging in a very authentic practice and usually have extremely rational reasons for their voting behaviour. We need to ask different questions. For example, what is wrong with

Labour's practice and programme that it continuously fails to attract a significant portion of the working-class vote?

LABOUR PARTY AND ELECTORAL POLITICS

One answer must focus on the nature of the Labour Party. It has been continually accused of not being socialist, of being reformist, labourist, social democratic or class collaborationist. Yet this does not answer our question. Rather, these criticisms provide us with reasons why a floating working-class voter might vote Labour rather than Conservative. In other words, if the Labour Party had been organically reformist, labourist, social democratic, it is much more likely to have attracted the floating voter than is the Conservative Party. If the Labour Party had succeeded in fusing its alliances into a predominantly social democratic practice it might well have replaced the Conservative Party as the most successful electoral party of the century. Its failure to construct such an organic entity has to do with the ravages of the class struggle within the Party, between different fractions of the working class, and, most particularly, with the effect of that struggle on the construction and practices of public sector institutions.

However we might view parliamentary democracy, whether we see it as a farce, a ruling class weapon or institutionalised class collaboration, it is undoubtedly one of the major realities of our politics which we cannot wish away. It has a history and it has itself been forged in struggle: it represents a focus of working class emotion and experience. To ignore or belittle parliamentary democracy is to ignore or belittle a large part of that working class emotion and experience.

The need for socialists to recognise the centrality of parliamentary democracy has been argued by Hindess (1983). He is unequivocal in his presentation of the view that socialists have to be concerned with working for an electoral and parliamentary majority. While he does not suggest that socialism can be achieved by working through the ballot box alone, he considers the alternative strategy, ignoring parliamentary democracy, to be ineffectual. To achieve anything, he argues, socialists must start from present political realities and this means constructing political support in the labour movement and elsewhere from existing centres of power and bases of political organisation. And it means working with others in the labour movement who may not identify themselves as socialists or who may be different kinds of socialists. The implication of his argument is clearly spelt out: if there is no serious attempt to work through the ballot box, there can be no hope of social and economic reform, of socialists running government or of subjecting the economy to more public control.

For us, this represents an entirely reasonable statement of materialist political practice. We intend to pursue Hindess's argument further.

The key starting-point of this argument is that effective political power requires that socialists seek electoral and parliamentary majorities on the basis of the forces that exist. This means that they must not propose Utopian ahistorical programmes of action, based on the forces which 'ought' to exist, and which can gain the support of but a handful of fervent believers. In contrast, it means, in order to be effective, that socialists must always carry out an analysis of the historically specific situation, so that programmes can be created which recognise the forces that exist, and which therefore enables alliances to be put together that will be necessary for electoral victory.

We believe that our analysis of class fractions is important here. For certain small fractions of the working class can see their own experience of politics as being, somehow, the universal experience of the working class and, at the same time, as being the 'authentic' working class experience. Yet this political experience is, at any one time, marginal and fragmentary. Furthermore, the contradictory nature of the political consciousness involved is clearly expressed in the conflict between the perception by the members of a class fraction that their experience is universally true for the whole class and the perception that their experience is the *genuine* experience of the class. The problem with universalising a 'rump' working class experience around, say, the declining smoke-stack industries, is that it misundertands the crucial sets of experience of millions of people separate from that fraction.

If political practices based on a belief in the existence of a universal class experience are ruled out, then building alliances has to involve reaching beyond friends and comrades who share the same fragmentary experience of a particular fraction. Many socialist social workers have at times wanted to see their colleagues reaching out to form alliances with the local working-class communities they serve, but this turns out to be extremely traumatic and hard to achieve. It is traumatic because failures to unite with other fractions of the working class are a set back and lead to feelings of weakness and marginality and it is hard to achieve because, up to now, social workers have failed to establish any durable organisational base for such an alliance. In these problems we find some reasons for socialist workers not to be too hasty to reject the importance of electoral politics. It does provide the potential as an organisational base for such an alliance and it has already achieved some success in unifying fractions of the working class.

Socialism has not been, and cannot be, achieved by the ballot box alone, as Hindess indicated. Yet alliances made in order to win an election may not survive government or may require negotiation in order to persist. That renegotiation may take place around policies and programmes within parliament or it may take place outside parliament. By their very nature, alliances are vulnerable to changing conditions of existence; if they are not looked after, updated, and developed they will eventually break up. Political alliances are not natural relationships that are eternally self-reproducing. Quite the reverse, they are socially constructed, socially maintained and socially destroyed. Complacency, apathy, thoughtlessness, lack of sensitivity and lack of imagination are ways in which personal relationships may suffer and break down; they are also ways in which political alliances may be socially destroyed.

Indeed, we would argue that the energy needed to maintain an alliance is probably greater than that needed to construct it in the first place. The alliance that won the 1945 Election for the Labour Party has been progressively weakened over the

last forty years and the various explanations for that weakening are important. There is the influential 'class betrayal'
argument which sees Labour's leaders delivering the Movement (party and unions) into the hands of Capital, wittingly
or unwittingly. As Miliband (1979) puts it:

> But the Labour Party is also a party whose leaders have
> always sought to escape from implications of its class charac-
> ter by pursuing what they deem to be 'national' policies:
> these policies have regularly turned to the detriment of the
> working classes and to the advantage of Conservatism. Nor
> can it be otherwise in a society whose essential character-
> istic remains class division. (p. 348)

There are variations on this theme but Miliband's presentation of it has been and remains influential on the left. This
explanation and its variants are essentialist, élitist, undialectical and profoundly pessimistic. The essentialism implies that
Labour has a 'true' character which has been abandoned by
its leaders. The 'true character', of course, is socialist and
class-based and can be found by selecting the necessary
evidence from Labour's history. We can find some socialism
in the Labour Party's constitution or the Movement's struggles and practices. But although the Labour Party has changed
since it was created:

> It has always been a more or less organised coalition of
> diverse political groupings and organisations, reflecting a
> variety of political concerns and ideologies. It would be
> difficult to argue that socialism, however understood, has
> ever been the dominant element in that amalgam . . . It
> would be no less plausible to construct a history of the party
> as a reformist organisation whose basic objectives are not so
> much to create a socialist Britain as to win seats in parlia-
> ment and local government, to gain representation for the
> working class. (Hindess, 1983, p. 92)

Such a history, of course, would be no less essentialist than the
former. A concrete, materialist history must point to the
contradictory alliance of practices that have made and make

up the Labour Party and the Labour Movement for that matter. 'Class betrayal' is also essentialist, says Hindess, 'Because it reduces analysis of a complex field of practices, objectives and interpenetrating arenas of struggle to a simple tale of an essential spirit combating alien infection' (Hindess, 1983, p. 93).

Once you have selected out the socialist essence in Labour's history, says Hindess, it is placed outside analysis and used as a means of locating deviation – everything outside the essence is a form of deviation or betrayal. This process is undialectical because it undermines the class struggle within the Party and Movement by forcing groups into increasingly rigid positions, making alliance formation and development extremely difficult. It is as if the contradictions within the Party and Movement are so difficult to live with, that political rigidity is the only relief possible from the pain of political uncertainty. If there is a materialist truth here, it is that living with contradiction is inevitable and necessary for the development of a materialist political practice.

'Class betrayal' is also élitist in the sense that it assumes that the working classes (in all their complexity and differential historical experience) are conned by their leaders to accept 'national policies'. Nationalism may not be a particularly mature practice in the socialist scale, but it is an extremely powerful one, particularly for the working class of world history and it is a necessary precursor to more complex politics. There is a danger that it can overspill into Fascism or national socialism or forms of authoritarian populism (Thatcherism) which are perversions of liberal democracy, but in *none* of these cases are the workers conned – they are supporting a degree of nationalism which they deem to be relevant to the conditions in which they find themselves. Those conditions include the failure of socialist politics to provide a more realistic alternative. There may also be a problem of the manner in which the alternative is presented (arrogance, essentialism, élitism, one-dimensionality, for example). 'National', 'regional' and 'local' policies will most likely be contradictory both in their legislative form and in the institutions that are constructed to implement them. The way in which we prosecute the class struggle around them will decide the 'advantage' at particular times and in particular conditions. The fact that we live in a class divided society does not mean the working classes can never win aspects of the class struggle. 'Class betrayal' represents the politics of despair, not progressive materialist political practices.

The 'class betrayal' argument does not exhaust the variety of political practice on the British hard left but it is a good example of the dangers of essentialism and myth that abound, particularly amongst those organisations that have strategies for a left Labour government. Hindess (1983) is aware that such organisations exhibit great diversity but argues that they also share a number of positions:

> They are concerned with the non-insurrectionary socialism of the Labour Party and trade union left in which the primary objectives of socialist strategy is seen as the achievement of a left-wing Labour government committed to a series of radical policies thought to be capable of obtaining wide-spread popular support and of providing the precondition for a longer term process of socialist reconstruction. (p. 148)

Hindess suggests that in one form or another they will construct a history of leadership betrayal in the Labour Party and combine it with democratic reform as a means of combating it. His criticism of the 'betrayal' argument has force, as we saw above, and it will follow that an 'essentialist history' will infect the demand for democratic reform of the Party. In other words, the demand for democratic reform will be fatally flawed at its conception. An essentialist history:

> Has the effect of appearing to establish a direct link between democracy and accountability within the party and its pursuit of socialist policies . . . This link between democracy and socialist policies clearly depends on a particular conception of the essential socialism of the rank and file. Because of that essential socialism it is possible to know in advance what kinds of policies would emerge from informed discussion within the Labour Party . . . In effect, for this conception, policy positions appear not so much as the

products of discussion and investigation, but rather as expressions of the essential character of the movement. (Hindess, 1983, p. 102)

Put another way, in this problem, we have a 'socialist' working class wanting to control a 'treacherous' leadership and do away with the autonomy of its political representatives. The answer is seen to lie in the construction of democratic accountability by letting the 'socialist' masses reselect their MPs, establish 'socialist' electoral colleges and allow the 'democratically' elected (block votes) NEC to control the manifesto. However, if the working class is not socialist and the leadership not treacherous, what has been created? This is not to argue that democratic reform of the Labour Party is impossible, but it must be carried out in the context of a concrete history of the party – not an ideal one – and most importantly:

It will require a constructive politics of persuasion and alliance starting from the present political concerns and objectives of the various sections of the PLP and those in the unions, civil service and elsewhere who play a significant role in forming the policies of the parliamentary leadership. (Hindess, 1983, p. 107)

In the field of local Labour Party politics it is, of course, quite possible that the 'local democracy' of the rank-and-file activists would construct representation which could be entirely out of touch with a wider 'democracy' between the party and the local working class. Under these circumstances very hard-left local councillors can adopt arguments about their 'electoral mandate' that sit very ill within their overall politics. Such an argument does, however, give them electoral power.

Finally, of course, the 'essential history' produces 'essential policy'. Policy will express the essential socialism of the rank and file, and the consequence of this is that 'expressive policy' will subvert the conditions in which it is discussed within the party. Everybody will agree on the necessity for 'informed debate', but instead of properly preparing the members with the relevant materials and the complexity of the arguments, most Labour Party branches will be reduced to hurried, over-formal branch resolutions which will mean little or nothing to the average member, let alone the average voter.

Organisations that have strategies for a left Labour government share two more themes: a belief in the unity-in-disunity of the left and a belief in the existence of a mass base for socialism (which is thought to be inherent in the structure of British society). A prerequisite for such a left government would be the unity of left forces which is disunited because of the treacherous leadership. This fragmentation is to be overcome by a party that can provide socialist leadership to the whole movement by uniting the diverse left groups, unions and social forces in alliances of one sort of another. The left unity of the 1980s would be an alliance of the oppressed – the traditional working class and the new social forces (women, ethnic minorities and the elderly – one wonders where *they* all were before 1945?). But this unity is unreal.

We are united by oppression, but do we see that unity as real? If we correlate income and employment with gender, race and age, do we get egalitarian distributions? We get stratified profiles for all three variables. It is the stratification that is perceived as real – we experience the profound maldistributions of resources as between men and women, black and white, old and young.

We may console ourselves with the assumption that there is a 'mass base for socialist politics which could be realised by the left so as to sweep a left Labour government into office on a wave of popular support' (Hindess, 1983, p. 96). But like left unity this is 'both presupposed and to be constructed'. It 'turns on a notion of working class interests as determined by the capitalist character of the economy . . . However politically divided and however uninterested in socialism they may appear to be, the working class are expected to share a fundamental interest in the removal of capitalist exploitation that can be tapped for socialist politics' (Hindess, 1983, p. 96). As Hindess (1983) implies, to conceive of interests as structurally given is to take them out of politics altogether and to locate them in the realm of abstract socialism. In fact, the 'interests' of the working class were written down long ago by the gurus of the movement. They may differ over what to do about these 'interests' but they are seen as being inscribed on tablets of stone. The problem with the notion of the mass base and this conception of 'interests' is that they are a recipe for complacency, righteousness, ritual incantation and the occasional holy day of obligation when we can parade with our battle flags and pretend we are a mass movement united around our clearly understood 'interests'.

A mass base may be constructed, but it is not given. To use the mechanism of a given mass base, and given interests, is to create the conditions in which fragmentation of the labour movement becomes the most likely future rather than socialism. This applies to all parties that hope to organise working-class people. If we wish them to achieve political goals, they must construct a 'concrete materialistic history' of the forces to which they relate and make a concrete analysis of the actual situation. For us to use essential categories and to operationalise these given relationships, is to construct the road to disunity.

We have been hard on us all. But such an analysis of the very separateness of much socialist politics is necessary for the study of social workers' trade unionism that we have undertaken. Given the glaring absence of mass democratic socialist politics, it is in this sectarian terrain that much of the politics of social workers' trade unionism has been carried out in the 1970s and, to a lesser extent, in the 1980s.

RANK-AND-FILISM

Rank-and-filism was a potent political doctrine in social workers' trade unionism in the 1970s and remains important in the 1980s. The doctrine was closely linked with the International Socialists (now the Socialist Workers' Party) who were actively mobilising different groups of workers in rank-and-file organisations in the early 1970s. In local government, the rank-and-filist ideology was expressed most strongly through the NALGO Action Group, which was an organisation with socialist supporters in social services and elsewhere. Its activities in the early 1970s drew the following pungent comments from NALGO's official historian:

The early 1970s were notable for the rise in strength and activity of the NALGO Action Group (NAG). Appealing very much to younger members who wanted an outlet for their ideas and enthusiasm, and a chance to challenge the establishment, NAG had shown great vitality and energy in pursuing its causes . . . it grew, spreading steadily from London, where it began, into all districts. Its magazine, brightly and cleverly written, became steadily more vituperative in its comments on NALGO policies and personalities . . . It became obvious that a number of its leading figures were using it to promote extreme left-wing views. (Newman, 1982, p. 552)

In 1975, the National Executive Committee (NEC) of NALGO became concerned about the role of left-wingers in the NALGO Action Group. There were allegations that International Socialists was the parent organisation and a working party was set up to look into the matter. In fact, whilst some NAG supporters were members of International Socialists, and said so, it is interesting to note that left-wing members of the Labour Party and members of the Communist Party allied themselves with the International Socialists at this time to make up an uneasy alliance of rank-and-filists. The issue fizzled out in 1976 and the NALGO NEC decided to take no further action against the NALGO Action Group.

The most coherent statement of the rank-and-filist doctrine has probably been provided by Callinicos (1982) who has described it as:

[The] basic orientation on the self activity of the working class, on socialism from below, rather than socialism from above of the Labour MPs and trade union leaders. (p. 1)

He locates a national rank-and-file movement (NRFM) within the tradition of the First World War shop stewards' movement and the National Minority Movement launched by the Communist Party in the 1920s. Its aim is identified by him as the widening of support for revolutionary politics in the context of bourgeois democracy. His definition of 'bourgeois' democracy is very broad indeed and, importantly, encompasses the role of the trade union movement:

> By 'bourgeois democracy' I mean as well as the institutions of universal suffrage, regular elections, and the associated rights of free speech, association, etc., the existence of a mass, legal trade union movement. Trade unionism provides the political form of bourgeois democracy with their economic and social substance. (Callinicos, 1982, p. 2)

The class struggle that produced our democratic institutions and that is currently being waged in their defence against bourgeois onslaughts is transformed into its negation. Why does this happen? Because, for example, trade unions are constructed within the 'framework of capitalist relations of production':

> They seek for example higher wages, rather than striving for the abolition of the wage structure itself, even though the latter is essential to the extraction of surplus value from workers. The trade union struggle, in other words, is concerned with improving the terms on which labour power is exploited, not with ending that exploitation. (Callinicos, 1982, p. 3)

Unions should try to abolish a system that by and large they actively or passively support. The contradictory nature of trade unions is said to contribute to the separation of economic and political struggles. Such a separation is said to defuse the working class, which is channelled into reformism rather than revolutionary practice: 'Trade unions, bourgeois democracy, and the separation of economic and political struggles thus mutually reinforce each other' (Callinicos, 1982, p. 3).

This structure of dependence is said to be the product of a growing economy which can improve living standards, allied to the formation of a 'conservative labour bureaucracy'. Trade union leaders and officials are presented as class collaborators from the 1920s to the formal incorporation of the trade union bureaucracy in the war years, and the subsequent post-war consensus. Trade union officials are seen as corrupted by office and by the bargaining process:

> It is the existence of this reformist bureaucracy that gives rise to rank and file organisations. The distance of trade union officials from their members – their distinctive interests as a layer committed to the pursuit of class compromise inevitably brings them into conflict with the mass of trade unionists. (Callinicos, 1982, p. 6)

But what do rank-and-file organisations have in common and how do they differ from official trade union structures? Callinicos (1982) once again:

> Rank and file organisations, then, are bodies of workplace delegates subject to direct election and recall by the workers they represent. Both their workplace basis and the direct control of delegates by the rank and file distinguish these forms of organisation from official trade union structures. The latter are very often organised on geographical rather than workplace lines and are in any case highly centralised. The officials even where they are elected often hold office for life. Rank and file organisations, on the other hand, arise directly and spontaneously from the daily struggle on the shop floor, and often in conflict with the trade union officials. Usually no-one plans their formation in advance. (pp. 6–7)

The rank and filist organisation may be recognised, therefore, by the fact that it has emerged spontaneously and unplanned, and because the organisation works through directly-elected and fully accountable delegates from the shop floor.

In some areas, substantial numbers of social workers were, and still are, influenced by ideas like these outlined above, but the rank-and-filism in social work was not solely directed by the International Socialists. Nor is the rank-and-filism in social work as coherent and articulate as the doctrine above. It is, rather, a contradictory, unevenly articulate practice that many live as an everyday experience and orientation.

RANK-AND-FILISM AS AN EVERYDAY EXPERIENCE

It is clear from our analysis of social work trade unionism that many of the leading activists were and are critical of official trade unionism. We would say they have a 'rank-and-filist' ideology. There have been many different positions amongst militant trade unionists in Britain and it is easy to obliterate these differences and thus obscure the material conditions in which distinctive ideological practices develop. So we need to ask what specifically did rank-and-filism amongst the social workers of the 1970s mean?

While individual social workers had, and still have, enormously varied ideas with respect to their trade unionism, the 1970s activists who were in the thick of the action tended to be preoccupied with social relations inside trade unions generally and little concerned with the specific conditions (which includes class relations) within which social work trade unionism has to operate. Social worker rank-and-filists' position on trade unions consisted broadly of three separate criticisms:

1. The official union organisations had authoritarian characters.
2. The union leadership was constituted by a privileged and conservative strata of 'bureaucrats'.
3. The trade union organisation always ended up collaborating with the employers in the exercise of control over union members.

It was seen as wrong that union officials – both national and local – should negotiate with employers and decide union policy while they had only a tenuous contact with the ordinary members. This was authoritarian because the members were not directly involved and decisions were made without even really consulting them. A social services activist in the mid-1970s expressed this criticism as follows: 'Everything seems utterly remote from the ordinary members. You vote these people in but they don't really come back to the members. They can vote against what their members feel if they want to.' She approved of reporting back procedures because, as she put it, 'You suddenly find that your union people have negotiated this for you and you weren't even aware that they were negotiating.'

A field social worker explained the lack of rank-and-file influence in the union in terms of a difference of view between the union centre and the rank and file. In various disputes, he said, 'the central office or the NEC conducted the campaign and they refused to do what a lot of rank-and-file branches wanted. They see things differently. They are full time officials. They are not faced with a gut reaction as someone in the situation is.'

The rank and filist of the 1970s was concerned that official trade unionism was out of control as far as the bulk of the membership was concerned. A social services activist working in an area team gave the following report of membership feelings:

> The general feeling amongst my membership, and I think it's quite right, and that is whatever they decide, whatever they ask the delegates to do, the great union machine will roll on regardless . . . It's like a great machine and I really feel that the rank and file have got really very little control over that. The only sort of control they really have is in terms of pushing their leadership reluctantly in directions they really don't want to take.

Any executive role for union bureaucrats was viewed as essentially undemocratic by rank-and-filists since union democracy was, by definition, decision-making by the rank and file. And its worth stressing that this bureaucratic authoritarianism was often seen in local as well as national terms. One social services departmental representative made the following complaint about a local full-time official:

> Our main complaint in the last year was that the particular official who was sent down didn't like being told what to do. He had a different view of his role from us. He came down as the man who was going to sort things out as opposed to the man who was there to do us a service. We called him because we felt he could do our job for us but we found that

he wanted to make all the important decisions himself and in a sense disregard our views.

But authoritarianism had another connotation for rank-and-filism. It meant the use by union leaders of the union's resources and procedures to thwart and demobilise the rank and file. Hence the union bureaucrats were seen as managing the flow of information in a way that controlled the rank and file. And they were seen as having set up procedures to make the taking of industrial action very difficult. These union procedures caused delay and took the momentum out of rank-and-file action – which was especially injurious to the spontaneity which rank-and-filists sought to develop. The following assessment of district officials by a London social worker is an almost perfect example of the archetypal rank-and-filist position:

> On the one hand you don't see a district official enough. He doesn't really know what's going on. He tends to be thrust in certain dispute situations knowing very little about it and his main criteria seems to be restoring the status quo as quickly as possible, almost regardless of the issues con-cerned . . . On the other hand, district officials try and take the initiative and the impetus from shop floor workers. They move into situations and say, 'Don't worry, I'll deal with it'. This has arisen in the libraries where the post of chief librarian was downgraded in a recent review. They feel very angry that their post has been downgraded such that it's lower than in any other London Borough now . . . So there was a branch meeting . . . and they felt very militant about it in terms of wanting to take action. District Office moved in and said, 'Look, we'll get the dispute approved officially at national level – it'll probably take a week or two'. That was about six or seven weeks ago and still nothing has been done and they don't know what's happening because they can't contact the district official. So in that sense you see too much of them. When you've got things at branch level you know what's going on – you can regulate it. You know what the issues are. When it goes up

to District Office level you lose track of it and as a result you can lose impetus. People start to become very disillusioned. Quite often the issue isn't really solved to the satisfaction of the members because the members have never been properly consulted. Its been whisked out of their hands.

In principle, authoritarianism can be orientated to widely differing ends and values. Rank-and-filists, however, were concerned about the reactionary and conservative character of trade union authoritarianism. One field work activist believed that there were occasions when a full-time official could be useful in sorting out local cases, but his reaction to a question on the usefulness of the advice of an official was less positive: 'Advice? Yes. The thought doesn't please me too much. The advice is inclined to be "do nothing".' This conservatism was seen as stemming from the material interests of the trade union bureaucrats. Whereas the rank-and-filists considered trade union organisation to be an instrument of workers' struggle, they imputed to the union bureaucrats an interest in union organisation as an end in itself.

The rank-and-filist critique of the conservative nature of official trade unionism takes as its point of departure the difference in work situation and life-style of the ordinary member and trade union official. A day centre worker said that she thought union leaders weren't really interested in the problems of the rank and file union members. When asked why she thought this was the case, she said, 'Because they're not their own problems. They've got job security and a much higher salary and just more interesting jobs. They live in a completely different situation.' The point is, however, that the official was seen as having not only a different job and life-style but that these were superior to those of the members. The union bureaucrats were privileged. And it was this privileged position which led to conservatism. According to one field worker, they were concerned not to do anything that would jeopardise their position:

They are not interested because their perspectives are so different for a start from their membership – they are full-time officials. They probably ride around in big cars, have big expense accounts, they mix with members of the CBI, government ministers. They are in a completely different world. And when they enter this sort of world it becomes most important to them. Anything to rock the boat they are basically antagonistic towards. But obviously they can't let membership get too much out of check because that will really disrupt things. By monitoring things they can at least stay on top. If the interests of the union membership was against their personal status and position, they would fight the interests of membership.

The union bureaucrats, because of their material interests, are seen, therefore, as playing it safe or making decisions which reflect their priorities rather than those of the membership. The official trade union is then 'bureaucratic' because the 'union bureaucrats' are running it with their interests paramount. In other words, the official union organisation has become an end in itself.

The reactionary and conservative nature of official trade unionism is seen as, in due course, leading to collaboration with management in the exercise of power over workers. Official union structures start out as means of workers pursuing their immediate and material interests, which for rank-and-filists in social services departments was often seen as involving action to counter arbitrary and incompetent management decisions. In the process of trade union organisation becoming an end in itself, there was, according to rank-and-filists, an evolution in the relationship between official trade unionism and management. This evolution has been a process of mutual accommodation: official trade unionism gains management recognition and secure collective bargaining procedures, which are important for the stability of union organisation and in return the official trade union organisation co-manages the workforce and takes on the role of manager of discontent. One field worker explained that they had been reluctant to call in a former full-time official because of his behaviour in this respect: 'We didn't know whether he was going to start taking management's side. So you'd bring him in as a heavy gun and then he was a heavy gun on the wrong side.' The ordinary member was subjected to the joint authoritarian control of both trade unions and management. Indeed, some rank-and-filist activists saw the ordinary member as the victim of a whole plurality of bureaucracies, each in the hands of the bureaucrats:

> Union leaders are part of the bureaucracy and therefore have more in common with Labour Party leaders or management then their rank and file. They are in the position of having too much to lose because they are full-time paid officials and even though they themselves were rank and file members once they are now out of touch with rank and file members.

In summary, the rank-and-filists of social services departments were often critical of the limitations of official trade unionism because they saw the union officials as relatively immune from rank-and-file pressure and as opposed to direct action by the 'shop floor'; also because they saw them as collaborating with the employer. In effect, they viewed union bureaucrats as an authoritarian braking mechanism on rank-and-file militancy.

RANK-AND-FILISM AND INDUSTRIAL DEMOCRACY

In the mid-1970s the British trade union movement began to seriously consider a revision of its traditional policy on industrial democracy (TUC, 1974). Whilst significant resistance existed within the movement towards any change of policy, there was sufficient support for the Labour Government elected in 1974 to set up the Bullock Committee to look into legally backed arrangements for worker directors. Nothing really came out of this initiative, partly because of the opposition of private sector employers, but the increased interest in the issues of industrial democracy generally led to discussions about the application of industrial democracy to local government. In view of the fact that local government is one of the most democratically controlled areas of the British economy, it is surprising that the debate on industrial democracy in local government was so late in starting. There is, of course,

the complication that the political democracy of local government may seem compromised by industrial democracy, but,
then again, the existence of collective bargaining already
provides this complication.

The idea of industrial democracy in local government was
explored by the Labour Party and the TUC jointly, and by
NALGO and the TGWU separately. Their discussions and
proposals have never been acted upon at national level and
the matter has, possibly temporarily, been put to one side.
Industrial democracy remains, therefore, a potential change
in the local government system of industrial relations, but a
potential change that could lead to very major developments
in industrial relations. Where do the rank-and-filists stand on
industrial democracy?

The rank-and-filist analysis leads to a deeply ingrained
pessimism about the possibilities of formal arrangements for
industrial democracy. In the context of an analysis of the
overarching authoritarian control structures of the trade union
and employer bureaucracies, worker participation means nothing more than worker participation in the organisation of their
own oppression. The authoritarian consequences of these structures are not, in other words, to be dodged by means of
industrial democracy.

Some of the activists were not totally opposed to worker
participation, but all saw limitations in it, and most wanted to
see workers' control. A field worker expressed reservations
about worker participation, even though he supported it on
the grounds that people would start to become active in
decision-making at work:

> As I said before, I'm very much in favour of increased
> contact with management even if this makes things more
> efficient from a management point of view. But I don't think
> that management would be able to go far enough to corre-
> spond to the interests of their workforce because, as I said, I
> see the two sides as ultimately conflicting.

But workers' control was different. It overcomes the fundamental conflict because, he said, it 'implies a complete change
in social structure'.

Other rank-and-filists went further in criticising worker participation:

> It means cutting your own throat. I don't like the term. I think it's a sop to any real form of control by rank and file members unless it is backed up by real power in the decision-making . . . individual schemes have to be looked at carefully. Usually it's a false trail giving the illusion of power but no real power.

Various fears were expressed about the dangers of worker participation:

> It would serve to devalue the position of stewards as a deliberate tactic of management. The steward would no longer appear to improve the conditions of the employee.

And:

> It might reduce shop stewards' power because employee participation in many cases would just involve a few union officials and shop stewards would find they were considered irrelevant. Management wouldn't want to negotiate with them because, after all, we've got these worker directors or whatever . . . I think it's a bad thing. I think the shop stewards are often far from perfect but of all union people they are closest to the membership.

In both these views the danger seen in worker participation is that of undermining shop steward organisation, which was seen as not only the most representative form of union leadership, but also crucial for the exercise of real power by the rank and file. And this would mean the end of worker resistance:

> It's [that is, worker participation] like the social contract. I suppose that union leaders and union representatives are making government or management policy more effective because there's no resistance to it. Resistance is having to be organised at the rank and file level.

THE RANK AND FILIST PRESCRIPTION

Given the rank-and-filist critique of official trade unionism as conservative and collaborationist, the social work activists in the early days had a number of options: to ignore official trade union organisation; to disorganise and destroy union organisation; or to work within trade union organisation. The first inclination of social work activists was to be part of NALGO but to ignore it. In other words, the initial acts of rank-and-filism had a tendency to consist of autonomous action by grass roots social workers. Later, there was a movement towards the option of working within the official union structure in order to rectify the tendencies towards conservatism and collaborationism. Undoubtedly there were those in NALGO who saw the social workers as seeking to undermine the union, although it is hard to find any real evidence that social workers were ever a primarily destructive force. Nevertheless, at times, they may have given this impression. And it has to be remembered that social work trade unionism could have degenerated into a purely disorganising force within NALGO.

Rank-and-filism placed its hopes for a progressive union leadership almost entirely on the shoulders of shop stewards. In the specific setting of local government this aspect of rank-and-filist thinking was often manifested as an attack on local Whitley structures and the staff side representatives on them. Social work activists argued for shop stewards to have the power to negotiate on behalf of the ordinary members. The local Whitley structures were characterised as too removed from the membership and the union's staff side members were accused of being insufficiently under the control of the rank and file members. In the strongholds of rank-and-filism the call was for the recognition of shop steward committees and the abolition of the Whitley system. This view was expressed succinctly by one activist as follows, 'Shop stewards' committees should be able to negotiate directly with management on issues that affect their members. At present the staff side system tends towards a lack of contact and accountability.' Another activist, a steward representing social workers and administrative staff, gave the following reason for wanting to be able to negotiate on major issues that were actually dealt with by staff side, 'Staff side, most of whom are not from within our department, are often out of touch with our problems and their representation suffers accordingly.'

The relationship between shop stewards and the 'shop floor' was seen as protecting stewards from the tendencies towards conservatism and collaborationism. Not only was there more likely to be direct and personal contact (although the dispersed nature of social services workforces in urban areas meant that contact was problematic even for shop stewards), but also the stewards were working on behalf of the members who elected them. Under the staff side system, a relatively small number of staff side representatives had the entire branch membership as their constituency and individuals might be given responsibility to negotiate, say, upgradings for specific departments. The shop steward committee was seen, therefore, as closer to the membership and under its control.

There were contradictions around this. For example, shop stewards in social services departments often argued that the representatives to the branch executive should be chosen by shop steward committees. This preference for indirect representation obviously reduced the say of the rank and file in the selection of union representatives. But it was, of course, a reflection of the internal power struggles between stewards and others in the branch. The shop stewards, fearful of the collaborationism of official union organisation, and being, in effect, a rival power base, sought to monopolise delegates to the branch executive.

Another contradiction was the commitment to shop floor accountability as a means of inhibiting bureaucratisation. The contradiction in this case was due to their own assessment of their relationship with the shop floor. One activist, for example, argued that he worked very hard on behalf of his members and put himself out for them:

It's a question of stimulating people and that's it. It's not just a question of response – which is, if you like, the 'soft sell' approach. It's a question also of being prepared quite often not to accept the 'no'. Because people always say no at first and they eventually come round to yes, I think.

The actual relationship with the shop floor could be very unrewarding at times. The same activist confessed:

> I go through these great periods of time of great depression when I feel I'm just doing all the donkey work and achieving nothing. But when one does achieve something I think people do appreciate – makes it all worthwhile.

In other words, the rank-and-filist shop stewards were seen by themselves as the active element in the relationship, the instigators of shop floor activism, and thus it was not logical to expect the shop floor to be intrinsically likely to provide the antidote to bureaucratisation.

Direct action had at least two rationales in the rank-and-filist schema: it was valued as both the most authentic form of struggle and as a valuable experience for the education of ordinary members. Authentic because it was seen as, on occasion, the only type of action that would have any effect:

> We get slagged off for being political but in local government politics do affect our work. And, if we are not being militant trying to get some interest among our members to fight the cuts, we are going to find people made redundant, reductions of services, and non-filling of vacancies so that the workload increases, which is against our members' interests.

Possibly it was also seen as the most authentic form of struggle because the previous two decades had witnessed the rise of the modern shop steward movement (predominantly in engineering and other manufacturing industries) which was associated, in popular conception at least, with rising levels of strike activity. The other advantage of militancy was often described in terms of educating members. Thus the following comment, 'And for those members involved, [industrial action] can raise their level of union consciousness quite a lot.'

Whilst the rank-and-filists saw official trade unionism as over-keen to avoid direct action, and as too fond of the constitutional approach even where it was not working, we must not caricature the rank-and-filist position. There was a readiness to use direct action but that does not mean that all other methods were shunned. This is expressed well by an activist in fieldwork services:

> I would say politically I was fairly militant. But I don't believe in going along, shouting around and thumping the table, and ordering people out . . . I believe things and see things for reasons. And I believe that in some instances it is possible to persuade people that my arguments are reasonable . . . But I certainly think it pays to be hard in representing your members. I think that that is necessary and that is good. There are instances where management will back down . . . I would in the first instance try and be reasonable . . . I'd probably be a militant although I wouldn't automatically be a militant. I wouldn't pick up the phone and start shouting down it or threatening. I would start off on a reasonable line, stating the case, and, if I got nowhere by being reasonable, I'd become hardline.

The value placed on spontaneous action was often implicit rather than explicit, and suggested by the tone of what was said rather than the content; for example, activists would place special emphasis on the fact that a stoppage had been spontaneous and had succeeded because the members had felt strongly about it. This seemed to be bound up with a widely expressed view that the membership was potentially very powerful. To put the view in a somewhat poetic way, the membership was regarded by many as a slumbering giant. A shop steward representing day centre staff and residential workers suggested, 'Management appears to have more power but ultimately workers do – if they are prepared to use it.' Another steward echoed this view: 'Management have more power at present because they are the major tools of the council and because workers are not prepared to use their potential at present.' The 'slumber' of the membership was, however, liable to interruption. The following judgement of a

social worker suggests some lack of predictability of the inter-
ruptions:

> Workers have full potential power in all work situations (for
> example, workers produce cars and workers provide service
> to clients). In fact, workers allow management to have
> considerable power . . . This does, however, erupt in certain
> specific situations – often leading to industrial disputes.

Against this background we can understand in more detail
why many rank-and-filists were distrustful of the jointly agreed
procedures. They were worried that these spontaneous eruptions of the rank and file would get choked by the procedures.
The procedures, which were seen as bureaucratic and labori-
ous, would defeat the membership, who wouldn't have the
staying power. Eruptions, after all, generally have a limited
duration. And, of course, official trade unionism, in its role as
co-manager of the workers, would be involved in this process
of bureaucratic quelling of the eruption.

In the earlier phases of rank-and-filism, spontaneity assumed the form of unofficial and unconstitutional action, which
was an attempt to outflank and by-pass the procedures which
stifle the initiative and vigour of grass-roots action. The problem
with spontaneous direct action is that it is difficult to realise on
a mass basis. The rank-and-filists found that they had to
choose between isolation or involvement in the bureaucratic,
official unionism that they were trying to evade. Isolation led
to impotency, whilst the involvement compromised spontaneity. They chose the latter course and, since their militancy
continued, showed not only had they originally overestimated
the power of small groups of grass-roots workers, they had
also underestimated the scope for militancy within official
trade unionism.

If rank-and-filism, in its earliest (and simplest) form, is
opposed to official union organisation, is it resigned to the
fragmentation implied by multiple centres of grass-roots activity? In a way, it is; since the ideal is often seen as a
federation of grass-roots organisations. But even then the
problem is in mobilising the rank and file to form such a
federation. Initially, and subsequently, there is a consciously

exemplary character to action by the most developed rank-and-filist organisations. At heart there is an expectation that the rank and file will grow by a kind of competitive militancy. Vanguardism is meant to spark off more grass-roots initiatives as other workers realise the validity of direct, spontaneous action. (The implicit assumption, of course, is that there is a dormant, but natural, militancy that can be awakened in other grass-roots organisations.) There is, therefore, an awareness, in this respect at least, of the uneven development of the rank-and-file movement. The most vanguardist elements are, therefore, always in danger of becoming intolerant or impatient of the groups that are not so advanced in terms of militancy. This, of course, creates a tension within any federation movement which can lead to early disintegration.

The fact is that social work rank-and-filism changed. The nearest it ever got to a federation of rank-and-file organisations was the All-London Social Workers' Action Group (ALSWAG). The durability and significance of federational forms of rank-and-filism were never really tested (and the full consequences of the implicit challenge to official union structures did not have to be faced). Rank-and-filism instead began to work more within the official union structures, which is not to say that it was absorbed and sanitised by official trade unionism; official trade unionism had also changed.

Trying to summarise the principles of rank-and-filist trade union practice by social workers is difficult, partly because the principles underwent change, and partly because rank-and-filism was a more complex and richer vein of ideas than we have been able to capture in our description of it. Nevertheless, in social work trade unionism in the mid 1970s, there were five main principles:

1. Formation of autonomous groups of workers at the grass-roots level.
2. Development of shop stewards as grass-roots leaders.
3. A preference for direct action (that is, strikes and other forms of industrial action).
4. Exploitation of spontaneous rank-and-file militancy.
5. Encouragement of further rank and file initiatives by accentuating the exemplary aspect of direct action.

All these are characteristics which would fit into the wider
theoretical model above.

HOW 'PURE' WAS RANK-AND-FILISM?

The social work activists who were prominent in the rank-
and-filist developments of the 1970s often voted for the Labour Party. For many, however, this was a reluctant choice.
Many were to the left of the Labour Party and were not totally
enamoured of its performance in office. One of the more
jaundiced comments came from a steward representing administrative workers, 'I don't think the Parliamentary Labour
Party has much allegiance to the working class the way they
carry on.' Some were critical of the Labour Party for its
ineffectiveness as a vehicle of socialism: 'I'm not a Labour
Party supporter. Because I don't think they are going to
achieve socialism by their way of going about things.'
    The qualified approval that many of them gave to the
Labour Party did not stop them being critical of the subordi-
nation of membership interests to Labour Party electoral
needs. To take just two examples, both from field workers:

> NALGO should be affiliated to the Labour Party to try and
> get it out of people's heads that NALGO isn't a political
> organisation. It would get through to certain people that,
> however cautiously, NALGO is affiliated to something
> vaguely socialist. What I am against is that the union
> leaders seem to be in the business of keeping the Labour
> Government in – rather than looking after the interests of
> their members.

And:

> The higher echelons of the unions are selling out to the
> Labour Government. We've been told that that we have got
> to accept cuts in the standard of life. I think to a certain
> extent there's been a brainwashing exercise. . . .

Rank-and-filism came to encompass a broad left political

alliance, which included Labour Party supporters, International Socialists supporters, Communists, and others. Why didn't political differences amongst these groupings prevent social services' rank-and-filism from becoming a hegemonic force? One answer is that the early 1970s was a time of rapid social change and the union bureaucracy was willing and able to adapt. As a consequence the union leadership did not crack down organisationally and ideologically on rank-and-filism, however anxious they were about it, and however concerned that it was a narrow-minded and dogmatic tendency that would lead to disunity. The leadership was also quite relaxed about the political character of rank-and-filism, notwithstanding the setting up of the working party to investigate the NALGO Action Group in 1975. So rank-and-filism encountered a degree of tolerance from the leadership, in the absence of which the rank-and-filists would have found it much more difficult to generate support for their ideas.

Another answer is that there was a substantial measure of agreement amongst the groups comprising the broad left alliance that the time was ripe to pursue more democratic involvement by ordinary members in the running of the union. This provided a shared point of principle about which the various groups could unite.

But what sustained rank-and-filism in social services – so that it was not just a five minute wonder – was the capacity of many social workers to learn from their practical trade union experiences. Instead of dogmatic adherence to the pure principles of rank-and-filism, many showed themselves able to develop union tactics, strategies and organisation in the search for effective action. This willingness to modify trade union practice, to take account of objective reality, usually accompanied a more durable broad left alliance. Where this willingness was lacking, and where rank-and-filists took principled stands, then the alliance had a tendency to break down or become weaker as more pragmatic socialists sought to work within branch organisations which had become more open and less reactionary. Rank-and-filists continuing a 'principled' line could only see in this action a contemptible form of opportunism.

Rank-and-filism undoubtedly showed its capacity for imaginative struggle. Likewise, mature socialist democracy may well require the degree of accountability suggested by rank-and-filism, but if it is to work it also requires mature socialist democrats. Our democratic forms can always be improved – democracy should be regarded as a process and a struggle. But pure rank-and-filism is no more than a strategy for mobilising a cadre force at the cost of losing the mass membership. The end result is a highly motivated, highly trained cadre force in conflict with the mass membership who experience the cadres as arrogant and élitist.

We would suggest that it is only perhaps in a transition to socialism or, more likely, in socialism as such that you can overcome these specific problems of arrogance and élitism. These problems are relative to specific conditions – they do not possess universal meanings and are not trans-historical. The arrogance and élitism of one social formation may be the expected normative practices of another. The practice of rank-and-filism in a capitalist society can and does lead to the isolation of the cadres. Likewise, of course, socialist societies may produce their own arrogant and élitist practices which must be challenged. Social worker rank-and-filism has certainly worried about the 'distance' between trade union officials and their members. But in reality, although some officials may well pursue class compromise, from the 1970s onwards union officials were becoming more sensitive to the needs and potential of their members. Far from being 'class collaborators' they are likely to be to the left of their members and frustrated by membership apathy and instrumentalism. Officials are quite well aware that the centralised structure of their organisation can undermine the quality of democracy and representation and will assist in promoting mechanisms that improve organisational responsiveness and communications, as mentioned above.

The NRFM as it surfaced in public sector unions in the 1970s did have some mobilising effects and did contribute to change, but it would be foolish to argue that that mobilisation and those changes (partly traced in our earlier analysis) could be explained simply as the result of the practice of rank-and-filism.

DEMOCRACY AND TRADE UNIONS

Running through the historical account of social work trade unionism are different political practices within NALGO. We can see them operating in a number of other unions also. Social workers who were members of the Labour Party would exhibit the range of political practices observable in the party but would be dominated by social democratic activists. The latter have had a changing matrix of alliances with various Communist groupings and various Trotskyite groups. Socialist union practice in the post-war period and particularly in the last fifteen years has largely turned on the nature and outcome of the alliances between these groups.

One of the problems that has faced social workers is that of relating to the range of occupational groups organised by NALGO. Social democratic NALGO, so to speak, would attempt to cope with the problem emanating from the range of occupational groups by pursuing largely industrial or economic issues around which they could expect to forge the widest alliance. On the whole, this probably worked for a majority of the membership in the sense that their apathy and inertia was a form of democratic control. We would suggest here that social democratic political practice represents a form of 'negative control' (Nicholson et al., 1981). Social democratic trade unionism copes with large numbers of members 'doing nothing', but so long as the social democratic leadership is reasonably efficient, or is reasonably effective, it will be able to reproduce itself by mobilising sufficient support in elections and ballots. This form of democracy, through 'negative control', consists of membership acquiescence when the leadership gets it right, and membership refusal to act when the leadership is in error. Neither leaders nor led are particularly proud of or positively want this form of democracy. Most union leaders, and NALGO's will be no exception, will ideally want an engaged membership that participates fully and intelligently in union affairs and structures. In reality, such participation will be, at best, spasmodic and probably incited by crises over pay, conditions and authority.

Social democratic trade unionism is normally characterised by low levels of membership participation, centralised bargaining and knowledge, and high levels of bureaucratism. Such a practice may 'work' after a fashion as long as it is matched by national governments: national social democracy reinforces that of the unions. The relationship between government and unions will be close and in the public sector will be expressed by good employer' policies which will facilitate union growth and practice. Change the nature of the government's political practice from social democracy to authoritarian populism and the relationship with the unions will go into crisis. 'Good employer' policies are fundamentally social democratic and, as such, antithetical to authoritarian rule. Much more in keeping with the latter is the doctrine of 'the sovereign employer':

> The concept of the sovereign employer (which strictly speaking precludes public sector collective bargaining as being incompatible with the absolute authority of the legislature) held sway in Britain in the pre-Whitley era but since the 1920s has been modified to do little more than provide the justification for certain reserve rights and powers of the executive in relation to the operation of the Whitley Councils and arbitration tribunals in the public sector. Thus the Treasury document 'Staff Relations in the Civil Service' states:
> 'The Government has not surrendered, and cannot surrender, its liberty of action in the exercise of its authority and the discharge of its responsibilities in the public sector.' (HM Treasury, HMSO, 1965)
> However, the constitutional aspect of the argument have been given something of a second lease of life by a number of confrontations between the government and public sector unions during the 1970s. (Thomson and Beaumont, 1978, pp. 150–1)

Whilst Thatcherism has not quite reinstated this doctrine, given a third term of office it could move more substantially in this direction. The authoritarian can meanwhile exploit the weaknesses of social democratic practice. There are the easy targets of overly centralised institutions in the public sector (including the unions), alienated service delivery, alienated service consumption, and an apparently unrepresentative union leadership. The fact that there may be substantial production of unalienated public service, often with imaginative and courageous leadership, can easily be masked by authoritarian subversion of the media. Social democratic leaders meanwhile can be lampooned as the straw men (there aren't many women amongst them) who lead phantom armies with pathetic, outdated shibboleths. True or false, it is difficult to strike back authoritatively from the shifting sands of 'negative control'.

TRADE UNIONISM AND PROFESSIONALISM

Social workers, of course, are not just trade unionists but also professionals and this adds a further complexity to social democratic unionism. Professions have an important body of knowledge and skill which we cannot ignore but which must be used with care and sensitivity. The Utopian would want either to jettison such knowledge and skill because of its bourgeois values and pretensions or to largely avow as a basis of power and authority. The social democrat would be caught between these poles and solve the dilemma of the relationship between the trade union and the profession by radically separating them so that the former dealt with issues such as wages and conditions and the latter with issues of professional practice and policy. This mirrors the social democratic separation of politics and economics.

Democratic socialist trade union practice would not ignore, would not avow and would not separate. It would attempt to progress issues of professional practice and policy through the union, both nationally and locally. Such a practice can be seen in NALGO, as described in our earlier chapters, but it is unevenly developed. There certainly seems to be national support for a unity of the practices (trade union and profession) but locally the branches display the full array of different practices outlined above. Given the current political attacks on social work, and the confusion in the ranks, it is vital that the tendency to the unity of the practices is accelerated.

BUILDING DEMOCRACY IN THE UNIONS

Events during the years since 1979 have brought home to
many trade unionists the need to devote more time and
resources to overcoming the weaknesses in trade unionism
and the urgency of helping to develop a stronger and more
united movement. There were plenty of signs before 1979 that
the trade union movement had to update its conservative
attitudes and organisation. There are many things that need
doing, but we have emphasised the problems facing trade
unionism in one particular area, that area being the inad-
equacy of democratic practice in the unions. This, of course,
was an issue that concerned the rank-and-filist social workers
who supported the NALGO Action Group. It is a matter
which many trade union leaders recognise as being of importance. But what are the steps needed to build stronger democratic attitudes and practices and which will lead to more and
more ordinary members being well-informed and actively
involved in the control of their union?

Of course, the trade unions are democratic. There is more
to their democratic government than the 'negative control' we
have referred to earlier. We can observe important, though
limited, democratic socialist practices. Thus, there are trade
union activists who are aware of the dangers of democracy
as purely 'negative control' and unions which continually
struggle to mobilise their members, to encourage constructive
activity, and to provide relevant information and education
from a very small resource base. But the movement's claim to
be democratic does largely rest in practice on the working of
its constitutional machinery of union government, with its
system of delegate conferences and election of representatives,
which, even when buttressed by the democracy of negative
control, is a very limited base for democracy. Furthermore,
the trade union movement has not been developing in union
members an appetite for democracy, a consciousness of being
engaged in a struggle to widen the reach of democracy in a
world dominated by autocracy, and a sense of remaking
society. There are massive difficulties in the way of achieving
progress in this area, but the message of recent years is that
the unions will only thrive when they have re-established the

social purpose implied by the commitment to real and full democracy.

The planning of the building of democracy in the unions has to be done, however, without the illusions of sectarian Utopianism. This raises questions concerning the nature of democratic discipline within the trade union movement. From our analysis of social work trade unionism, it will be seen that we consider this to be a very important issue for the strength and solidarity of public services trade unionism. We believe that arguments about priorities and methods should take place in trade unions, indeed they are essential to democratic decision-making, but arguments have to be within an agreed framework or the unions become disorganised. There must, therefore, be an element of discipline in union decision-making, which prevents sections of members pursuing their self-interest or principles to the point of weakening and dividing the union. On the other hand, internal union discipline must be kept within limits otherwise democracy will be supplanted by autocracy.

What, then, can be done by the unions to increase the democratic character of their organisations? This has to be a matter of starting from where the unions are now. Hence, building democracy has to be within the constraints of the current resources of the trade unions, but it also has to be directed at the trade unionists in their workplaces, since by and large they are not involved in the national level machinery of the union. Their involvement is largely confined to the local level, and even there it is rare for the involvement to be well-informed or active. It is at least arguable that ordinary members can more easily be brought into an active democratic role in local union affairs than in national ones, and that the growth of local democracy provides the essential platform for a replenishment of the democratic spirit at all levels of the trade union movement. The efforts of the unions to produce a renaissance of local democratic involvement in union affairs could take a multitude of forms, but we would suggest that, for public services unions, there are three particular issues that need to be addressed: political education, industrial democracy, and the representation of women members.

Political education

The extension of political education in trade unions is part of the answer to the problem of how more union members can be encouraged to engage in active democratic practice – the existing provision of political education by the trade unions is totally inadequate for the scale of the educational task involved. Whilst the labour movement has agreed in theory with the need for political education, there have been few practical steps to ensure its provision. There is political education in existing programmes mounted by trade unions, but courses tend to be dominated by TUC funding and steered towards the acquisition of skills and information related to collective bargaining, grievance handling and other matters such as health and safety at work. These courses are entirely necessary but are no substitute for political education, which is needed for the development of a spirit of democracy in the trade unions.

The aims and content of political education will be matters for individual unions to determine but it will obviously need to address the low level of political knowledge amongst the bulk of the membership and the content will need to relate to the particular circumstances of the membership's working lives. Thus, courses in political education for public services workers will need to raise their political knowledge so that they are able to form judgements which are less at the mercy of systematic bias and distortion in the mass media.

Social workers, in particular, have suffered at the hands of the press, television and radio and must see how valuable would be a political education that fostered an appreciation amongst other NALGO members of the media representation of their role. If we look at the media's treatment of social workers we find that an ill-prepared debate is going on which seems to be largely concerned to blame social workers for everything from child abuse to encouragement of welfare scroungers. It is as if social workers are the collective finger in the dike: as our society slowly comes apart at the seams, social workers are sent in to stop the flood, and as they are usually around when the flood occurs, they are a convenient group to blame. The media, it seems, lacks the concepts to understand the social world in other than individualistic or stereotypical terms. Whereas social democracy constructed the social worker as the cure for all the social problems which were generated by social relations in our society, the media made the social worker into the problem itself.

Political education has to be about making everyday decisions and making them competently and confidently on the basis of more adequate political knowledge. This means that ordinary union members have to be encouraged not to leave judgements about politics to the politicians or the media. It also means that political education is about teaching people to recognise the nature of a political practice when they see it or confront it. It is about providing them with the opportunity to practice applying that conceptual competence to our society, to our workplaces, to our unions, our associations, to our lives. Only when this competence has been adequately developed are women and men able to recognise the way in which information and arguments are being presented in order to exert political influence. Only then are they able to make up their own minds about the choices they have and, indeed, whether or not choice exists at any particular point.

For public services workers, political education courses must examine the nature of their services, including the fact that services are both economic and political acts and that the political dominates. They need to understand that the services of the public sector are only possible in the first instance as the result of political decisions and strategies. They also need to understand that the very size and scope of the public sector has been the product of a long process of class struggle and that any increases or reductions in the sector will also be part of that process.

This education needs to deal with the debate about public services in general and about particular public services. It needs to raise with groups such as social workers questions concerning their relationship to their service, and their relationship to other services and other public services workers. The trade union movement helped through its political practice to create the public services. Through its political education it now needs to help those workers employed in these services to become conscious of the potential of working in a democratically-managed sector of the economy which is orientated to socially beneficial objectives.

Industrial democracy in local government

Political education will help to foster more active democracy amongst the bulk of ordinary union members, but practical experience provides the best form of education. Women and men have very little experience of democracy in their lives and thus it is not surprising that a democratic ethos is not more strongly established in the trade union movement. It is true that the trade unions are collectives which are run on democratic lines, but we have to recognise that the day-in, day-out experience of people as workers and as citizens who receive and use public services does not involve direct democracy as an experience.

Can the public services' trade unions play any part in creating a practical school for democracy? We believe they can, if the unions were to take up again their ideas for industrial democracy in local government, especially if these ideas were to be developed in the direction of joint management of services so that the focus was on sharing in the control of service delivery on a service-by-service basis. In our view, this would be the strongest basis for the active involvement of ordinary union members in democratic arrangements. The organisation of service delivery seems to us to be an area that would allow the most immediate scope for a constructive policy of sharing in control.

Women and democracy in trade unions

Union democracy, in its fullest sense, means union government by and for the mass of ordinary members. In large-scale union organisations there is inevitably going to be some reliance on indirect forms of democracy, that is, on elected representatives. There ought also to be direct involvement of ordinary members in managing union affairs, especially those affairs which are of local significance. But these matters of constitutional machinery and formal organisation should not distract us from the point that democratic unions pursue the priorities of the mass of ordinary members, and that unions which do not pursue such priorities cannot fully lay claim to the title of democratic. Do the priorities of unions reflect the aspirations of the mass of ordinary members, which includes enormous numbers of women as well as men?

In the 1970s, within NALGO, rank-and-filists, including those in social services departments, were among the first people to campaign around priorities important to women trade unionists. The 'Working Women's Charter', which was an important focus for this campaigning in 1974 and the years that followed, included amongst its objectives: equal opportunities and equal pay; a national minimum wage; provision of day care for children; maternity and paternity leave; free contraception; and free abortion. Supporters of the charter were active in a number of unions and trades councils. In NALGO, the charter's supporters sought to get it discussed and accepted as branch policy. In the case of the Tower Hamlets branch, which was one of the earliest to have a discrimination sub-committee, the charter was endorsed and union representatives attempted, in 1976, to take a step towards realising one of its objectives. They unsuccessfully raised as a bargaining demand with the council the provision of a crèche for the children of staff.

At national level, the union was also taking steps to remedy the neglect of priorities important to women members. In 1974, the NALGO conference approved a National Executive Council decision to set up a working party on equal rights. According to the official historian of NALGO, a one-day conference convened by the Equal Rights Working Party in December 1974 'was quite a revelation to some present who had not realised the intensity of feeling of women on the subject' (Newman, 1982, p. 499).

The Working Party's 1975 report made many recommendations, including the setting up of a National Committee on Discrimination (subsequently renamed the National Equal Opportunities Committee) to monitor progress on equal opportunities. Newman, the official historian of NALGO, says of the report, which found evidence of discrimination and evidence of members prepared to defend it, that it 'was a devastating appraisal of the situation of women at work, in society and within NALGO' (Newman, 1982, p. 499).

In the case of women's aspirations, therefore, whatever conflicts there were between NALGO's leadership and rank-and-filist activists, in this respect there was some measure of similarity of purpose. Both began in their own ways to respond to the exclusion of women's priorities. Efforts have been continued both nationally and locally in the years following. In 1981, NALGO conference passed a resolution calling for positive action to counter discrimination against women at work and under-representation of women in the union. Its structure of equal opportunity committees has been developed and encouraged at district and branch levels of the union. Branches have carried out educational work (for example, Haringey) and have been slowly negotiating agreements of specific relevance to equal opportunities (for example, Islington NALGO negotiated time-off facilities for parents with sick children).

Do NALGO's priorities now reflect the fact that 51 per cent of its members are women? Despite all the efforts of the past decade, the union's progress in establishing in practice its policy of equality has been limited. Priorities have not substantially changed. The union is especially concerned about the persistence of under-representation of women in the work of the union, that is, in the leadership of the union at its various levels. Despite the fact that many of the leading trade union activists in social work have been women, the general situation in NALGO is one of failure of women to take part in the representation of members in numbers commensurate with their overall strength in the union. A survey in 1981 showed that only 30 per cent of shop stewards and 17 per cent of branch secretaries were women. Equally worrying was the finding that only 20 per cent of conference delegates were women (see NALGO, 1983).

There are no easy solutions to the problems for union democracy caused by this deep inequality of the sexes. And it is no excuse to say that there is no formal inhibition to the greater involvement of women members in union leadership. Any union which wants to achieve a full democracy has no option but to continue examining all its practices and struggling for positive change. In these circumstances, some variants of feminist critique, ones that see inequality as being essentially a function of male domination, and not soluble through socialist struggles, will be attractive to those women who are, quite rightly, impatient for change. But for most women this essentialist feminist ideology will not connect with their experiences: they share with the bulk of men in trade unions that relationship with union leadership which we have earlier characterised as 'negative control'.

How long will it be before the required positive change of union practice occurs? That depends partly on national political events, but assuming that we see, in the near future, the return of a Labour government that determinedly pursues social policies necessary to liberate women from carrying the main burden for the domestic labour of caring, cooking, cleaning, and so on, the time should be sooner rather than later. But it also depends on what happens within trade unions. Democratic practice will not be strengthened by an élitist form of active feminism which is unconcerned with democratic relationships. If there is a political tendency that can hope to release the democratic potential in trade unionism, it is a democratic feminism. This is a feminism that rejects privileged accounts of the world, that rejects oppression and exploitation, and that rejects apathy and 'negative control'. It is a feminism that reaches out, that does not exclude, that is critically constructive of our institutions, that can and does build alliances with both men and women across the complexity of the working class.

Amongst the tasks facing democratic feminism may be numbered the following: it has to help in making the union more accessible to both men and women by transforming the rituals and procedures of trade unionism; it has to make the union more accessible to parents by pressing for more union meetings during the working day and more child-care facilities for meetings in the evenings and at weekends; and it has to demand well-prepared and well-informed debate about the range of issues that concern all sections of the membership, both women and men.

While we have stressed the difficulties that lie ahead of trade unionism in this area, there is equally no doubt that the feminist movement, in all its complexity, has had an impact on the trade union movement's conception of democratic practice. The unions will never again be able to turn a 'blind eye' to the poorer treatment of women in our society nor to their obligation to do all that can be done to create a truly democratic trade union movement on the basis of equality.

CONCLUSION

When we examine democracy in this society, then, we find it lacking. This is not because of the abstract and idealistic reasons adduced by the backward-looking right-wing thinkers who present us with an anarchic authoritarianism which is barely rational. Our democracy is inadequate because too many of us struggle for it within the unimaginative practice of social democracy, which we experience as the alienated form we have described in terms of 'negative control'.

There are some who struggle for democracy in Utopian forms which radically separate them from the masses they would represent and lead. For this Utopian democratic practice eventually isolates its proponents and they end by denouncing and abusing the masses they would lead.

If we mean to achieve democracy, then we have to be aware that learning to be democratic is a struggle which contains no short cuts, and that advances to democracy are always partial and vigorously resisted by social forces whose interest does not lie in the realisation of a fully democratic society.

In this chapter we have explored the contemporary politics which provides the setting for social work trade unionism. We have explored it through the frame of reference provided by democratic socialism. It is evident, therefore, that we have been looking at social work trade unionism not as neutral and disinterested observers, but as people with a definite point of view. In our last chapter, we will outline what we consider to be necessary for an overall programme for social workers. When we say necessary, we do, of course, mean necessary to achieve democratic socialist trade union goals bearing in mind the possibilities, as far as we can see them, in the situation facing social workers.

7
A Programme for Social Workers' Trade Unionism

INTRODUCTION

It is one thing to analyse social workers' trade unionism, and it is another to come up with a constructive programme for it. In previous chapters we have examined the practical trade union experiences of social workers, and have attempted to deal with these in terms of our ideas about class and trade union politics. There is no doubt that the democratic socialist position we have been developing here does provide a distinct point of view on issues and controversies in trade unionism, but can it also provide the basis for the identification of realistic and credible goals and strategies for the advance of trade unionism? In this last chapter we will attempt to answer this question by outlining a programme for social workers' trade unionism.

We should make it clear that it is not a programme for all time, but it assumes that certain social and political conditions continue to prevail; for example, that the current system of local elections for councillors in local government remains intact and that the scope of the powers of local government are not further eroded by central government. Moreover, a democratic socialist trade union programme for other groups of workers would not necessarily be the same as the one outlined here; the specific situation of each group has to be taken into account when drawing up programmes.

Any attempt to advise people directly about political or social action by means of explicit programmes must meet a number of prerequisites. Firstly, such programmes have to recognise the existing conditions and tendencies for change if they are not to be merely wishful thinking. Secondly, they must also be realistic in terms of the assumptions they make about individual motivation. Thirdly, they must be based on the recognition that nearly all trade union organisation and trade union aims have developed with a very specific relationship to sectional organisation and consciousness. If programmes succeed in meeting these prerequisites, there is a chance that they will be constructed and presented in such a way as to connect with real social forces, and thus go beyond the level of ideas on paper.

The task of constructing a programme which connects with social forces is especially difficult in this case. For the production of a trade union programme on the basis of an argument developed in a book is quite different from the production of a programme using the democratic machinery of a trade union. In the former case it has to be an appeal to trade unionists, enforced by arguments and evidence, but ultimately having no democratic status. A programme constructed within the democratic machinery of a trade union is a set of ideas that trade unionists have developed as part of their own self-government. So we are very conscious of the difference between these words in a book, which we have written, and a programme which has been adopted by a trade union.

THE PROGRAMME

We would characterise our programme for the trade unionism of social workers with the words 'democratic socialism'. It is democratic in three different ways: firstly, because it involves the democratic activity of the workers through their trade unionism; secondly, because it involves a role for local government as a form of representative democracy; and, thirdly, because it provides for citizen involvement in the day-to-day organisation of the services provided by social workers. It is a socialist programme because it recognises that it is only within a fully socialist society that the contradictions between these three different sorts of democracy can ever be fully tackled. However, as previous chapters show, we recognise that we live in a capitalist society and therefore our programme must underline that these three forms of democracy, for social worker trade unionists, will only take place within a framework of disagreements and contradictions. To construct a strategy around the democracy of the consumer, the worker and the local government employer will only happen with some considerable conflict. We recommend this programme in the knowledge that there can be no alternative which does not end in the ghettos of sectionalism.

Our programme for a progressive trade unionism for social workers is stated briefly here and is then followed by further discussion of each aspect of it. The programme has seven components:

1. Support for new forms of popular control of local authority social services to supplement the limited democratic accountability provided by elected members.
2. Decentralisation of social services with the aim of making them more accessible and responsive.
3. Introduction of industrial democracy in local government.
4. Extension of trade union concerns to include activities traditionally associated with professional associations – not least the development of voluntary ethical codes for social workers and the active encouragement and involvement in processes to advance the techniques and knowledge of social work practice.
5. Expansion of the union's organisation and resources in the publicity area to the point that it has a significant role in public education on conditions, constraints and problems in local government social services.
6. Formation of a national board, consisting of representatives of local and central government, trade unions and recognised community and pressure groups, to issue orders with statutory force on minimum standards of social services to apply nationally.
7. Support for the introduction into local government of full-time and paid elected members.

NEW FORMS OF POPULAR CONTROL

There must be more impetus towards popular involvement in the control of public services. The existing form of representative democracy in local government has very many gaps and imperfections. Elected members of councils represent too many people for their electorates to know them personally in any way, their elections are infrequent and dominated by national politics, they have to cover a broad range of activities and, therefore, become isolated and nominal representatives. Thus, it is essential to supplement these forms of democracy with tripartite structures of elected members, community representatives and trade union representatives to manage services in a way that achieves more popular control of social services. A variety of forms are possible, but we would recommend a series of geographically-based boards covering small areas within a single local authority. This arrangement would allow popular involvement in services at a neighbourhood level – these could be specific to social services or cover a range of local government services. An alternative form could consist of a series of tripartite boards each focused on a particular client grouping (for example, children, the elderly, the mentally ill, people with learning difficulties) and each involving appropriate local community groups. There could be a variety of powers delegated to these organisations but they would concentrate on management, while final democratic control, and the authority to delegate, would rest with the elected members.

DECENTRALISATION

An increasing number of local authorities have begun the difficult process of decentralising power from the town hall to much smaller units. This process has three major forms. Firstly, it may involve the provision of a specific service to a much smaller locality from a local office. The area social services team has provided one of the best examples of this process, where the service is delivered from a local unit which is itself much more accessible to local people. Increasingly, services are taken down to these local levels whether they are local housing management or libraries.

Secondly, and more controversially, the whole range of local authority services could be provided in a series of mini town halls. Under these conditions, professional workers, such as social workers, do not work as a completely separated team from the other local authority workers involved in the caring process. The office, again in the locality, will have a central reception and citizens will have under one roof the whole panoply of local authority services at their disposal. Whilst departmental structures would still exist within the upper level of council organisation, the local office would have, or be heading towards, no departmental divisions where it actually met the public.

The third and most important form of decentralisation would also involve the decentralisation of some power from council committees to local neighbourhood committees. This would involve a limited budget and powers over services, but would represent a real loss of power from the centre. It is this reform that is most important for our programme for action, for it is the decentralisation of power which provides the possibility of a much richer democratic experience for local citizens. It is this process that will provide the best possibility for local government trade unionists to involve themselves with organised local sections of the public.

Decentralisation is taking place in all three of these forms, but in several places real shifts in power are envisaged. For example, in both Islington and Birmingham, two local authorities with Labour majorities, but with very different sorts of Labour Parties, important changes in the structure of power have begun. In some places, local branches of NALGO and some social workers have tried to resist the overall process. Whilst it definitely involves the disruption of working conditions for a period of time, in the long term we would argue strongly that local authority trade unions will gain enormously by this enriched local democratic form. We discuss below some of the reasons for local government trade unionists gaining as trade unionists from a growth of popular democracy.

INDUSTRIAL DEMOCRACY

A completely democratic society needs to achieve democracy both in civil society and in the area of social production. Political democracy is concerned with citizens as free and secure individuals in civil society and with people as consumers of collectively provided goods and services. Trade unions are concerned with people as producers. Trade unions, as democratic organisations of producers, should be involved in the democratic control of public services. We now have decades of experience which shows that to exclude trade unions would, if there was no aspect of industrial democracy, be detrimental to full democracy. The dictatorship of the consumer and the resulting degradation of the worker would be the end result of such a form of popular control. For where the consumer is sovereign, work remains only as a means to an end, that end being the satisfaction of the consumer's wants and desires. The producer is exploited and subjected to poor working conditions, so work becomes an alienating and unfree experience.

Without industrial democracy there will be three continuing problems. Firstly, there will be the problem of the persistence of a bureaucratic organisation, which allows no democratic input. We must remember that the involvement of local government trade unions is the involvement of the very people who are themselves the bureaucrats. Involving them through their union will serve to break open the bureaucracy. Secondly, there will be passive resistance by social services staff to democratic control. If we fail to involve trade unions it is inevitable that there will be very great resistance from social workers to other peoples' democratic involvement in running the service. Thirdly, without industrial democracy, techniques and knowledge of social work practice will be developed by a management which tends towards the worst kind of professional élitism or, even worse, 'scientific management'.

The last of these problems, which is essentially concerned with labour as a social process, has not received sufficient attention from social workers. At present the social division of labour in social work is very demeaning for many of those involved in it. One only has to look at the present occupational differentiation within social services, with the splits between manual and non-manual workers and between professionally qualified and unqualified staff, to see how harmful has been the development of social services occupations so far. The social distance between these various, hierarchically divided occupations (especially the gap between manual and non-manual) and the limited opportunities for workers to develop their vocational skills, add up to a very 'alienated' labour process in social services. The trade unionism of social workers should be more involved in the development of the occupational structure of social services, and on a progressive rather than a reactive basis. This means that there needs to be a direct involvement by the union in the development of social work techniques and knowledge, in the certification process of social workers, and in national and local bodies concerned with advising on, or setting, social services standards.

The democratic involvement of producers in the control of social services is needed to ensure that the design of work in social services is fitted to the human needs of the producers. This will provide the base for trade union intervention at a national level. In the past, the absence of a trade union intervention – at least on any macro scale – has meant that the development of social work practice has been influenced by external political and legal events which have left no room for any real vocational self-government. We are thinking here of the effects of Seebohm-instigated changes, the 1983 Mental Health Act, and the almost random effects of joint funding and other non-traditional sources of revenue.

In the 1970s, both NALGO and the TGWU made detailed proposals for industrial democracy in local government. In 1977, a report by NALGO's National Executive Committee suggested employee representatives in the full council and in council committees. A year earlier, the TGWU had suggested joint union–management boards to run departments, whilst the council was to be left in charge of policy-making. These bipartite boards would not be enough in the light of the need to increase popular involvement but it shows that some thinking in this area already exists.

In our view, the failure to develop industrial democracy is a serious impediment to the emergence of more satisfying forms of social work practice – forms which would lead to the development of the capacities of all social services employees. But industrial democracy cannot compensate for the imperfections that currently disfigure political democracy. This is because trade unions, the only viable channel of worker representation in any form of industrial democracy, is concerned with preserving the freedom of workers within the workplace and with raising their standard of living, and is not primarily concerned with the consumers' point of view. While trade unionists are also consumers, the sectionalist nature of individual trade unions makes it difficult for them to have paramount regard for the community interest as a whole or the interests of consumers of public services.

A joint working party of the Labour Party and the TUC Local Government Committee considered industrial democracy in local government in 1977. Unfortunately, nothing much has happened since then and so the active trade unionists amongst social workers would need to mobilise support in their trade union and in the wider labour movement for the realisation of industrial democracy as soon as is politically possible. We base this part of our programme on the overall analysis we have made about local government. We reiterate that local government is a different form of employer than private capital, therefore we are not engaging in the overall discussion about industrial democracy in capitalist enterprises. Within local government the trade union movement must involve itself in industrial democracy.

TRADE UNIONISM AND PROFESSIONAL CONCERNS

We do not think it is advisable for public service workers ever to give up collective bargaining or their right to strike. These are essential for the preservation of free and independent trade unions. Therefore, the maintenance of effective collective bargaining in the public services is important.

There are, however, two major issues around the use of industrial action. Firstly, NALGO members and other workers in local government cannot materially affect the profits of their employers (there are no profits!) and so the power of the strike weapon is very greatly diminished. Secondly, social workers, we have argued, have to pay special regard to the effects of their union action because of their relationship to other workers as consumers who work in the private sector, and to the general public who both pay for and consume the service. In effect, social workers, because they cannot expect or rely on spontaneous solidarity from these groups, must actively form alliances with them.

The formation of an alliance is not an act of pure willpower. Still less is it the passing of a series of resolutions. An alliance has the nature of a bargain in which both sides expect to gain. An alliance constructed on the basis of one side giving but getting nothing in return will be unstable – even unreal. Recent national strikes have demonstrated that this simply will not happen. Social workers cannot expect unconditional support from the general public or from private enterprise workers. They have to offer something in exchange. Moreover, consequential on the negotiation of the alliance, the social workers will be changed.

Very often in the past trade union activists in social work have talked about solidarity with local communities but at most alliances have been built in respect of a single issue such as homelessness. We have suggested above an organisational form which will institutionalise the alliance of producers and consumers and the political representatives of the local community – the tripartite board. But for this form to be stabilised it needs the activists we have discussed above to change. An alliance built on the current trade union practice would founder, so what change needs to occur if that alliance is to stand a real chance of working?

We suggest that NALGO could seek to develop in respect of its social services membership a professional ethical code and a capacity to initiate or carry out activities to advance the techniques and knowledge of social work practice. It could do these things itself or in conjunction with other vocational bodies organising social workers. An ethical code, which would dictate the moral conduct of social workers in relation to the community, would also create a stronger overlap with the concerns of the local community. Just as the traditional professional associations' ethical code served to stabilise the professional's relationship to the consumer, so the ethical code of NALGO's social services membership would stabilise the democratic alliance of producers and consumers.

But it must be recognised that such an ethical code would make a material difference to the way NALGO defended and advanced the interests of its social services membership. NALGO would have been changed. The local community, however, would then see that the union was concerned with consumers' interests. The commitment to the development of the techniques and knowledge would show further their concern with consumers' interests by demonstrating a concern to improve the service to the local community.

Programmes have to be realistic in terms of their assumptions about individual motivation. Is it, therefore, Utopian to think that public services can be developed in the ways suggested above? We are certain that this is not Utopian. A large number of social worker trade unionists have experienced eight long years of Thatcherism. They have frequently made calls for 'general support' of welfare and have found that this has not happened. Many of them realise that it will take considerable alliances to rebuild their welfare organisations. Many people employed in local government – not just social workers – are daily engaged in serving their local communities and they, in addition to their concern about pay, job security, working conditions, and so on, already display a commitment to community service, and this can be built on.

To sum up, the genuine (but undemocratic) concern of traditional professional bodies with their clients' welfare and with the advance of their techniques can be usefully imported to public service trade unions under the move towards more democratic socialist forms of trade union practice.

PUBLIC EDUCATION

We have stressed that public service workers have to pay special regard to the effects of their union action on consumers – the general public. The fact that public service workers share with private sector workers the experience of having to sell their labour in order to live is not sufficient to guarantee the sympathy and support of the latter for public-sector trade union struggles. Public services are not provided on a capitalistic basis and so militant action – or even passive resistance – cannot put pressure on an employer by turning off the flow of profits. Such actions may lead to political pressures but the public service trade unionist risks incurring the hostility of the general public. Margaret Thatcher has tried to highlight public service trade unionists as pampered and cynically exploiting the general public. Involvement in local tripartite boards may lead to representatives of the local community becoming better informed and more sympathetic to public service workers. The development by NALGO of ethical codes and activities to advance the techniques and knowledge of social work practice may provide the necessary change in trade union practice to cement the democratic alliance.

A third crucial development, which is needed to break down destructive images of public service workers and to educate the general public about its role in the popular control of local government services, is for NALGO to commit even more resources to publicity, and not only at a national level. The union needs to develop its organisation and resources so that continuous publicity can be directed at the general public. The public's ignorance about their services, including both the problems faced by public service workers and the achievements of local government, needs to be dispelled.

Recent struggles for local government carried out by local authorities themselves have demonstrated the effectiveness of public campaigns in changing public attitudes. Trade unions at a branch level need to apply this lesson and play a fuller role in the public life of their locality. This education work will become even more important as the popular control of local government services increases. Paradoxically, the more public service unions educate the public and reduce its ignorance of the difficulties of delivering public services, the more real will be the democratic control of public services.

NATIONAL MINIMUM STANDARDS

One of the main results of the changes in the 1970s was that social workers have come to be seen as responsible for social problems in general. Many social workers recognised that there could never be sufficient resources to abolish all social problems in a capitalist society but, institutionally, there is no recognition of this fact. One possible union response to this could be to press for a new statutory agency to be set up to decide national minimum standards in social services.

These standards might specify the minimum frequency of visits by social workers to children on the at-risk register, the ratio of social workers to clients with a learning difficulty, the maximum size of a hostel for people with a mental illness, and so on. The agency could be set up on a similar basis to a wages council, with representatives of the employers (local government) and trade unions, and a third group composed of representatives of central government and voluntary organisations which lobby on behalf of sections of the general public who have an interest in the service provided. In this way NALGO would be involved in the negotiation of national minimum standards, which would inevitably help to define the general expectations of the services provided by social workers. Such standards would also be valuable in union attempts to open a dialogue about public services with the general public, since there would be more measurable and comparable data on the services.

FULL-TIME AND PAID ELECTED MEMBERS

An implicit assumption in all this discussion is that democracy would be a lot healthier if the collective consciousness and public-spiritedness of the mass of ordinary people were greater than they are now, and many of the measures described above should help to foster these attributes. But there is an easy, practical measure to increase local democracy that does not depend upon changing ordinary people. The measure we have in mind is that of making elected members into paid, full-time elected representatives of the local community. Indeed, it is hard to believe that there is so little value placed on the principle of democratic control that in the late twentieth century we still have part-time, amateur elected members. Considering the enormous social capital tied up in public services and the numbers employed there can be no sensible or rational reason for hampering democratic control by keeping the elected members as part-time representatives of the local community. If they were full-time they would have more opportunity of finding out what local people want and ensuring that the services met what was wanted. In whose interest is it to impede democracy in this way? Certainly not the public service unions' – they should campaign vigorously for full-time elected members.

CONCLUSION

Nothing we say, or fail to say, should be construed as opposed in principle to the use by public service unions of strike action and other forms of industrial action. There will always be times and places where such actions are necessary. The thrust of our arguments are, however, that public service unions, because of the context in which they operate, cannot afford to base their entire strategy around industrial militancy. The class analysis we presented earlier suggests that indiscriminate recourse to industrial action will not automatically be greeted by class solidarity from the working class; the working class is too differentiated in its relations to private capital for that to happen. A comprehensive strategy needs to be based on a programme which aims at the popular involvement of the public in the operation of social services, decentralised service delivery, industrial democracy and an 'ethical' trade unionism which is actively involved in the advance of techniques and knowledge in social work practice. And we cannot emphasise sufficiently how crucial it is for public service workers *as a matter of self-interest* to get the backing of the general public. Public service workers need a better informed and better educated general public to be democratically involved in the popular control of services.

Bibliography

Allen, V. L. (1971) *The Sociology of Industrial Relations: Studies in Method* (London: Longman).

Bain, G. S. (1970) *The Growth of White-Collar Unionism* (Oxford: Clarendon).

Bain, G. S., Coates, D. and Ellis, V. (1973) *Social Stratification and Trade Unionism* (London: Heinemann).

Benington, J. (1976) *Local Government Becomes Big Business* (London: Community Development Project Information and Intelligence Unit).

Blackburn, R. M. and Mann, M. (1979) *The Working Class in the Labour Market* (London: Macmillan).

Callinicos, A. (1982) 'The Rank-and-File Movement Today', *International Socialism*, 17.

Clegg, H. A. (1976) *Trade Unionism Under Collective Bargaining* (Oxford: Basil Blackwell).

Cockburn, C. (1977) *The Local State* (London: Pluto).

Cook, F. G., Clark, S. C., Roberts, K. and Semeonoff, E. (1976) 'White and Blue Collar Workers' Attitudes to Trade Unionism and Social Class', *Industrial Relations Journal*, vol. VI, no. 4.

Creigh, S. and Makeham, P. (1980) 'Striker's Occupation: an analysis', *Employment Gazette* (March) pp. 237–9.

Crompton, R. (1976) 'Approaches to the Study of White-Collar Unionism', *Sociology*, vol. 10, no. 3 (September).

Crompton, R. (1979) 'Trade Unionism and the Insurance Clerk', *Sociology*, vol. 13 (September).

Davies (1986) 'Social Work and Deskilling' (CNAA Ph.D. thesis).

Drain, G. (1975) 'Drain Speaks!', *Tower Power*, (published by NALGO's Tower Hamlets branch), no. 23 (January).

Fowler, A. (1980) *Personnel Management in Local Government* (London: Institute of Personnel Management).

Hawkins, K. (1981) *Trade Unions* (London: Hutchinson).

Hibbs, D. A. (1978) 'On the Political Economy of Long-Run Trends in Strike Activity', *British Journal of Political Science*, vol. 8.

285

Hindess, B. (1983) *Parliamentary Democracy and Socialist Politics* (London: RKP).

Hyman, R. (1975) *Industrial Relations: A Marxist Introduction* (London: Macmillan).

Hyman, R. and Fryer, R.H. (1975) 'Trade Unions: Sociology and Political Economy', in J. B. McKinley (ed.) *Processing People: Cases in Organizational Behaviour* (London: Holt, Rinehart and Winston).

Hutber, P. (ed.) (1978) *What's Wrong with Britain?* (London: Sphere).

Johnson, T. J. (1972) *Professions and Power* (London: Macmillan).

Jordan, B. and Parton, N. (eds) (1985) *Political Dimension of Social Work* (Oxford: Basil Blackwell). See chapter by Leeds Social Workers' Action Group: 'A Trade Union Base for Action'.

Jones, C. (1983) *State Social Work and the Working Class* (London: Macmillan).

Kelly, M. P. (1980) *White-Collar Proletariat: The Industrial Behaviour of British Civil Servants* (London: Routledge and Kegan Paul).

Kitching, G. (1983) *Rethinking Socialism* (London: Methuen).

Lane, T. (1974) *The Union Makes Us Strong* (London: Arrow).

Lane, T. (1982) 'The Unions: caught on the ebb tide', *Marxism Today* (September).

Lenin, V. I. (1970) *What is to be Done?* in V. I. Lenin (1970) *On Trade Unions* (Moscow: Progress Publishers).

Lockwood, D. (1958) *The Blackcoated Worker* (London: George Allen and Unwin).

Marx, K. and Engels, F. (1942) *Manifesto of the Communist Party*, in *Karl Marx: Selected Works*, vol. I (London: Lawrence and Wishart).

Maybin, R. (1980) 'NALGO: The New Unionism of Contemporary Britain', *Marxism Today* (January).

McIlroy, J. (1984) *Strike!* (London: Pluto).

Miliband, R. (1979) *Parliamentary Socialism* (London: Merlin Press).

Newman, G. (1982) *Path to Maturity: NALGO 1965–1980* (Manchester: Co-operative Press).

Nicholson, N., Ursell, G. and Blyton, P. (1981) *The Dynamics of White Collar Unionism* (London: Academic Press).

Offe, C. (1984) *Contradictions of the Welfare State* (London: Hutchinson).

Price, R. and Bain, G. S. (1983) 'Union Growth in Britain: Retrospect and Prospect', *British Journal of Industrial Relations*, vol. XIV, no. 3.

Rose, R. (1985) *Public Employment in Western Nations* (Cambridge: Cambridge University Press).

Seebohm Report (1968) *Report of the Committee on Local Authority and Allied Personal Social Services*, Cmnd 3703 (London: HMSO).

Stewart, J. (1983) *Local Government: The Conditions of Choice* (London: George Allen and Unwin).

Strauss, G. (1954) 'White-Collar Unions are Different!', *Harvard Business Review*, (September–October).

Thomson, A. W. J. (1983) 'The contexts of management behaviour in industrial relations in the public and private sectors', in K. Thurley and S. Wood (eds), *Industrial Relations and Management Strategy* (Cambridge: Cambridge University Press).

Thomson, A. W. J. and Beaumont, P. B. (1978) *Public Sector Bargaining: A Study of Relative Gain* (Farnborough: Saxon House).

Thompson, E. P. (1968) *The Making of the English Working Class* (Harmondsworth: Penguin).

Townsend, D. (1983) 'Rarely in the field of industrial conflict can so much have been claimed by so few from so many', *Community Care*, November 17.

Walker, P. (1981) 'Burgess: Militant at the top', *Community Care*, July 2.

Webb, A. and Wistow, G. (1982) *Whither State Welfare?* (London: RIPA).

Younghusband, E. (1978) *Social Work in Britain: 1950–1975*, vol. I (London: George Allen and Unwin).

Documents and Reports

British Association of Social Workers (BASW) *Annual Report 1983/84* (16 Kent Street, Birmingham B5 6RD).

British Association of Social Workers (BASW) *Memorandum, Articles and Bye-laws* (no date).

CIPFA (1983) Finance and General Statistics 1983–84 (London: CIPFA).

Economic Progress Report, no. 131 (March 1981) and no. 182 (January–February 1986). (London: the Treasury).

Joint Manpower Watch Group (various dates) Press Notices on Joint Manpower Watch (issued by Department of the Environment, 2 Marsham Street, London SW1P 3EB).

National and Local Government Officers' Association (NALGO) (1976) Working Party on Communications, *Report*. Presented to the National Executive Council.

National and Local Government Officers' Association (NALGO) (1977) *Advice to Branches on the Introduction of Steward Systems*. Circulated by NALGO headquarters to secretaries of district councils and branches in October 1977. An accompanying letter, dated 5 October 1977, was written by Geoffrey Drain, then General Secretary.

National and Local Government Officers' Association (NALGO) (1983) *Organizing for Equal Opportunity*. A brief guide to equal opportunities and structure in NALGO.

National and Local Government Officers' Association (NALGO) (1984) *The Personal Social Services*.

National and Local Government Officers' Association (NALGO) (1985) *Residential Workers' Dispute: Report by the National Local Government Committee to the 1985 Local Government Group Annual Meeting*.

288 BIBLIOGRAPHY

Tower Hamlets Case Con (1972) *The Great East End Housing Disaster*. A report published by Tower Hamlets Case Con.

Trades Union Congress (TUC) (1974) *Industrial Democracy*. A statement of policy by the Trades Union Congress, published in July 1974.

Scheme of Conditions of Service (the 'Purple Book'). A national agreement negotiated by the National Joint Council for Local Authorities' Administrative, Professional, Technical and Clerical Services.

Index